Like my friend Mark Clark, I was rais  When I was eighteen years old, I actua out of being a Christian! I will never forget that conversation because I realized that the reason he could be talked out of his faith so easily was because it had no solid foundation. That's why I am praying that Mark's new book will be read by millions. Mark is one of the next generation's best communicators. This book is just like Mark—honest, inspirational, and encouraging. Read it and pass it on!

Ray Johnston, Senior Pastor, Bayside Church; author
of *The Hope Quotient, This Changes Everything,*
and *Jesus Called—He Wants His Church Back*

I'm a big fan of Mark Clark. His new book, *The Problem of God,* is important. I love books that will bless and deepen seasoned saints and also speak provocatively to seekers and skeptics. Every emerging generation needs fresh voices to help illuminate our path with Jesus; I believe Mark Clark is one of those voices.

Daniel Fusco, Lead Pastor, Crossroads Community
Church; author of *Upward, Inward, Outward* and *Honestly*

If you ever wished there was an apologetics book that was academically sound, logically compelling, and actually fun to read, your wait is over. Mark Clark brings his own engaging, fun, and refreshing voice to some of the key objections to the Christian faith. He does the almost impossible task of making a usually dry subject not only easy to understand but enjoyable and compelling, without losing any academic integrity. This book is a must-read for Christians and skeptics alike.

Carey Nieuwhof, Author and Founding
Pastor, Connexus Church

I'm so grateful for Mark Clark and his ministry! In *The Problem of God*, Mark has created a very practical and personal resource. It provides an accessible paradigm for understanding and answering common objections to God, Scripture, and the historical person of Jesus without needing to be a philosopher, language expert, or historian. This book will equip followers of Jesus to have informed conversations with their friends and neighbors and deepen our own conviction that Jesus is Lord.

Bruxy Cavey, Pastor at The Meeting House;
author of *(Re)Union: The Good News of
Jesus for Seekers, Saints, and Sinners*

THE PROBLEM OF

ANSWERING A SKEPTIC'S
CHALLENGES TO CHRISTIANITY

MARK CLARK

For Sienna, Hayden, and Isabella:
Your love for Jesus inspires me every day. My hope is that
this book will go with each of you as you grow closer to him
in the midst of both the beauty and the teeth of this world.

CONTENTS

Foreword

By Larry Osborne

It's no news flash that the prevailing worldview in North American today is decidedly post-Christian, dominated by secularism, science, and an intensely privatized spirituality. As with every culturally dominate worldview (including that of the Christian era), it impacts the way that we evaluate competing truth claims. We all start out with a set of presuppositions and paradigms that we assume to be fact based—but in reality, are seldom tested, at times illogical, and in some cases blatant falsehoods.

That's why before we dismiss Jesus, the Bible, and Christianity as mere ancient myth, antiquated literature, or a set of oppressive and failed moral standards, we need to first test our assumptions against the facts and then let the facts speak for themselves.

The same goes for those of us who call ourselves Jesus followers. Our faith doesn't magically make our assumptions about Jesus and the Bible true. Faith can't turn a falsehood into truth. Rightly understood, it's not a blind belief in the unbelievable; it's a rational belief based on a preponderance of evidence. If we trust God and the Bible enough to do what they say, it should be because we've put them to the test and found them to be trustworthy. Anything else is mere credulity.

Whether you self-identify as a skeptic seeking answers to what Christians believe, an antagonist wondering why they believe such nonsense, a Christian looking for well-reasoned answers to the tough questions you've been asked, or you fall somewhere else on the continuum, I guarantee that you'll find the following pages to be enlightening and beneficial in your spiritual journey.

What you won't find is a collection of straw man arguments that convince none but the already persuaded, or the soulless answers that read like a well-researched term paper. Instead you'll find a thoughtful examination of the legitimate and sincere questions that skeptics, antagonists, and agnostics have long asked about Jesus, the Bible, and the Christian worldview.

In many ways, Mark Clark was born to write this book. When it comes to the deeper questions of life, truth, and spirituality, our personal experiences always have a profound impact upon the lens through which we see and interpret things. Clark is no exception. His upbringing, cultural context, and life experiences have uniquely prepared him to speak to both skeptics and Christians.

In one sense, he's the last person anyone would have expected to become an articulate Jesus follower—an atheistic upbringing, drug abuse, Tourette syndrome, and a series of profoundly negative church experiences as a new Christian are not your typical career path to ministry.

But with the clarity of 20/20 hindsight, it all makes perfect sense.

From the very first time I met Mark, I've been impressed with his ability to powerfully communicate to both those who believe and those who doubt. His deep knowledge of the Bible empowers him to reach Jesus followers. His personal journey and struggle with the questions that skeptics ask enables him to both validate and answer their concerns with a clarity and persuasiveness. It's no wonder that despite its location in one of the most secular and diverse cities in

North American, huge crowds flock to his church and tune into his podcasts each week.

If you've assumed that science and faith are inherently at odds or must exist in two distinct, unconnected, parallel universes, you'll find his chapter "The Problem of Science" to be eye-opening and helpful.

If you've struggled with the arguments for and against the existence of God, the historical reliability of the Bible, or the origins of the Christ myth, you'll find answers in these pages.

And if you've failed to find satisfaction in the clichés that too easily dismiss the real and genuine issues that surround the conundrums of evil and suffering, hell, and the exclusiveness of Christianity, you will find rich and satisfying answers in these pages. Not easy answers. But rich, satisfying, and intellectually honest answers.

This is a book I will buy in bulk and keep on hand to pass out to both my skeptic and Christian friends who are honestly asking the tough questions about Jesus, the Bible, and Christianity that deserve careful and thoughtful answers.

LARRY OSBORNE

2017

Acknowledgments

Thanks to my wife, Erin, the brains and strength behind the operation, whose sacrifice and love keep me going.

To my mom and Al, for loving me well and giving me the opportunity to explore Christianity at a time when I looked more lost than ever. I miss you, Al.

To William Redpath (Bobbie), for being the first person I ever saw Jesus in and for being the most godly man I have ever known and likely ever will know. Yours are the shoulders of faith I now stand on.

To Village Church, for being the best church a pastor could be a part of. Keep living out your faith and letting God use you every day, even among the skepticism of the world and your own quiet doubts.

To all those writers and thinkers who have written similar books to this one—C. S. Lewis, Timothy Keller, Nancy Pearcey, Ravi Zacharias, Alvin Plantinga, etc. This book is but a pastoral application of ideas I learned from you, some of my greatest teachers, though I've never met you.

All of the problems of heaven and earth, though they were to confront us together and at once, would be nothing compared with the overwhelming problem of God: That He is; what He is like; and what we as moral beings must do about Him.

A. W. TOZER, THE KNOWLEDGE OF THE HOLY

INTRODUCTION

I was raised in a staunch atheist household. We never went to church. We never owned a Bible. We never talked about God. My father was such an ardent atheist that he demanded my mother spell my brother's name, Mathew, with only one *t* so as to not be biblical. He then named me *Mark*.

Clearly he didn't see the irony.

I heard about Christianity for the first time at a summer camp when I was nine years old. I was fascinated by the concept of God. Not enough to make me want to go to church or read my Bible or whatever else religious people did. But I found myself going back to the camp every year. Singing songs, meeting new friends, talking about God, and then coming home to a *very* different life. I experimented with drugs at a very young age. A guy from our neighborhood cooked up hash and offered it to a bunch of us kids in the neighborhood. I came back to drugs as a teenager. I partied, got high, and stole money (from cars or the purses of my friends' mothers) so I could continue to party and get high. A cycle I enjoyed until I bumped up against God again. And then it all changed.

My parents divorced when I was eight years old. Shortly thereafter, I acquired a psychological disorder called Tourette syndrome, which later developed into Obsessive Compulsive Disorder. So, growing up, I would adopt a habit—a face twitch or swearing randomly to myself for months at a time—until another habit came along and replaced it. Because of the Obsessive Compulsive Disorder, I would superstitiously pound my hands together or smack my face, for instance, because if I didn't do these things, I was convinced something bad would happen to the people around me. If I didn't hit that post three times in the airport or tap my foot against the seat, the plane would go down, etc. It all sounds crazy now. But it was the reality for much of my life. To anyone observing, becoming a pastor would have seemed like the last job I'd ever get. People tend not to come to churches when the preacher drops an f-bomb every few minutes.

My father was a classic deadbeat dad. He couldn't hold down a job, didn't know how to raise my brother and me, and divided his time between drinking and yelling at football games. He died of lung cancer when I was fifteen. I never got to say goodbye to him because he never told us he was sick. He was forty-seven years old. There were eighteen people at his funeral. As I stood over his casket, my mind was flooded with questions about God. I was a skeptic then, and in many ways, I still am. The longer you're a Christian, the more you come to realize that faith requires skepticism. Believing in one thing means you have to challenge and exclude other things. As G. K. Chesterton once said, "To believe in everything is the same as believing in nothing." I didn't want to believe in everything—that everyone was right about God no matter what their views about him. That seemed weak and absurd. That whole view, now very popular, seemed too convenient, and I am skeptical about convenient things. I had chosen instead, at that point, to believe in nothing. And maybe that's you. A skeptic. A doubter. At some level, it's all of us. Christians don't believe in Thor or Aphrodite, for instance. Christians have varying levels of doubt and skepticism about a lot of things. In the same way, you may not believe in God at all or you might reject some of the Christian ideas about him. That was me. But as I stood in that very lonely funeral home, I began to ponder where exactly my father was; I asked myself what I believed. About God, humankind, eternity, and morality. About my father.

Where did he go?

Somewhere? Nowhere?

At age seventeen, a few days from starting to deal drugs myself, I met a guy named Chris. He was a former drug dealer at my school who had become a follower of Jesus and had been totally transformed. I was intrigued by his life, his questions, and his passion for God. We met in woodworking class, and he challenged me to examine my doubts, read the Bible, pray, and think about the implications of what I believed. I knew one of two things would happen if I did that: I would either lose the small amount of faith I had possessed since my days at summer camp or that faith would explode and come to define me.

So I began to research and wrestle with the existence of God scientifically, historically, and philosophically. I had lingering questions about suffering and evil that came from my own experience—my sickness and the loss of my father. I wrestled with the reliability of the Bible, the legitimacy of miracles, and the dark history of the church, filled as it was with judgment, violence, and hypocrisy. I wrestled with the doctrine of hell and how God could allow my father, who to my knowledge never became a Christian, to go to a place of everlasting torment, since this didn't square with my understanding of justice, love, or Jesus. I set out to explore these things and lean into my doubts rather than away from them. The more I explored, the more I saw the power and soundness of Christianity. I saw science and philosophy were not *opposed* to faith at all. Historically, Christianity stood apart from other world religions in its legitimacy.

Later that year I gave my life to Christ. After I got serious about following Jesus, there still was one step I could not bring myself to take: attending church. It's ironic looking back on this, given that I now spend my life serving and building a church as a pastor. Initially I was afraid and disinterested in church altogether. I thought it would be an old man up front preaching from a big dusty Bible, the building old and smelling like mothballs. A friend finally convinced me to go . . . and it was exactly like that! But I stayed anyway. I'm not really sure why. I guess because I found others like me, wrestling in the place where faith and skepticism meet.

To have faith in something, I require a certain level of information. Like you, I don't believe every claim that comes my way simply because someone tells me it's true. I want evidence. I have always been that way. It was no different when I came to faith in Christ. Every idea and claim about God or humankind had to have *evidence* behind it, or I wouldn't accept it. I grew up in an exclusively non-Christian social world, where if you believed something with conviction, you would have to test it so you were able to defend it when challenged—an informed faith rather than an assumed faith. And that is what this book is all about.

Starting a Church for Skeptics

In 2010, when I was twenty-nine years old, I found myself planting a church. How I got to this point is a long story, but the short version is that when I was nineteen, God called me into pastoral ministry through a series of seemingly disconnected events. I didn't know what that would look like initially, but I started attending a Bible college, worked as an intern in a few different youth ministries, developed a passion for scholarship and philosophy, married my high school sweetheart, and moved to Vancouver to pursue a master's degree in New Testament Studies. This move was originally intended as a three-year stop on my way to doctoral studies at Oxford.

The longer we lived in Vancouver, however, the more our

hearts stirred for it as a city, and we developed a passion for the local church. While working on my master's thesis, I felt God calling me to start a church that would reach people like me—skeptics who either didn't grow up in the church or who had walked away from it altogether. I wanted to reach people who lived in the real world of television, Reddit, post-secondary institutions that cut their teeth on anti-Christian convictions, and workplaces with colleagues who have never been to church. I wanted to reach people who doubted the existence of God, who thought Christianity was judgmental and narrow-minded, and who spent their time reading Richard Dawkins and Thomas Friedman, not the latest Christian bestseller.

My wife and I, along with a small team of amazing people, started dreaming of a church where the Bible was taught and, at the same time, where skeptics and cynics could come, be challenged, ask questions, and maybe even get some answers. We envisioned a place where every week we would talk about God's profound answers to the questions we are all asking in life—the questions that have come to define our post-Christian culture. So, that's what we did. It was a risk, because Vancouver is the third least churched city in Canada, located in the country's most secular province.[1] How does one speak into and reach a culture like that? The best way I had come up with was to do what the apostle Paul did. He went to strategic areas of his time—Athens, Corinth, Ephesus, Rome—and spoke into the marketplace of ideas, showing how the gospel and the biblical story interfaced with those ideas, interacting with the thinkers and philosophies of the time, and showing how Jesus is the one true God, and the center of all things (see Acts 17–20).

By God's grace, that risk has paid off in ways I never could have imagined. Village Church launched in January 2010 in an elementary school gym with fifty people, and it has since grown to a multisite church of thousands of people, many of whom are skeptics (un-churched and de-churched people with lots of hang-ups about Christianity), but who are meeting God in powerful ways. The transformation and growth we have seen in every demographic has been beyond our every expectation.

This is why I am hopeful.

I have seen the answers and evidences we will explore in the coming pages actually change people's lives in amazing and tangible ways. The last time we did a formal sermon series based on the questions raised in this book our church grew by eight hundred people in a week. This would be a minor miracle in the Bible Belt of the American South. In Canada, it is unheard of. Why would almost a thousand people show up at a church one Sunday who weren't there the week before? How does a church go from a group of thirteen people in a living room to thousands across multiple locations in just a few years? It is a movement of God that we can neither explain nor control. But I think it is also because we are addressing the common questions of the human mind and working to give answers to them, week in and week out. And that is connecting to a sincerely skeptical culture.

What's amazing about all of these people finding faith in Jesus in our modern day is this: years ago it was theorized that by the time my generation grew up, faith and religion would be dead in the Western world because of the development of technology, science, and human knowledge in general. But this has turned out not to be the case after all. While these developments have certainly changed the conversation, people are not abandoning spiritual questions in the Western world. Rather, they are entering into and welcoming many spiritual experiences that they weren't open to a generation ago. Everyone from Howard Stern to Jim Carrey now claim to meditate and connect to the transcendent. Ace Ventura *meditating*? I'm not going to lie; I never would have predicted that. But I should have, because spirituality rings true, even virtuous, to people of all ages and stages of life. My desire is to take that conviction and show that that impulse is ultimately meant to lead us to somewhere more defined. Indeed, to *someone*.

All those people, skeptics just like you and me, who showed up to our church during the series where we explored the questions in this book didn't just come and then leave. They stayed. I believe this is because Christianity answered their questions, and their longings, better than anything else. They saw that it presents a rational and distinct view of origins, meaning, morality, and destiny beyond any other worldview, religious or secular, in the marketplace of ideas. That the Bible, Jesus, and everything else that orbits around Christianity actually hold up under historical, scientific, philosophical, and even literary scrutiny. And when they realized this, they were willing to give their lives to it.

So, this book emerges out of the intersection of these two worlds: my skeptical life and my skeptical church. The questions I have asked myself, and the questions of real people, like you, who I am reaching out to every day the best I know how, *do* have answers. There *is* hope. There *is* meaning to it all. If you have the courage to doubt your doubts, to suspend your disbelief, even for a moment, there is a possibility you will see something really is on the other side of the veil. And in coming to see that, I believe you will experience the same transformative reality that I and so many others have—forever changing your life.

Problem: a question raised for inquiry, consideration, or solution; an intricate unsettled question.

CHAPTER 1

The Problem of
SCIENCE

The trouble about argument is that it moves the whole struggle on to the Enemy's own ground. . . . By the very act of arguing, you awake the patient's reason: and once it is awake, who can foresee the result?

C. S. LEWIS, THE SCREWTAPE LETTERS

How often have we turned on the television and heard the host say, "Tonight we will be talking about faith versus science. Our first guest is a former University of Oxford professor, evolutionary biologist, and bestselling author. He believes that science, not faith, holds the answers to all questions. On the other side of the aisle we have Joe Smith, who will speak for the legitimacy of faith and Christianity. Joe homeschools his kids, thinks Oprah is the Antichrist, and lives in a swamp."

Something like this plays out every day on television, social media, and even university campuses across the Western world. Joe and the Oxford professor represent the widely embraced caricatures of the opposing sides of the faith-science debate. Christianity—and faith in general—is seen as naive, simplistic, and incompatible with human reason. It might have a place in a carefully isolated sphere of life, but science should occupy *all* of life. Science is based on truth and evidence, while faith is based on hopeful thinking and legend. Science is a search for objective evidence that leads humanity forward, while faith looks back to ancient teachings, outmoded holy books, and irrational conclusions in the face of overwhelming evidence otherwise.

Confronting the Myth

The dichotomy between faith and science, however, is misguided. It is created by a culture that thinks only in sound bites and extremes, rather than bothering to investigate the place where truth is usually found: in the *both/and*, in this case, of faith *and* science working together rather than the *either/or* choices presented to us time and time again, wherein the two are mutually exclusive. This is a cultural myth written and preached by one of the most powerful and pervasive structures of thought the world has ever known—*secularism*. Secularism teaches that because there is no God and no spiritual reality in the universe beyond what we can test (naturalism), beliefs in such ideas should be marginalized from public life and discourse. Secularists believe that religious beliefs have been categorically proven false by modern developments in science and technology, and they can now be dismissed.

Secularism has held philosophical sway in Western culture since its ascent during the Enlightenment (1600–1800 AD). Its modern form is represented most popularly by thinkers such as Richard Dawkins, Sam Harris, and the late Christopher Hitchens. They argue that science and naturalistic evolution have provided enough evidence to deduce atheistic conclusions to all of our foundational questions—those of origins, meaning, morality, and destiny. Furthermore, they assert that people who don't submit themselves to a purely naturalistic outlook are primitive and irrational. "Faith is like a mental illness," Richard Dawkins has said, "a great cop out, the excuse to evade the need to think and evaluate evidence."[2] Sam Harris agrees, saying, "We have names for people who have many beliefs for which there is no rational justification. When their beliefs are extremely common, we call them religious. Otherwise, they are likely to be called mad, delusional, or psychotic."[3]

Notice the dichotomy: science is about *thinking, evidence,* and *rational justification,* while Christianity and faith in general are about evading evidence and clinging to nonrationality. But what if secularism and naturalism are the views that are outdated? What if the worlds of faith and reason are not opposed to each other at all but actually belong together in a beautiful and life-changing symmetry that makes sense of the evidence, even more than atheistic explanations do? That is precisely what I have come to see after years of examination. I have been led *toward* Christian faith by reason and the study of science, history, and philosophy—and away from a modern, secular, atheistic worldview. I have come to see that Christianity isn't a *less* rational worldview ("spiritual" versus "logical"), but a *more* rational one.

The Plantinga Effect

Such a conclusion is not mine alone but is the experience of many in the academic disciplines of science, philosophy, and the like, which is a story we don't hear very often. For instance a few years ago, Quentin Smith deplored the way Christians were taking over philosophy departments in universities across America, warning his colleagues "that the field of philosophy is being 'de-secularized,'"[4] a movement that came about largely because of the work of one man—Alvin Plantinga, a theist (one who believes in God) and a Christian who is considered by many to be the greatest living philosopher.[5] Plantinga argues for the existence of God at such a high and convincing level that Smith says, "In philosophy, it became, almost overnight, 'academically respectable' to argue for theism."[6]

This trend is but one of a plethora of examples, including many occurring in the fields of history and science, where the walls that had separated faith from reason are crumbling. And this resurgence in the credibility of theism is not occurring as the product of naive ignorance but as the direct *by-product* of reason and intelligent exploration by top thinkers in their respective fields. So much so, in fact, that the sentiment of many now reflects not a Dawkins-like derision of Christianity but the opposite—a mockery of the misinformed tenets of atheism. Philosopher David Bentley Hart captures this fundamental shift well, saying, "I do not regard true philosophical atheism as an intellectually valid or even cogent position; in fact, I see it as a fundamentally irrational view of reality, which can be sustained only by a tragic absence of curiosity or a fervently resolute will to believe the absurd,"[7] concluding that atheism "must be regarded as a superstition."[8]

The Myth of the Church vs. Science

Contrary to the popular narrative of our time that posits faith, and the church specifically, against science, the reality is the church has never been its enemy, and any disagreements between the two, which have of course existed at times, have been gravely exaggerated. When atheists speak of the church's "persecution" of scientists, for instance, they tell stories about people being burned at the stake for scientific theories that displace God; about Galileo, Copernicus, and Giordano Bruno being tortured for holding "heliocentric" views of the universe. Thrilling dramas, but untrue. Historian David Lindberg, speaking about the medieval era wherein these supposed persecutions of science took place, writes, "There was no warfare between science and the church."[9] Historians agree the science *versus* religion story is a nineteenth-century fabrication.[10] The church did not persecute Copernicus or Bruno or Galileo for scientific theories. As historian

Thomas Kuhn points out, "Bruno was not executed for Copernicanism but for a series of *theological* heresies centering on his view of the trinity."[11] A gruesome reality but not one based on the conflict of religion and science. In fact, Galileo was a friend of the church for most of his life—a practicing Catholic. In 1616 he came to Rome and met with the pope multiple times. As time went on, he did become more critical of the church and its views. The church did persecute Galileo for a time, demanding he recant some of his heliocentric views, but he was never charged with heresy and placed in a dungeon, or tortured, as has become popular mythology among skeptics. He was sentenced to house arrest and then released into the custody of the archbishop of Siena, who housed him for five months in his palace. Galileo then returned to his villa in Florence, continuing his scientific work and even publishing before dying of natural causes in 1642.[12] The traditional picture of Galileo as a martyr of intellectual freedom is wrong. Any persecution he faced serves as an "'anomaly' historian Thomas Lessl writes, 'a momentary break in the otherwise harmonious relationship' that had existed between Christianity and science. Indeed there is no other example in history of the Catholic church condemning a scientific theory."[13]

Another modern example of this historical revisionism by skeptics is the story of the medieval church believing that the Bible taught a *flat earth*, and then reacting in outrage when science came along and proved that the Bible was wrong. This is simply not true. From the time of the ancient Greeks, people knew the earth was round. They observed that the hull of a ship sailing from shore disappears before the top of the mast, and would see the reflection of the earth on the moon during an eclipse.[14] They knew the earth was round. The so-called flat-earth conflict is simply part of nineteenth-century propaganda. And so, Oxford professor Alister McGrath concludes rightly, "The idea that science and religion are in perpetual conflict is no longer taken seriously by any major historian of science. . . . One of the last remaining bastions of atheism which survives only at the popular level—namely, the myth that an atheistic, fact-based science is permanently at war with a faith-based religion."[15]

The Garden of Christianity

It's not just that Christianity is not at war with science, but historians now acknowledge that "the thing we presently call Modern Science was [actually] conceived and born, and flourished in the matrix of Christian theism"[16] itself. Christian theology was the garden out of which modern science grew because it presented a world with distinct form, complexity, and design. Christianity challenges us to experiment with what we see, believing there is order and uniformity to the universe. No other worldview, philosophy, or religion of the ancient world offered the unique perspective Christianity did. This is why modern science didn't emerge prior to the seventeenth century. The foundational philosophical thinking in many cultures inhibited progress toward a scientific outlook:

- Animism deifies nature and claims there is a god in trees, water, and rocks. Such a worldview inhibited scientific investigation because one cannot subject deified objects to objective analysis.
- Buddhism says that the universe itself is an illusion; therefore, there's no point in doing any kind of scientific inquiry because all of your conclusions are going to be an illusion as well.
- Polytheistic religions explain events by citing the actions of the gods; thus there is no point in investigation. It is not necessary to ask why water bubbles up in the ocean because the answer is metaphysical: Poseidon is stirring it up.

Though several great civilizations of the ancient world (Mesopotamia, India, China, Egypt, Greece, Rome) developed some significant technological advancement, these societies lacked the philosophical framework necessary to birth the experimental enterprise known as modern science.[17] Christianity offered a number of fundamental variables that laid the groundwork for scientific inquiry. Kenneth Richard Samples cites ten such variables:

> (1) The physical universe is a distinct, objective reality, (2) the laws of nature exhibit order, patterns, and regularity, (3) the laws of nature are uniform throughout the physical universe, (4) the physical universe is intelligible, (5) the world is good, valuable, and worthy of careful study, (6) because the world is not divine and therefore not a proper object of worship, it can be an object of rational study, (7) human beings possess the ability to discover the universe's intelligibility, (8) the free agency of the Creator makes the empirical method necessary, (9) God encourages, even propels, science through his imperative to humans to take dominion over nature, and (10) the intellectual virtues essential to carrying out the scientific enterprise are part of God's moral law.[18]

From these, science drew on the biblical mandate to use reason to explore and to investigate.

In contrast, consider Judaism and Islam. They, for the most part, are worldviews that emphasize not reason so much as *jurisprudence*, the study and interpretation of law: in their case, the study of the Torah, the Mishnah, and the Qur'an. That is their rich history. But Christianity's history is in theology and philosophy. The heroes of Western Christianity are people who wrote and taught doctrine and creeds: the apostle Paul, Thomas Aquinas, Augustine, John Calvin, and Jonathan Edwards. The popular picture of Christians being scared of science and deep thinking has simply never been true. In fact, the

University itself is a twelfth-century *Christian* invention. Harvard, Princeton, Yale, Dartmouth, and Brown all began as Christian institutions.[19] Detailed scientific and literary analysis has not only been an emphasis of Christianity since its inception, but Christianity had a part in *their* birth.

Everyone Has Faith

But isn't faith blind belief? Isn't it something *religious* people have versus the rest of humanity, say atheists or agnostics, who believe in facts and evidence? Not at all. Everyone, even the most convinced atheist, has a faith position. Everyone believes in something and makes assumptions about reality that can't be proven even through science. One might say, "I don't believe in God. I follow where science and history lead us, objectively, without a predetermined agenda. I don't have faith in anything." Such a person is not being honest with himself. Everything we believe is filtered through a grid, or worldview, that has been adopted over time (constructed from a myriad of variables: where and when we were born, our family, our education, media, etc.). We are frequently unaware of these presuppositions, but we must see that all of them are, to a certain degree, *faith-based* conclusions rather than beliefs adopted through empirical proof.

For instance, I recently read a story about a nurse who was a follower of Jesus. The doctors with whom she worked were adamant that the hospital was a purely secular place—in other words, there was no room for "faith" to play a role in caring for patients. One night the staff was discussing a patient who was on life support. In debating whether to take him off or not, one doctor said to another, "Well, at least we know if we do that he won't be suffering anymore." Everyone in the group nodded in agreement. But the nurse wondered to herself, *How do you know this?* That belief (the idea that the person would not be suffering anymore once he was dead) in and of itself is a metaphysical statement about what the afterlife is like. The group of doctors was speaking out of a faith position for which they had no *proof.* How did they know that this person wouldn't be suffering *more* than he was now? They believed this wholeheartedly, but based on what evidence? It is a faith position. Everyone has one.

The problem is that many of us are blind to the everyday conclusions we draw without proof. Many of us are also blind to our own blindness. For instance, Harvard University biologist Richard Lewontin wrote an article published in the *New York Review of Books* in which he admitted that he and the scientists with whom he works prefer naturalistic and atheistic explanations for everything they study, which is itself no surprise. But what he wrote next was telling: the reason he prefers such explanations for things, he said, is because he and the scientific community "have a *prior* commitment . . . to materialism. It is not that the methods and institutions of science somehow compel us to accept a material explanation of the phenomenal world, but, on the contrary, that we are forced by our *a priori* adherence to material causes. . . . We cannot allow a Divine Foot in the door."[20] What Lewontin is admitting here is staggering. What drives his science is not *facts* but *philosophy.*[21] His faith position predetermines his science, not the other way around. That is how many in our modern world live, most without even knowing it or thinking about it.

Beyond that, however, philosophers point out the contradiction of the whole premise of purely naturalistic science as a philosophy, contending rightfully that the assumption that we can believe only what can be proven by scientific methods must be abandoned because that conviction itself cannot be proven by science. "The faith which the positivists displayed in natural science," philosopher Nicholas Wolterstorff argues, "was not itself arrived at scientifically,"[22] so shouldn't *it* be doubted?

The fact of the matter is we all have a faith position, an interpretation of reality that does not have *definitive* proof. This faith position exists for all of us to help frame reality and give life meaning—to answer our deepest questions regarding identity, environment, origins, and purpose. In their book *The Transforming Vision*, Brian Walsh and J. Richard Middleton point this out, saying that everyone has a worldview whether they realize it or not, and that it is the way we answer four basic questions:

> (1) *Who am I?* Or, what are the nature, task and purposes of human beings? (2) *Where am I?* Or, what is the nature of the world and universe I live in? (3) *What's wrong?* Or, what is the basic problem or obstacle that keeps me from attaining fulfillment? In other words, how do I understand evil? And (4) *What is the remedy?* Or, how is it possible to overcome this hindrance to my fulfillment? In other words, how do I find salvation?[23]

We all have arrived at answers to these questions, even if many of us can't pinpoint the influences that came together to form our beliefs. Every construct of reality answers these questions differently (compare how an atheist would answer them versus how a Buddhist would, for instance), but never, Walsh and Middleton say, are the answers "merely a vision *of* life. [But] always a vision *for* life as well."[24] And that is the tricky part. If we answer these big questions with an eye to the latter first, versus the former, we may influence what kind of truth we allow in.

Alternate Beliefs

Skepticism is itself a set of narrow-minded and dogmatic *beliefs*, a commitment to a lifestyle of consistent doubt. In choosing not to commit to any one belief about spiritual or ultimate things, skeptics feel that they are being open minded, but miss the inherent irony that to *not* commit to one set of beliefs about spiritual matters *is* itself a choice to commit to a set of beliefs about spiritual matters.[25] The problem is that people often lack the self-awareness to recognize this contradiction. Secularism is a set of alternative doctrines and beliefs to theism, beliefs that have not been proven and substantiated enough to be taught as the *only* or exclusive way to think as a human being. Some thinkers go as far as to believe, as Sam Harris once wrote, that "Atheism is not a philosophy; [nor] even a view of the world; it is simply an admission of the obvious."[26] I have encountered this perspective a thousand times in talking to atheists and agnostics in my life and have done my best to point out how naive and blind it is.

In his book *The Reason for God*, Timothy Keller points out that doubts are simply a set of *alternate beliefs*. "You cannot doubt un-provable Christian Belief A," he wrote, "except from a position of faith in un-provable non-Christian Belief B."[27] Take, for instance, the skeptical doubt that Jesus Christ really rose from the dead. Why do people reject this? Because they already hold a prior belief that when people die there is no coming back from the dead. This reflects the thinking that came out of the seventeenth-century Enlightenment, and continues to be the script most of us read from the cradle to the grave in the Western world. But a belief in the finality of death and a belief that nothing can defy the laws of nature are both *unprovable* conclusions.

Interestingly, many non-Christian scholars believe miracles such as the resurrection *are* possible given certain recent scientific discoveries. For instance, the science of quantum mechanics has shown that some aspects of Newtonian physics, which have informed naturalistic assumptions for years, are fundamentally misguided. It turns out the universe is far more complex (and connected) than we once thought. Science itself has evolved and gone beyond the *observational* evidences of Newton and Darwin. The objection to supernatural activity has been shown to come "from a rigid application of the modern world-view's definition of reality . . . [which] is but one of a large number of humanly constructed maps of reality . . . impressive because of the degree of control it has given us; but it is no more an absolute map of reality than any of the previous maps."[28] New developments in science show that the old constructs are ill informed. This alone should cause any skeptic to be careful when making dogmatic statements about the impossibility of miracles. Concluding that miracles *can't* happen is not a neutral point of view. As New Testament scholar Craig Keener has pointed out, "To rule out even asking questions about divine activity is not neutral, but . . . an act of cultural hegemony."[29] In other words, it is an accepted belief informed by powerful Western institutions that shape how we all think every day.

We must all admit we have faith-commitments, and we are all people of faith. The real question is: What is the content of my set of beliefs? And flowing from that: What is that content *based on*? And finally: Is my faith position the *most valid* to hold if I were to carefully examine all the best available evidence?

Evolution and Our Cognitive Faculties

I talk to many people who say, "The reason I reject Christianity is because I already believe in evolution," but they can't readily explain why they have adopted such a framework, or faith-position, even though it lacks large amounts of evidence to support some of its central tenants (a first cause, the explanation for the existence of the human eye, the problem of the Cambrian explosion,[30] missing links in the fossil record, etc.). For instance, noted Harvard paleontologist and atheist Stephen Jay Gould admits, "The extreme rarity of transitional forms in the fossil record persists as the trade secret of paleontology. The evolutionary trees that adorn our textbooks have data only at the tips and nodes of their branches; the rest is inference."[31] He admits that the fossil record does not show species gradually transforming from one kind to another, but each kind appears all at once and fully formed.

Much has been written about these holes in evolutionary theory, which should collectively cause us to at least be cautious before accepting the worldview uncritically and carte blanche. Darwin himself cited the holes as "the most obvious and gravest objection, which can be urged against my theory."[32] All well documented and legitimate, however, there is another fundamental weakness in evolutionary theory worth exploring, which is immediately relevant to our study and is often not discussed in popular debates, and it comes from the sphere of *philosophy*. Explanations for life and origins that preclude God have long been frustrated when trying to explain where and why certain *cognitive developments* originated in humans. For instance, how did creatures "with the evolved physical and cognitive capabilities of contemporary humans come to create the vast body of scientific knowledge that now exists, including evolutionary theory itself?"[33] We used our brains, of course (our cognitive faculties and rational thought). And this is the challenge for evolution, because if evolution is true, everything, *including our minds* (and what they conclude) requires a naturalistic explanation. And that's a problem.

Evolution argues that what presently exists in us, whether a physical trait or emotional, is nothing more than what was and continues to be *useful for survival*, not what is necessarily *true*. Yet people believe in God, for instance, though belief in God is not *necessary* for survival. In fact, "religion seems useless from an evolutionary point of view. It costs time and money, and it induces its members to make sacrifices that undermine their well-being for the benefit of others, who are sometimes total strangers."[34]

So how did belief in God survive? The skeptic says, "It survived as an *untrue belief* that does not correlate to reality. It is simply about our comfort in the face of suffering, etc. We have fooled ourselves into believing in a metaphysical reality and have called it *God*. Our cognitive faculties are telling us to believe something that isn't true." Naturalists celebrate this explanation for the existence of a God-consciousness, but it doesn't answer the question, because *if we can't trust our belief-forming faculties to tell us the truth, then why would we trust them to tell us the truth about anything, including evolution itself!* All knowledge depends on the validity of reasoning. If certainty "is merely a feeling in our own minds and not a genuine insight into realities beyond them . . . then we can have no knowledge. . . . Unless human reasoning is valid no science can be true."[35] Thus, a strict naturalism refutes itself because, "If my mental processes are determined wholly by the motions of atoms in my brain, I have no reason to suppose that my beliefs are true . . . and hence I have no reason for supposing my brain to be composed of atoms."[36] And so, the whole idea that we are *rational* creatures at all goes against the idea of us being products of evolution. Given unguided evolution, it is not likely creatures such as you and I would ever develop *true* beliefs. We would only develop beliefs that helped us survive. And if that is true, then we have a reason not to doubt only our belief in *God* but to doubt our belief in everything, including naturalism and evolution itself! All of which is a weakness philosophers have pointed out for years.

"Atheists have a reason to doubt whether evolution would result in cognitive faculties that produce mostly true beliefs," Mitch Stokes argues. "And if so, then they have reason to withhold judgment on the reliability of their cognitive faculties . . . [and] this ignorance would, if atheists are consistent, spread to all of their other beliefs, including atheism and evolution. . . . [A]theists who believe the standard evolutionary story must reserve judgment about whether any of their beliefs produced by these faculties are true. . . . Believing in unguided evolution comes built in with its very own reason not to believe it."[37]

Alvin Plantinga concludes the same thing, arguing that it "is improbable, given naturalism and evolution, that our cognitive faculties are reliable. It is improbable that they provide us with . . . true beliefs over false."[38] This is a problem for the atheist because our cognitive faculties have produced our beliefs in evolution itself, and the entire scientific method. In other words, "Atheistic man uses his mind to create a worldview that nullifies the use of his mind."[39] Charles Darwin himself recognized this problem and feared it when he wrote hauntingly: "Within me the horrid doubt always arises whether the convictions of a man's mind, which has been developed from the mind of lower animals, are of any value or at all trustworthy."[40] The problem being, of course, that Darwin's theory itself was the conviction of man's mind, and thus by his own logic, he couldn't trust it.

The Myth of the Secular Society

A generation ago people believed that the deeper science delved into the world (via cosmology, biology, and other disciplines), the more secularized society would become. In other words, the more educated we became, the less likely people would be to believe in God. The reality, however, is proving just the opposite. In fact, the growing trend toward belief in God in academia has given rise to talk of the "myth of the secular society."[41] In his book *A Primer on Postmodernism*, Stanley Grenz points out that if you watch the original *Star Trek* series, created in the 1960s, there is very little religion in its portrayal of the future. The underlying message, which was the assumption of modernity, was that humanity would progress to a point of not believing in God. So, as the crew on the *Starship Enterprise* cruises the galaxies, with few exceptions, spirituality is largely absent. However, if you watch *Star Trek: The Next Generation*, created in the 1980s and 1990s, things are vastly different. People *are* religious and spiritual, and even some members of the crew are.[42] What happened in the span of twenty years?

As science delved more deeply into the workings of the universe, people discovered rational, logical reasons to believe in the existence of God. As Allan Rex Sandage, said to be the greatest observational cosmologist of all time, has said: "It is my science that drove me to the conclusion that the world is much more complicated than can be explained by science."[43] Theologian Lesslie Newbigin agrees, pointing out that statistically "the correlation between academic life and irreligion is much higher in the social sciences and the humanities than it is among the natural sciences—physics, chemistry, and biology. Atomic physicists are much more likely to believe in God than sociologists."[44]

The NOMA Principle

Science has come to terms with the fact that nothing it deduces about reality can really disprove the existence of God. Why? Science studies the natural, *physical* world. But the existence of God is what is called a metaphysical question (the word *meta* is the Greek word meaning "after" or "beyond"). God is a being found beyond the physical world, thus the question of his existence is beyond what physics can evaluate. Whatever power atheists think lies in science, it by itself can't speak to the question of God's nonexistence. Harvard professor Stephen Jay Gould, the most celebrated atheist, evolutionary biologist, paleontologist, and historian of science of the last generation, understood this fact deeply, arguing that "Nature just is" and "we cannot use nature for our moral instruction or for answering any question within the magisterium of religion. . . . To say it for my colleagues and for the umpteenth millionth time, science simply cannot, by its legitimate methods, adjudicate the issue of God's possible superintendence of nature. We neither affirm nor deny it. We simply cannot comment on it as scientists."[45]

Gould went on to argue for what he called the NOMA principle, the idea that science and the question of God's existence are "non-overlapping magisterial authorities [NOMA]." In other words, one can't use physics to prove a metaphysical being *doesn't* exist. But it could, as we have seen, be helpful in giving us evidence that he does exist. This is contrary to modern mythology, which teaches that physics and science are enemies to faith.

So what if science actually points humanity *to* God instead of disproving his existence? In Romans 1, Paul wrote: God's "invisible attributes . . . have been clearly perceived, ever since the creation of the world, in the things that have been made" (v. 20). In other words, the Bible teaches that science is not the enemy of faith but simply one of the means by which we look into nature and learn about God. God constantly woos us through what he made—stars, trees, and microorganisms. He constantly preaches at us, saying, "I want to know you. Here I am."

Paul says that the issue we have is not the *lack* of evidence but the suppression of it. "For although they knew God," Paul says, "they did not honor him as God or give thanks to him, but they became futile in their thinking, and their foolish hearts were darkened" (Romans 1:21). The problem is not that the evidence isn't there; it's that we overlook the signposts because we would rather believe something else.

If that describes you, I hope that you are willing to consider that God has not given up on trying to get your attention. When the sun comes up tomorrow morning, it isn't only because of the earth's rotation, but because God is love, and behind all the wonderful beauty of scientific study of this world, he wants us to discover the God who made it.

CHAPTER 2

The Problem of
GOD'S
EXISTENCE

*Frodo began to feel restless, and the old paths
seemed too well-trodden. He looked at maps, and
wondered what lay beyond their edges: maps made
in the Shire showed mostly white spaces beyond its
borders.*

J. R. R. TOLKIEN, THE LORD OF THE RINGS

When I was a kid, I used to get pulled behind my friend's bicycle on Rollerblades. I would hold on to a long rope tied to his bike seat, and he would pull me around the neighborhood. My mother once saw us doing this and said, "I want you to stop. You are going to get hurt." My reply? "How do you know I will get hurt?" *Where is the evidence?* Unless I saw some, I refused to believe her premise. I continued to be pulled behind the bike, day after day, until the bright midsummer afternoon I came swinging around a corner and there in front of me was a car driving toward me full speed. I threw myself flat on the ground, skidded across the asphalt, and came to a stop directly underneath the car. My back and legs were ripped up, and it took weeks until the pain of all the cuts and bruises subsided. As I laid there in pain on the asphalt, one thought hit me: *evidence.* Finally, I had it firsthand and was willing to believe. I've always been that way; I still am.

The debate about the existence of God centers on the question of evidence. Things we now take for granted as true (e.g., gravity) were all at one time hypotheses that needed proof/explanation before the scientific community and the general public accepted them as fact. If someone proposes an idea to us, we consider its validity based on the evidence to support it. We then take that evidence and deduce certain things about the world, even if it causes us to rethink views we previously held. Finally, we change the way we live in light of that new belief. This is foundational to life and progress.

If we are going to believe in God, then we must ask what the evidence is for his existence. What proofs and clues are there that an all-powerful, eternal, infinite being actually exists? If the evidence is there, we must have the courage to rethink what we may have previously believed and then change our lives accordingly. And if it isn't, then we must look that square in the face and be willing to abandon belief in God. So, are there evidences of his existence? Modern science and philosophy overwhelmingly say yes. Alvin Plantinga points out that there are "two dozen (or so)" philosophical arguments for God's existence. For the sake of our exploration, we will boil down the evidences to two broad categories that philosopher Immanuel Kant (1724–1804) named "the moral law within and the starry hosts above."[46] Or, as Plato framed it, "There are two things that lead men to believe in God: the argument from the existence of the soul, and the argument from the order of the motion of the stars" (Plato *Laws* 12:966e). In other words, anthropology and cosmology. People and the universe. Together they will help us realize that it may be *more* rational to believe that God exists than that he does not.

The Evidence of Morality

First, the evidence that comes from people, or the soul, as Kant put it. C. S. Lewis, an Oxford professor and philosopher, was a skeptical atheist most of his life. He opens his book *Mere Christianity* by pointing out why he began to believe in God in the first place—the existence of morality. "Every one has heard people quarrelling," he says,

> They say things like this: "How'd you like it if anyone did the same to you?"—"That's my seat, I was there first"—"Leave him alone, he isn't doing you any harm"—"Why should you shove in first?"—"Give me a bit of your orange, I gave you a bit of mine"—"Come on, you promised." People say things like that every day, educated people as well as uneducated, and children as well as grown-ups. Now what interests me about all these remarks is that the man who makes them is not merely saying that the other man's behavior does not happen to please him. He is appealing to some kind of standard of behavior, which he expects the other man to know about. . . . It looks, in fact, very much as if both parties had in mind some kind of Law or Rule of fair play or decent behavior or morality or whatever you like to call it, about which they really agreed.[47]

I watch my kids and their friends playing together every day, and from my observations I've deduced that human beings are exactly the way Lewis describes. "You got to sleep with Mom and Dad last night, so I get to sleep with them tonight!" my seven-year-old says. "It's my turn on the trampoline, you had your turn!" the youngest cries. They're constantly appealing to an unspoken, yet agreed upon, understanding of the universe—that there is an objective standard of fair and that we should follow *rules*. But who told them about these rules? Lewis's point is that no one really did, nor did anyone have to.

They are predisposed to believe them. This is built within them, and of course, this does not just pertain to children, but to all of us.

Recently my family and I were at the Seattle zoo and had lined up at a dinosaur exhibit so my kids could climb up on a large plastic Stegosaurus and get a picture taken on it. We got to the front of the line and were just about to walk up to the dinosaur when a woman and her family cut right in front of us. My wife stared daggers at the woman and demanded, "Excuse me, what are you doing?" The woman snapped back, "What did you say to me?" as her children romped on top of the dinosaur's head. "You just cut in front of us. That's what I said," my wife retorted. "I didn't cut in front of you," the woman said, pushing out her hip. By this point, all of our kids were up on the Stegosaurus yelling at each other, the wives were yelling at each other, and the other dad and I were just standing there looking at each other. "Hey," I said. That's all I could muster.

There's a moral code that says, "Don't cut in front of me." And we all agree on it. We all know it's wrong to cut in line. But *where* did we get this transcendent view of morality that spans across cultures and time? When did we all agree on these foundational morals? Christianity says that they came from God. In order to have a moral law, you need a moral law *giver*. Someone who decided cutting in line is wrong and hardwired it into us as human beings—a reality that separates us from the animals.

Skeptics push against this explanation and say that morals *do not* transcend culture but are merely a product of it. In other words, what one person believes about right and wrong is true for her but not necessarily for everyone, and thus we should not impose our morals on other individuals or cultures. I understand where this sentiment comes from, and I believed it with all my heart for many years. But over time I came to see that philosophically—and practically—this idea doesn't make any sense and is logically bankrupt.

When a person embraces this relativistic understanding of morality, they no longer have a leg to stand on. You can't get angry when somebody cuts you off; you have no reason to scream at them. You can't say one view on abortion is right over another or that polluting the environment is *wrong*. The best you can say is that you don't happen to agree with it. But logically, it is not clear why a moral relativist should care what anyone else believes.

But, of course, we all know this is wrong. We feel like we should care. We *know* it's wrong to cut people off. We know it's wrong to drop napalm on babies, to hate someone because of his or her race, or to murder innocent women and children. Even if you travel to a culture that takes joy in those things, you would still deem them *wrong*, would you not? But why? Lewis and Kant say because there is a law, or rule, that transcends our cultural values and our human experiences. There is an absolute right and wrong in the universe.

WHAT IF THEY ATE YOUR SISTER?

Many skeptics push against the idea that a moral law is evidence for the existence of God. Their solution is to say that our moral values are not objective at all but come from our evolutionary development. In other words, they are socially constructed, a product of our culture and upbringing. A commitment to this view of morality, however, forces people into a strange corner. For instance, I used to work at a Michaels arts-and-crafts store in college, and one of my coworkers was an ardent and articulate atheist. He and I would often get into discussions about God and Christianity while working at the cash register or hanging wreaths or putting away googly eyes. One day he said to me, "I believe all morality is culturally constructed, relative, a product of our evolution, and that it's wrong for our Western ideals to be projected onto other cultures." To test how committed he was to this belief, I asked him: "If we went into a village in the middle of a jungle somewhere, and we brought your sister along, and they captured her, tied her up, tortured her, and then ate her alive because that's what their culture believed in, how would you feel about that? What would your response be? If you are true to your worldview, you could not say they had done something decisively *wrong*. You could only say they did something *you* didn't like but that is nonetheless morally acceptable."

He sat there for a minute or so weighing his options. And then he looked at me and said, "As much as it would hurt me to say it, I would *not say* they did something wrong, only something I personally disagreed with." This is the fundamental problem with moral relativism and why it is a *less rational* option to adopt into a larger framework of life and society as a whole. It is not sustainable as a way to order society and is self-contradicting at its core. Despite what my friend said that day, I know he was lying to me. Moral relativists still care. We all care.

In the 1960s and 1970s, the inconsistency of moral relativism was on full display. In one breath, that generation, committed as they were to a sexual revolution, was saying, "No one is going to tell me what I can do with my body. I'll do whatever I want with it! Morality is relative to the person who concludes it. Stop trying to impose your old-fashioned, traditional views of sex on me!" And yet in the next breath, they were protesting the Vietnam war which they saw as morally *unjust* and, in so doing, were imposing *their* views on everyone else, whether others wanted to hear them or not. But who were they to decide that the war was immoral and impose their views on the government? When you remove objective morality from the picture, can't those in power kill whomever they deem an enemy? What absolute moral law were the protestors citing to say otherwise? By its own ethics the "flower power" of the 1960s and 1970s should never have tried to impose its moral views on others.

But they did. So where did they get their convictions of what "just" and "unjust" wars are? Where did the concept of an "unjust" war come from anyway? It doesn't make sense unless there really is an objective measure to compare our lives against. That's the point of the moral law. We *do* believe in right and wrong. We believe hurting a child is wrong. We believe raping and pillaging the environment is wrong. We believe all races should be equal. That there is such a thing called *justice* that tells us mercy is better than hate. That loyalty is a virtue, and that there is evil in the world. All of these convictions give meaning to our lives, but if there is no absolute right and wrong, all of them go away; they are but a mirage. Meaningless. Weightless. Worth abandoning with every other construct of modernity. Those are the stakes.

WHAT DAWKINS GETS WRONG

Even if you don't accept that objective moral values exist, let's assume for a moment that they do. What does that tell us about the universe in which we live? We can observe that humans appear to be wired with a sense of right and wrong. The apostle Paul contends as much in his letter to the Romans: "For when Gentiles, who do not have the law, by nature do what the law requires . . . [t]hey show that the work of the law is written on their hearts, while their conscience also bears witness" (Romans 2:14–15). By saying that the law is "written," Paul is implying that there is a writer. And that rings true not only as a biblical teaching but experientially in our lives.

It is important to note that I am not saying that belief in, or agreement with, a certain set of morals is necessary for them to exist. This is a point often misunderstood by skeptics. In *The God Delusion*, for instance, Richard Dawkins cites the thought experiments of Harvard biologist Marc Hauser in which Hauser proposes hypothetical scenarios about five people being saved from being hit by a train by the sacrificial death of one fat man, and five people in a hospital being saved by harvesting the organs of one healthy man in the waiting room, pointing out that 97 percent of people agree that it is immoral to kill the fat man and the healthy man in the hospital in order to save the many. He says the main conclusion of Hauser's study "was that there was no statistically significant difference between atheists and religious believers in making these judgments. This seems compatible with the view, which I and many others hold, that we do not need God in order to be good—or evil."[48] What Dawkins fails to understand is that Christians agree that you do not need to believe in God to be good or to *want* to be good. The study simply proves what Christianity actually proposes: that every person has what the apostle Paul calls "a law" written in their hearts, *whether they believe in God or not*. As John Calvin said: "There is no nation so lost to every thing human, that it does not keep within the limits of some laws. . . . Some notions of justice and rectitude . . . as they could not otherwise distinguish between vice and virtue."[49] Why then do human beings, and cultures, disagree with one another on what is vice and virtue at times? Why does a village believe in eating people if it's objectively wrong? Because, like mathematics, people sometimes get their answers wrong, but that doesn't mean the multiplication table isn't right or that it doesn't exist. Morals are not a matter of mere taste or opinion any more than math equations. Human beings may not get the moral math problem correct, but that doesn't change the fact that there really is a right answer.

IS THERE AN EVOLUTIONARY EXPLANATION?

The modern tendency is to argue that there is no objective moral law in the universe, that "whatever values we do have as a species, can be explained *without God*, because they came about through the process of evolution." There are many circumstances in life where we ensure our own survival by acting favorably toward others, skeptics say, not because of some kind of altruism but for selfish gain. Loving one's neighbor, for instance: the Darwinian explanation is that we want to ensure our own genes continue on through our children, thus we treat them favorably—we act with "reciprocal altruism" where we do good to others to benefit our selves.[50]

These moral urges were programmed into our brains "in ancestral times when we lived in small and stable bands like baboons," when we had the opportunity to be good "only towards close kin and potential reciprocators."[51] Any notion of absolute *good* is what Dawkins calls a "misfiring—a precious mistake."[52] The problem with this explanation for good, as many have pointed out, is if we inherit our morality from genes wherein survival is the utmost consideration, many of our modern moral constructs are unexplainable and even *counterproductive*. For instance, why would laying down your life for people you have never met be considered heroic rather than stupid? There is no good evolutionary explanation for why we would ever come to adopt many of the more selfless principles we have come to value as a species. As Timothy Keller points out: "For evolutionary purposes hostility to all people outside one's group should be . . . widely considered moral and right behavior. Yet, today we believe that sacrificing time, money, emotion, and even life—especially for someone 'not of our kind' or tribe—is *right*."[53] If we see a stranger fall in a river, for instance, we jump in after them or feel guilty for not doing so. Most people will feel this obligation; the question is: "How could that trait have come down by a process of natural selection? Such people would have been less likely to survive and pass on their genes."[54]

Not only do naturalistic explanations for the origins of morality and consciousness fall short, but they also have embedded in them ghastly moral trajectories. According to natural selection, there are, for instance, races within the human species that are deemed as more advanced than others and that, therefore, should be *favored* over others. This is illustrated by the full (and less commonly referenced) title of Darwin's most popular work *On the Origin of Species by Means of Natural Selection, or the Preservation of Favoured Races in the Struggle for Life*. Darwin's explanation of origins contains within it a prejudice against what he calls "un-favored races," for example, the mentally challenged, whom, he contended, should not be allowed to marry or reproduce because they will hinder our progress as a species: "Man scans with scrupulous care the character and pedigree of his horses, cattle, and dogs before he matches them," he says, "but when he comes to his own marriage he rarely, or never, takes any such care. . . . Both sexes ought to refrain from marriage if they are in any marked degree inferior in body or mind."[55]

While this idea seems staggering to us in the modern world, this kind of thinking was quite popular in the 1920s and 1930s as many progressives began to advocate for exactly these kinds of policies. It was perfectly normal for popular thinkers, such as J. B. S. Haldane, to contend for eugenics—the belief in the possibility of improving the quality of the human species by discouraging reproduction by persons having genetic defects or inheritable undesirable traits—since it was understood that this is where naturalistic Darwinian science leads. Haldane argued for "the optimization of the human gene pool by preventing certain types of people from breeding."[56] This was an attitude grounded in the best science of the time and with the best motivation—to ensure the survival and flourishing of the human race in a dog-eat-dog world. Bertrand Russell followed Haldane in his *Marriage and Morals* (1929), in which he contended for a compulsory sterilization of the mentally deficient, asserting that the State should be empowered to forcibly sterilize all those regarded as "mentally deficient" by appropriate experts. By reducing the number of "idiots, imbeciles, and feeble-minded," he said, society would benefit to a degree that outweighs any dangers of sterilization's misuse.[57]

These were widely held views among the British and American intellectually elite in the period between the two World Wars—the era of the rise of scientism as a worldview. During these years there were three International Eugenics Congresses (London 1912, New York 1921, New York 1932) that argued for "birth selection" and for the genetic elimination of those who were deemed unfit.[58] Similarly, Adolf Hitler took Darwinism to its natural conclusion. In his 1925 book *Mein Kampf* he wrote: "If nature does not wish that weaker individuals should mate with the stronger, she wishes even less that a superior race should intermingle with an inferior one; because in such cases all her efforts, throughout hundreds of thousands of years, to establish an evolutionary higher stage of being, may thus be rendered futile. . . . He who does not wish to fight in this world, where permanent struggle is the law of life, has not the right to exist."[59]

Why don't we adopt this way of thinking? Why not take a worldview like naturalism all the way to its intended end as these thinkers did? Why not pick and choose which parts we like and which parts we don't? The very fact that something within us is repelled by racism, sexism, and unequal treatment of the poor and disabled begs the question that such convictions would have to come from *somewhere*, for they are not *natural*. Naturalism by itself would lead us to conclusions similar to Haldane and Russell, would it not? The existence of such contrary-to-nature convictions is a very strong evidence for the existence of God—a mind who placed within us a moral law, which includes the love of all people and the passion to even lay down our very lives for perfect strangers when necessary, knowing full well we personally may not benefit at all. Such is what it means to have the heart of God stitched into our being.

The Evidence of Cosmology

The second evidence of God's existence we will explore comes from the world of cosmology—the "starry hosts above" as Kant called them. From the times of Aristotle, Plato, and Aquinas, a concept known as "contingency" has been a very important part of science. The idea is that if something *begins* to exist, its existence is dependent on something outside of it that preexisted it, *causing* it to come into being. You are sitting where you are right now reading this book, but you didn't *always* exist. Your existence is contingent up your parents—existing, meeting, falling in love, lighting some candles one night . . . you get the picture. Everything that *begins to* exist has to have a cause; on this, scientists and philosophers—both atheists and theists—agree. David Hume, the eighteenth-century Scottish skeptic, even admitted, "I never asserted such an absurd proposition that anything might arise without a cause."[60] So what is the noncontingent, infinite, uncaused *something* that has always existed, that had no beginning? For most of history the atheist and agnostic response has been simple: "You don't need God to start the universe; the noncontingent eternal thing is *the universe itself.*" This is precisely how most people, even today, answer the question of origins. This was always difficult to dispute, because there was little evidence to the contrary—until 1929 that is, when Edwin Hubble made what has been called the greatest scientific discovery of the twentieth century. He discovered that the universe itself actually *began* to exist.

THE BIG BANG

Working out of his laboratory in California, Hubble looked through his 100-inch telescope farther than anyone had ever looked into space and observed something incredible. He saw that galaxies were moving rapidly away from each other in a universe vaster than anyone had ever imagined. And as the galaxies moved away from each other, the universe—and space itself—was getting bigger. Further scientific study concluded that the galaxies were moving apart because they were once flung apart by a massive explosion. By measuring the speed and distances of the galaxies' movement away from one another, Hubble was able to deduce what modern cosmology now confirms: all galaxies, stars, planets, energy, and matter had a common point of origin, approximately fifteen billion years ago, when all the mass in the universe was compressed smaller than a single atom. Our universe, he discovered, came into existence with a single cosmic explosion—the big bang:

> The number of stars involved in this galactic dispersal suggested an astoundingly vast universe. . . . Some galaxies were millions of light years away. . . . Hubble noticed that planets and entire galaxies were hurtling away from one another at fantastic speeds. Moreover, space itself seemed to be getting bigger. The universe was not expanding into background space. . . . Incredibly, space itself was expanding along with the universe. Scientists realized right away that the galaxies were not flying apart because of some mysterious force thrusting them away from each other. Rather, they were moving apart because they were once flung apart by a primeval explosion.[61]

According to the big bang theory, all space, matter, energy, even time itself, began to exist at a point in the past. This is important to understand, as people often think that big bang cosmology says that fifteen billion years ago matter and galaxies started receding from one another into existing time and space. But the reality is that the galaxies themselves are actually at rest in space. They recede from one another because *space itself is expanding.*[62]

In addition to the expansion of space itself, the *second law of thermodynamics,* which tells us that the energy in the universe is decreasing, also hints at the finite nature of the universe because it tells us that the energy in the universe is limited and dying. The universe is like a flashlight running on batteries. If it were eternal, it would have already run out of energy.[63] Simple science.

The big bang explanation of the origin of the universe is now accepted in all major fields of science. How that acceptance came about, however, illustrates how easy it is for us to deny evidence that points toward conclusions with which we are uncomfortable. Big bang cosmology was originally rejected by the scientific community—not because of some flaw with its data—but because, as associate professor of physics at Auburn University J–M Wersinger points out, it seemed to "give in to the Judeo-Christian idea of a beginning of the world, [and] it also seemed to have to call for an act of supernatural creation. . . . It took time, observational evidence, and careful verification of predictions made by the Big Bang model to convince the scientific community to accept the idea of a cosmic genesis . . . a successful model that imposed itself on a reluctant scientific community."[64]

Let's think about that reluctance for a moment. The observable beginnings of the universe and its limited energy are significant problems if one wants to argue that the universe is the uncaused, eternal something that has always existed. That's why many scientists were reluctant to accept the idea of a big bang. It did not match what they wanted to believe. But science has now concluded that the universe is not the uncaused source of all that exists because the universe itself has a birthday. It *began to exist* fifteen billion years ago, and whatever begins to exist has a cause. Again, this pushes us back to the question of what caused the big bang. What's a logical answer to that question? The logical explanation is that the cause is something outside the material universe. In other words, the cause must be *mind*, not matter, because matter itself began to exist at the big bang. What led to the big bang? Something immaterial that transcends the universe. That's where the evidence points us. And that's exactly what Christianity has been claiming from the beginning.

NOBODY TIMES NOTHING EQUALS EVERYTHING?

God seems to have stitched this evidence into history so that we could find it, follow the evidence wherever it leads us, and thus find him.

But that doesn't mean we all follow the evidence. Many people have attempted to deny that this cosmological evidence leads to God. There have now been almost ninety years of speculation since the Hubble discovery, and skeptics have produced different theories, and continue to work on more, about why the big bang doesn't necessitate a cause outside of itself. The most predominant theory is called the "nothing hypothesis." It's not hard to grasp. It goes like this. What caused the big bang? Nothing. Did it happen? Yes. What caused it? Nothing. It just happened.

Assuming we all want to be rational, reasonable people who use our minds and follow evidence wherever it leads us, it doesn't take a genius to realize that this explanation doesn't work scientifically, philosophically, or experientially. One night recently, I was awakened by our house alarm. I jumped out of bed and went running downstairs to see if someone had broken into our house. No one was there, so I shut off the alarm and went back upstairs. I looked at my wife and asked, "What caused the alarm to go off?" Her eyes still closed, she said, "Nothing. Now come back to bed." Now, you and I both know that she was being irrational at that moment. Nothing? Really?

Saying "nothing" doesn't work. That's what tired people say when they just want you to shut up and go back to sleep. It's a non-explanation. What she meant was that we likely weren't going to figure it out that night; it may have been a problem with the wiring or the phone line, one of the kids' windows popped open—who knows. The bottom line is this: it wasn't nothing. Something caused the alarm to go off that night.

So what is a rational, scientific, and theologically compelling equation to build our life on? Would you at least consider the possibility that a mind that transcends all space, time, and matter, created all things in a moment? My argument is that "it's better than nothing." This event, however it happened, is what Genesis calls "the beginning" (Genesis 1:1). God created the universe, starting with light and moving from there (see Genesis 1:3). As the astrophysicist Robert Jastrow says in his book *God and the Astronomers*, "Now we see how the astronomical evidence leads to a biblical view of the origin of the world. The details differ, but the essential elements and the astronomical and biblical accounts of Genesis are the same; the chain of events leading to man commenced suddenly and sharply at a definite moment in time, in a flash of light and energy."[65]

So,

> Whatever *begins* to exist has a cause.
>
> The universe began to exist.
>
> Therefore, the universe had a cause.

The award-winning scientist who mapped the human genome, Francis Collins, agrees: "The Big Bang cries out for a divine explanation," he says. "It forces the conclusion that nature had a defined beginning. I cannot see how nature could have created itself. Only a supernatural force that is outside of space and time could have done that."[66]

The Evidence of Design

The final evidence we will consider for the existence of God is that of the *design of the universe*. There is a strange and mysterious design to the cosmos, an anti-randomness, that points strongly to a designer who created and crafted the world with very intentional precision and balance. While much can be said about this, we will limit our discussion to two disciplines within human science: biology and astronomy. You can think of these as the microscope and the telescope, and both of them point us to a balancer, sustainer, and designer. Some will look at the evidence of this design and reject it as chance or luck. In my estimation, it takes a leap and measure of faith I can't justify to do that.

BIOLOGY

Scientists tell us that when one looks at the DNA of any living organism, it is packed with coherent and information-filled code. Not random but intelligent, structured information. An amoeba, for instance, has enough structured and meaningful data to fill thirty encyclopedias![67] This is such a profound and amazing evidence for the existence of an intelligent mind that it is what Francis Collins calls "the language of God." He points out that a genetic code is built into every living organism, down to the level of a single strand of DNA. Think about the complexity involved in this. Thirty encyclopedias of information packed into an amoeba, an organism composed of a *single* cell. The step toward God, an intelligent designer of the code, is not a very large leap of faith. When we observe the presence of intelligible, structured, coherent language or communication, we typically assume it is the creation of an intelligent life/mind.

ASTRONOMY

What about the evidence from the stars? The famous philosopher William Paley (1743–1805) pointed out that if you were walking along the beach and came across a piece of wood, you might say, "This must have chipped off a tree and ended up here—that is its origin." But if you continued on and found a watch, with all the complexity of its moving parts and pieces, you would probably deduce that someone had designed it—not that it had been produced over time by accident! Paley says that the same logic is true regarding the design of our universe.

There is something scholars call the anthropic principle, which has been called the "the most powerful argument for the existence of God."[68] This principle suggests that the universe is fine-tuned. The mathematical chances of our universe ever coming into existence are so tiny that they are at the level of the miraculous. But that's not all. The chances that all the life-permitting variables needed to line up perfectly to birth our universe within such a specific range are so low that mathematicians tell us they cry out for an explanation. The improbability of the existence of our universe begs us to wonder how it exists at all.

Scholars tells us that the chance of our universe coming into existence is one chance in 10^{138}. To put this into context, consider that 10^{17} is our best estimate of the number of seconds in the entire history of the universe, and 10^{70} is the number of atoms in the entire universe.[69] So the probability of the universe coming into existence in the way it has, fine-tuned for human life, is impossible. Astrophysicists tell us that there were around 122 variables that would have had to be lined up in precise values in order for our universe to come into existence, and if any of those was off by even one part in a million millionth "[m]atter would not have been able to coalesce. There would have been no galaxies, no stars, no planets, and no people."[70] Astronomer Fred Hoyle concludes: "A commonsense interpretation of the facts suggests that a super intellect has monkeyed with physics, as well as chemistry and biology, and that there are no blind forces worth speaking about in nature."[71]

In addition to the improbability of our universe existing in a way that allowed life to develop by random chance, there is also the question often overlooked by many skeptics, one that is difficult to explain without a designer in the picture. And that is: When did the laws of physics themselves *begin to exist*? It is one thing to say that 122 dials would have to be dialed in, but it is another to determine where these "dials" even come from. The "laws" that govern physical matter would need to exist *prior* to the big bang. They could not come into existence at the same moment as the big bang itself or else they would not do their work. In other words, certain conditions had to exist *prior* to the existence of the material universe.

This is an admitted challenge for atheists. I was once watching a debate with Richard Dawkins and when the question of the preexistence of the laws of physics was raised he admitted that "physics does not yet have its Darwin." What he meant was that the field of physics doesn't have a theory of origins for the laws of physics themselves. I believe that, in this case, the theist has a more rational answer than the atheist: mind came before matter; the universe itself was created according to the laws that predate the existence of it. This is the most, not the least *rational* explanation of first causes in the marketplace of ideas. All of which is why renowned scientist Stephen Hawking concluded: "If the rate of expansion one second after the Big Bang had been smaller by even one part in 100 thousand million millionths, the universe would have re-collapsed before it ever reached its present size into a hot fireball. The odds against a universe like ours emerging out of something like the Big Bang are enormous. I think there are religious implications."[72] Hawking isn't willing to accept an explanation of "chance." You shouldn't either, because "chance" is not an explanation; it is a non-explanation and certainly the *less* rational of the two options.

What If I Don't Want to Believe?

I believe there are several reasons why we can know with a high level of confidence that God exists. We have moral instincts, and the best explanation is that these exist because the one who designed us is righteous. We can look at the universe and the world around us and see that it is littered with evidence of design. The evidence itself is what forces us to rethink our presuppositions about the world. Our desire in life is to follow evidence, not run from it. So where is the evidence leading us when it comes to the nature of humankind and the universe itself? It's leading us to the conclusion that there is a *noncontingent, uncaused* reality that created all things. Mind had to exist before matter, which is the opposite of what atheism teaches (matter led to mind and consciousness, it says) but on point with exactly what Jesus taught us about God: "God is spirit," he said (John 4:24). This is part of the reason no one has to prove that someone "created God," as is the challenge on the playground ("Then who created God?!"). We have no evidence that God ever *began* to exist. The best we can prove is that the universe began to exist.

If you don't want to believe the evidence, the onus is on you for proving God's *non*existence, which is not as easy as it seems. When we reject the existence of God we create more problems than we solve—moral and philosophical problems, yes, but even scientific ones. A short time ago, I was studying in a Catholic monastery. I spent the morning in my room, and then left for lunch. When I left my room, the window was closed and locked; when I came back, it was open. I had all the evidence in the world that someone had opened my window while I was out. But imagine you were with me, and you said, "I don't believe your theory that *someone* opened the window. I don't know why, I just don't." Is that enough? Where is your evidence and what is your argument? "I just don't believe your evidence" is not an acceptable answer. To believe something, one must present *counterevidence*. So what are our options if we don't want to believe in God in the face of evidences to the contrary?

The first option is the "Lucky Us" hypothesis. It says, "Yes, admittedly, the chances were extremely low that our universe would ever come into existence, but lucky us, here we are! Just celebrate it!"[73] Proponents of this theory suggest ideas similar to a poker analogy. Imagine that you are dealt a poker hand that turns out to be a royal flush. Although it is highly unlikely and improbable statistically that you would be dealt that hand, you received it, so you celebrate. Lucky you! The problem with this analogy is that it does not compare apples to apples, because the statistics are not even close to comparable. For the analogy to work and the situations to be comparable, you would have to be dealt that perfect royal flush every hand *forever*. But if that were to happen, nobody would chalk it up to chance circumstance to be celebrated. It would take three hands before someone else at the table would accuse you of cheating. Because everyone knows that chance isn't a *rational* explanation at all. And that's what we are all after, aren't we? The most *rational* explanation.

A second option, extremely popular among skeptics, is what is called the "multiverse" theory: while it is highly improbable that our one universe would ever come into existence given the number of variables, the odds change if there are an *infinite number of universes*. Dawkins says that the anthropic principle can be answered "by the suggestion . . . that there are many universes, co-existing like bubbles of foam, in a 'multiverse.'"[74] In other words, what if instead of not just one set of 122 dials, there are an infinite number of sets? The chances therefore increase that one of those sets would actually line up to give birth to our universe:

> Our time and space did indeed begin in *our* big bang, but this was just the latest in a long series of big bangs. . . . If bang-expansion-contraction-crunch cycles have been going on forever like a cosmic accordion, we have a serial, rather than a parallel, version of the multiverse. . . . of all the universes in the series, only a minority has their "dials" turned to biogenic conditions. And, of course, the present universe has to be one of that minority because we are in it.[75]

This is a creative solution to the question of the origin of the universe, but unconvincing for three reasons. First, the multiverse and big crunch theories do not hold up under philosophical scrutiny. In his lecture, "Darwin, Mind and Meaning," Alvin Plantinga points out the bankruptcy of the multiverse logic saying that rejecting the anthropic principle based on the theory of a multiverse is tantamount to rejecting "the evidence for the earth's being round by pointing out that there are possible worlds in which we have all the evidence we *do* have for the earth's being round, but in fact the earth is flat. Whatever the worth of this argument from design, [multiverse] really fails to address it."[76] Second, modern science is pretty certain that there will never be a "big crunch" because of what it is learning about the universe. Ironically, Dawkins recognizes this very point: "As it turns out, this serial version of the multiverse must now be judged less likely than it once was, because recent evidence is starting to steer us away from the big crunch model. It now looks as though our own universe is destined to expand forever."[77]

Third, and most importantly, there is *not one shred of evidence* for either of these explanations—an infinite number of universes or a twenty-billion-year cycle. These belong to the realm of pure conjecture. These are faith positions with no evidence at all. And thus, ironically, in the end, atheism asks us to believe in an infinite number of metaphysical realities, for which we have no evidence, while Christianity asks us to believe in one (God), for which we do actually have evidence. These are just a few of the reasons why more and more people, including myself, find it *more* rational to believe in the existence of God than not to.

CHAPTER 3

The Problem of
THE BIBLE

We will have many fights. But they will be for the sake of Torah.

CHAIM POTOK, *THE PROMISE*

Many skeptics doubt that God exists because they doubt the legitimacy of the Bible. They have doubts about its accuracy, its trustworthiness, and its truthfulness. They see the Bible as outdated, irrelevant, and mythological. Because Christian faith requires belief in the Bible as the revealed word of God, without which we wouldn't know the specifics of God's character, the plan of salvation, etc. (what scholars call "special revelation" versus "general revelation," what we can know about God through nature), it is natural to ask: Can we trust it? Is it reliable? Does it tell us the truth? Or, as skeptics argue, is it an outdated text about irrelevant religions believed by people who bury their head in the sand and deny reality?

Questioning the legitimacy of the Bible is nothing new. In Luke 24, Jesus approaches a cluster of his own disciples shortly after his resurrection from the dead. They saw him brutally killed and don't yet know he is alive again. They are feeling defeated, and in response to their mourning, Jesus delivers some unexpected words: "O foolish ones, and slow of heart to believe all that the prophets have spoken!"

(Luke 24:25). When Jesus speaks of "the prophets," this was a Jewish way of speaking generally about the Bible.

In other words, the disciples of Jesus were the first skeptics of the Bible as it related to Christianity.

People often criticize Christians for blindly believing the Bible. Sam Harris, a popular atheist writer and speaker, says, "Tell a devout Christian that his wife is cheating on him, or that frozen yogurt can make a man invisible, and he is likely to require as much evidence as anyone else. . . . Tell him that the book he keeps by his bed was written by an invisible deity who will punish him with fire for eternity if he fails to accept its every incredible claim about the universe, and he seems to require no evidence whatsoever."[78] Is this true? In my experience, it is a gross representation of Christians I know, but also of the long history of Christian study and thought. The people I know aren't blindly believing in the Bible. They want to dig into the evidence and examine the Bible's claims. They want to know that Christianity, and the Bible specifically, is historically reliable, and that its claims accord with archeology and science rather than ancient mythology and fairy tales.

How did Jesus respond to his own disciples? Jesus showed these skeptical disciples *evidence* to prove they could trust the Bible (Luke 24:26–27). And when they were faced with the evidence, they retired their skepticism and exercised faith in Jesus. Are you willing to do that if the Bible can be shown to be trustworthy and reliable by the standards of historical research? Are you willing to consider that the Bible might be true and allow it to change your life, as it has millions of people throughout history?

Before I embraced Christianity as true, I wanted answers. I wanted assurances that it wasn't just a myth or a fairy tale. So I went searching. Here's what I found.

Modern Questions

Pastoring a church in the greater Vancouver area, one of Canada's most progressive, secular, post-Christian cities, I have no shortage of opportunities to talk to thoughtful, educated, and well-intentioned skeptics of the Bible. Their questions are regarding the authority, historicity, and trustworthiness of the Bible:

- Is the Bible historically legitimate? Hasn't it been proven false?
- Hasn't the Bible changed throughout history?
- Isn't there a long list of contradictions and mistakes in the Bible?
- Aren't the Gospels filled with legends that got worked in later?
- Isn't the Bible full of ancient and outdated moral teachings (regarding such things as stoning, chauvinism, homosexuality, etc.)?
- Isn't the Bible written by people who merely wanted power?
- Why does the church only include four Gospels and exclude others, such as the Gospel of Thomas?

While many in our culture respect the Bible as a good story, they do not consider it good history.

Has the Bible Been Changed?

Many people believe the Bible has been mishandled and that its original message and content has been changed, lost, and manipulated. But historians tell us that the Bible is actually one of the most, if not *the* most, reliable and credible documents from antiquity.[79] One of the reasons it has such credibility as an ancient document is that it has largely *remained the same* throughout history. The ancient Jews who wrote and copied the Bible cared so much about the content of each manuscript that you can compare two copies of the same passage, copied five hundred years apart and found in completely different geographic areas, and they are virtually identical.

The Jews who copied the manuscripts cared a great deal about what they were preserving. This was a precious book to them, the Word of God. The "scribes" mentioned throughout the Gospels were a certain class of Bible scholar who would write chapters and chapters of text, making copies of biblical books so others could read them, and the process was extremely laborious. It wasn't something they did alone in a dark room. Two other scribes would hover over the copier's shoulder as he worked, and if he made an error—even in a single Hebrew letter—they would correct the mistake, and then all three would have to initial the correction as it was being copied or the manuscript would be destroyed. Even today, many Jews retain this deep respect for the Scriptures.

We don't always appreciate how important the preservation of the Scriptures was to the Jewish people. A good illustration of this dissonance is seen in a question posed by celebrated Jewish author Chaim Potok in his novel *In the Beginning*. The main character, a young Jewish boy growing up in Brooklyn, recalls a life-changing event:

> . . . the night in the second week of October when we danced with the Torah scrolls in our little synagogue. It was the night of Simchat Torah, the festival that celebrates the completion of the annual cycle of Torah readings. . . . The little synagogue was crowded and tumultuous with joy. I remember the white-bearded Torah reader dancing with one of the heavy scrolls as if he had miraculously shed his years. My father and uncle danced for what seemed to me to be an interminable length of time, circling about one another with their Torah scrolls, advancing upon one another, backing off, singing. Saul and Alex and I

danced too. I relinquished my Torah to someone in the crowd, then stood around and watched the dancing. It grew warm inside the small room and I went through the crowd and out the rear door to the back porch. I stood in the darkness and let the air cool my face. I could feel the floor of the porch vibrating to the dancing inside the synagogue . . . the joy of dancing with the Torah, holding it close to you, the words of God to Moses at Sinai. I wondered if the Gentiles ever danced with their Bible.[80]

This is a beautiful reminder of the care Jews have always had for the Scriptures. The scribes who wrote both the Old and New Testaments had a deep passion for preserving the purity and accuracy of all their authoritative texts, making sure that they were not changed in any significant way through the passing of time.

Contradictions and Mistakes

Many skeptics believe the Bible contains contradictions and mistakes. One of the most popular websites for young skeptics today—and supposedly the largest gathering of atheists online—is Reddit.com. Reddit allows anyone sitting in sweatpants in his parents' basement to post an alleged contradiction he has found in the Bible. On the website users wax eloquent by citing Bible passages that seem to contradict one another and pulling out verses from the Bible that are deemed to be historical mistakes. Adding fuel to this fire you can find some New Testament scholars such as Bart Ehrman, who asserts in his book *Misquoting Jesus: The Story Behind Who Changed the Bible and Why* that there are more than 400,000 errors in the Bible. Ehrman claims that the "New Testament copies all differ from one another, in many thousands of places."[81] Sadly, this is the type of claim that has caused many Christians to doubt their faith and many skeptics to feel they are justified in their assertions of the Bible's errors. But what are the alleged errors? We need to look closely and contextually at the apparent contradictions and mistakes to see if they really are what skeptics claim.

When we do this, we find that many of the "'mistakes" people cite in the Bible are nothing new. They are not "errors" but passages that are misread or misunderstood and have been known and explained by scholars of all stripes for many years. And when Erhman claims that there are more than 400,000 errors, he isn't talking about 400,000 separate mistakes as he makes it sound. Rather, he is speaking about small variations between different manuscripts. In other words, there is occasionally a word here or there spelled differently in the original Greek or Hebrew when you compare one manuscript to another. Erhman's number, however, is not based on 400,000 different instances in the Bible, but on the *number of copies* that have been made of whatever text he is arguing is in dispute. So, if there was a problem in Matthew 16:4, for instance, and it had been printed in thirty different original manuscripts, Erhman counts that not as *one* problem but as thirty. Another New Testament scholar, Craig Blomberg, points out that based on Ehrman's own logic of counting a single mistake and multiplying it by the amount of times it was published, one could argue: "There are 1.6 million errors in the first printing of Erhman's book, since someone counted 16 typos and there were 100,000 printed!"[82]

Still, Ehrman is correct in pointing out that there are slight variations between manuscripts. So what should we make of these? Are they problems a Christian should worry about? Again, these are not what we typically imagine—long narratives or chunks of text containing stories and concepts detrimental to Christian doctrine. Rather, the variations are a word here or there in a verse here or there, and even these are not scattered equally throughout the New Testament but are clustered in certain areas. In truth, there are only *two disputed passages* in the entire New Testament that are more than two verses in length (Mark 16:9–20 and John 7:53–8:11). And Christians do not try to hide this information from anyone. If you pick up an English version of the Bible today, it will inform you of the dispute about these passages in the footnotes or right above the stories themselves, saying "The earliest manuscripts do not include this passage."

Two Case Studies in Contradiction

During my second year of Bible college, I started to doubt the legitimacy of the Bible myself because I found contradictions. I had read a parable in Luke and then noticed differences when I compared it to Matthew's version of the same story (take a look yourself and compare Matthew 25:14–30 with Luke 19:12–28). I came to believe that these differences were a result of the stories being made up or that the writers were getting the details wrong because the events themselves had never happened. Tired of wrestling with these doubts alone, I walked into my professor's office and threw my Bible on his desk. "There are all kinds of contradictions in here!" I said. He sat back in his chair and asked me what I meant. I paced around his office. "Look at this! Matthew writes that Jesus said one thing and Luke writes that he said another—so which is it? The Gospel writers couldn't even get their records straight. They made all this up!"

My professor sat forward in his chair, reached into his bag, and pulled out two cassette tapes (remember, this was the '90s). He threw the tapes on the desk. I had given them to him weeks earlier because I was preaching at different churches, and my sermons had been recorded. I wanted to get his opinion on how I was doing as a preacher. "You know what's interesting?" he said. "Preachers preach different sermons in different places at different times and sometimes they use the same illustrations, don't they? You did that a few times in these two sermons."

"So what?" I retorted. "Well, sometimes within those illustrations," he continued, "the preacher will change the details of the stories he tells—to emphasize a specific point here or there depending on the audience, just like you did." I still wasn't following his point. So he leaned forward and said it plainly for me. "Don't you think in Jesus' three years of ministry, he would have told these parables more than once? We know that's how the rabbis taught in the first century. Jesus would have told the same parables multiple times in different settings, possibly using a different emphasis each time. The differences in the Gospels exist because Matthew is likely using one version of the story told one day and Luke is using another."

As I thought about what he had said, I realized that I had manufactured a reason for my doubts by imposing a standard on to this ancient book that I didn't impose on my own speaking and communication. And I raise this because, more often than not, it's the source of most every supposed contradiction or mistake people find in the Bible. The critic is demanding a level of precision and perfection that we don't demand of other forms of ancient literature, or of *any* sort of literature for that matter. Let's look at a couple of examples:

1. JUDAS'S DEATH

First is the question of how Judas, one of Jesus' twelve disciples, died. This is a very popular criticism among skeptics. Matthew 27:5 says, "And throwing down the pieces of silver into the temple, he departed, and he went and hanged himself." But Acts 1:18 says, "[Judas] acquired a field with the reward of his wickedness, and falling headlong he burst open in the middle and all his bowels gushed out." So which is it? Did Judas hang himself or did he die by falling headlong into a field with his guts spilling out? In looking closely and contextually at the two stories, we see that this isn't a contradiction at all. These are actually complementary accounts. The story in Acts is simply filling in later details. He hung himself, and someone eventually cut him down or the rope broke, and he fell on the ground below and his bowels spilled out. That was his end. These accounts don't contradict each other. Acts 1 doesn't say Judas never hanged himself. It is simply expanding on the story. If the book of Acts said Judas died by a stab wound or drowning or of old age, *that* would be a contradiction.

2. THE ANGELS AT THE RESURRECTION

Another popular example is the difference in the number of angels at the resurrection site of Jesus. Matthew 28:5 says, "But *the angel* said to the women, 'Do not be afraid.'" In John 20:12, however, it says, Mary "saw *two angels* in white, sitting where the body of Jesus had lain, one at the head and one at the foot." So, what do we do with this? Well, basic mathematics comes in handy even in biblical interpretation. Where there are two, there is always one. There is no contradiction. Matthew's account simply tells us that one particular angel *spoke* to Mary. John is reporting *how many* angels were actually there: two. John cares about the number of angels, but that is not Matthew's interest or emphasis. He simply cares that one spoke and what it said. In order for this to be a contradiction, Matthew would have had to say there was *only* one angel present, but he doesn't say anything that contradicts John's account at all.

Are There Contradictions Between the Old and New Testaments?

Another common charge is the differences between the Old Testament and the New Testament. "Read the Old Testament," people say. "It says that you can't eat shellfish or pork, but you do! You get tattoos, and you work on the Sabbath! There's a command in Leviticus that says a man with crushed testicles must not be allowed to come into church (see Leviticus 21:20), but you don't check that, do you?" I'll always admit that we don't adhere to that particular practice at our church. But here the skeptics are right: we don't follow many of the rules of the Old Testament today as Christians. Why is that?

When we read the Old Testament, we are reading about laws and practices given to a *specific* nation: the nation of Israel. Even more, these laws and practices pointed to a coming time when they would be fulfilled by a new way of believing and relating to God. The Old Testament says that a Messiah will come and usher in a new kingdom. Strict adherence to the specific laws revealed in the Old Testament was only intended for a specific time and for a specific people—what scholars refer to as one epoch in salvation history.

The prophet Jeremiah, for instance, writing hundreds of years before Jesus, said:

> "Behold, the days are coming . . . when I will make a new covenant with the house of Israel . . . not like the covenant that I made with their fathers . . . I will put my law within them, and I will write it on their hearts."
>
> (JEREMIAH 31:31–33)

The Law of the Old Testament was given for a season of salvation history, one that would eventually give way to another season: one in which the Spirit of God would come to live in individual people, empowering them to be obedient to him in all things. The apostle Paul tells us that the Law was like a childminder or tutor that guides God's people for a time but is superseded by Christ and the Spirit (Galatians 3:23–29). Ironically, then, we would be operating contrary to the commands of the Bible itself if we tried to please God and earn our acceptance before him by following Old Testament rules in the present epoch. They were given to Israel to guide them through a particular season and era of salvation history, and to serve as a "shadow" and pointer to the fullness that would one day come in Jesus through his sacrificial death on the cross (Colossians 2:17). The New Testament makes it clear that the Messiah has come, has brought God's kingdom, and has instituted a new era with new practices and commandments. In Acts 10, for instance, the apostle Peter has a vision of a sheet, filled with animals that Jews were not permitted to eat, drifting down from heaven. A voice tells him: "I know in the past I told you not to eat these animals, but now, because of what has happened in Jesus, you can kill and eat because I've made all things clean" (Acts 10:13–16, my paraphrase).

This was not a minor event for Peter and for the other Jews who followed Jesus. They had ancestors who would have died rather than eat what God had deemed unclean. Several, in fact, were boiled to death for refusing to eat pork and other foods (1–2 Maccabees). This is why Peter, at first, objects. "By no means, Lord; for I have never eaten anything that is common or unclean" (Acts 10:14). But God's message is clear. Now that Jesus has come and completed his work, he has made all things clean. The rules have changed. Evolved.

In other words, you can't understand the Bible without understanding it as a story that progresses. With Jesus—his life, death, resurrection—and the transition to the era of the new covenant, which includes all ethnicities (a transnational movement not a geographic or localized one), an important shift took place. And by implication, there are rules in the Old Testament, given for a specific period and purpose and people, that no longer apply in the New Testament era. Christians no longer live under the rules of the kingdom of Israel but under the rule of Jesus Christ in his new kingdom. So before someone tries to argue that there are contradictions between the Old and New Testament, he or she needs to understand how the Bible is a progressive revelation that is not static but reveals the truth about God to us in stages, the latter stages of which overshadow and leave behind the former stages. This of course is far different than contradiction. It is the by-product of maturation.

Historical, Cultural, and Personal Trust

A number of criticisms regarding the *historical reliability* of the Gospels also are present in popular, skeptical culture. Basically, can one actually trust the biblical documents themselves given how long after the events they were written? In the face of this question most scholars—both secular and Christian—after having looked at the historical and literary evidence, agree that the Gospels, along with the rest of the New Testament, are "the best-attested documents in antiquity."[83] Let's explore why they have concluded this.

HISTORICAL TRUST: MANUSCRIPTS AND CONTENT

When trying to deduce whether an ancient document can be trusted, scholars must consider a number of factors. One of those is the *number of manuscripts* available of a particular document, because the more manuscripts there are, the more it can be compared and contrasted for possible contradictions, mistakes, and/or inconsistencies. In other words, the more, the better. Scholars point out that if we compare the number of New Testament manuscripts to other writings in antiquity that are accepted as accurate, we find that it is the most trustworthy set of documents in the entire ancient world. For instance: Thucydides lived from 460–365 BC and wrote extensively about Greco-Roman culture. Most scholars trust what Thucydides reported in his writings as historically accurate. We have in existence *eight* copies of his writings, the earliest transcribed 1,300 years after the events of which he wrote. There are *five* copies of Aristotle's *Poetics* dated 1,400 years after the originals. Caesar's *Gallic Wars* describe events that occurred in 58

BC, and the *few* manuscripts scholars have are from 1,000 years after his death. There are *two* ancient biographies of Alexander the Great that are seen as authoritative and fully accurate, the earliest of which was written 400 years after Alexander died. Historians trust all these writings as historically accurate. So what about the New Testament? Believe it or not, there are over 25,000 copies of the New Testament documents in existence![84] This is the greatest number of manuscripts by far of any writing of its kind from the ancient world.

Another complaint skeptics lodge against the Gospels is that they are written *too far* after the events they record to be trusted. Obviously, the closer to the event something is written, the more accurate it is considered, because less time has passed and thus less chance to be tainted with untrue stories, mythologies, or legends. Karen Armstrong's bestselling book, *A History of God*, for instance, says, "We know very little about Jesus. The first full-length account of his life was St. Mark's gospel, which was not written until about the year 70 AD, some forty years after his death. By that time, historical facts had been overlaid with mythical elements which expressed the meaning Jesus had acquired for his followers . . . rather than a reliable straightforward portrayal."[85] What do we say to this charge?

It doesn't take long to recognize how out of place this critique is on the stage of history. All of the above non-biblical examples were written between 400–1,500 years after the events they record, and they are accepted as accurate and respected texts of antiquity. The New Testament, however, was written as early as *fifteen to twenty years* after the life of Jesus (Paul's letters, for instance). Even the most liberal scholars contend that the Gospels were written between *thirty and fifty years* after the life and death of Jesus. This is why Sir Frederic G. Kenyon, former director of the British Museum, concludes that "in no other case is the interval of time between the composition of the book and the date of the earliest extant manuscripts so short as that in the New Testament."[86]

If the Gospels were written only thirty to fifty years after the life of Jesus, then we have good reason to trust them. If you're going to make up stories about miracles and events that you are claiming really happened, you have to wait until all the eyewitnesses are dead and gone. If you make up fictitious stories about Jesus, write them down, and then start shopping them around, and there are people alive who can discredit you, they will. For example, if I wrote a book claiming that Canada had dropped nuclear bombs on America in 1991, you would say "I was alive in 1991, and that didn't happen." Rumors that are started when people are still alive to refute them don't make it very far because they run up against facts. This is why when the apostle Paul argues for the historical basis for Jesus' resurrection from the dead, he says that over 500 people saw him, "most of whom are still alive" (1 Corinthians 15:6). What he is saying is, "If you have any doubts, go ask them—they're still around." As F. F. Bruce points out, "It can't have been so easy as some writers seem to think to invent words and deeds of Jesus in those early years, when so many of his disciples were about, who could remember what had and had not happened."[87] There were also plenty of people at the time opposed to Christianity, and therefore the "disciples could not afford to risk inaccuracies (not to speak of willful manipulation of the facts), which would at once be exposed by those who would be only too glad to do so."[88]

The New Testament, however, was written within the lifetime of all the eyewitnesses. During this time, some amazing claims were made about Jesus—claims that people could easily have discredited—everything from 2,000 pigs drowning (a big deal back then; Mark 5:1–20) to Jesus feeding five thousand people with a few pieces of bread and some fish (Mark 6:30–44) to his raising a Roman leader's daughter from the dead (Mark 5:21–43). These were *public events* in small towns that never would have gained an audience in written form if they hadn't happened.

✓

The Gospel writers also do something very unique: they write people's names into their accounts. We read those names and don't think much of them, but scholars point out that there is more going on than meets the eye working as credibility markers for the Bible as a whole.[89] In Mark, for instance, when he says "Simon of Cyrene" was carrying the cross for Jesus and that he is "the father of Alexander and Rufus" (Mark 15:21), Mark identifies them so that if readers have any questions about the event, they can go ask Simon themselves. Mark is able to say "Alexander and Rufus" because "Mark expected many of his readers to know them, in person."[90] These are a few reasons, among many, that the New Testament gains scholarly legitimacy over and above the more historically detached religious texts of Islam, Buddhism, or Hinduism.

Timothy Keller points out that the Gospels also gain credibility with what he calls "counter-productive content."[91] Skeptics often contend the Gospel writers were trying to *gain power* by showing how impressive Jesus is and how impressive they are by association. But if this were in fact their intent, they did a poor job because plenty of content in the Gospels is very counterproductive to that agenda. Take the story of Jesus in Gethsemane, for instance (Mark 14:32–42), where we see the supposed "God-Man" at the end of his life sitting in a garden sweating blood because of anxiety and fear. Afraid, he cries out to God, asking that the mission of suffering be taken away from him (vv. 35, 36, 39). This is not something you put in a story you are making up if you want Jesus to be the perfect hero, because it shows weakness and creates doubt.

Later, on the cross, Jesus cries out, "My God, my God, why have you forsaken me?" (Mark 15:34). There would have been immense pressure to omit that because it is confusing to spend fifteen chapters arguing that Jesus is God and then record him talking to himself, saying that he is forsaking himself. Furthermore, people regularly approach Jesus and ask him if he is God. When he responds that he is, they ask him questions, to which he says, "I don't know, only the Father knows" (Mark 13:32, my paraphrase). What? He claims to be God, who knows everything and made everything, and yet he *doesn't know* stuff? Why not take this out of the account? Take out the idea that Jesus "*could* do no mighty work there, except that he laid his hands on a few sick people" (Mark 6:5). What do you mean, *could not*? He's God. He can do whatever he wants, can't he? All of this is counterproductive to any agenda of power and making Jesus look like the perfect hero. But alas, it is present.

Peter and the other disciples look terrible in these stories. Peter is always making mistakes, saying the wrong thing, and even looking blasphemous. One minute he basically says, "I'll go to the death before I deny you, Jesus" (see Mark 14:31), and then hours later, he denies Jesus and runs away (14:66–68). Similarly, James and John beg to sit at Jesus' right and left in his kingdom (Mark 10:37), looking like conniving power-hungry children whom Jesus then rebukes. These pillars of the early church disobey, ask the wrong questions, teach the wrong things, lack faith, and over and over again show themselves to *not* be men of valor. Why? Because the Gospel writers are saying, "This is just what happened," and instead of cleaning up the accounts, they left them as they were.

CULTURAL TRUST: SLAVES, WOMEN, AND POLYGAMISTS

Skeptics also point out the *cultural* disconnect between the modern world and the Bible, arguing that the Bible is culturally regressive in a way that people shouldn't accept. People argue that it is pro-slavery and misogynistic. So is there a way to approach the Bible that engenders trust for what it says, even in modern times?

First, Timothy Keller says, when we read the passages that grate against us, we need to consider that the Bible might not always be teaching what we think it's teaching. In other words, be slow to judge something from another time and culture until you are sure you understand what it is saying in context. Take the common objection that "the Bible teaches slavery" because Paul says, "Slaves, . . . obey your earthly masters" (Colossians 3:22). From this one phrase one could conclude that Paul, and all other Christians, affirm and support slavery. But this is anachronistic. When North Americans hear the word *slave*, we typically think of the African slave trade in which an owner could beat his slave, kill him—basically do whatever he wanted with the slave and the slave's family. But was this the norm in the Roman empire of the first century? Historians tell us that first-century Roman slavery wasn't like that at all. Slaves were not identified by race, and they weren't owned in the same way that African slaves were owned in the Americas. They weren't segregated from society, killed on a whim, or tortured. In fact, "85–90 percent of the inhabitants of Rome and Italy were slaves or of slave origin in the first and second centuries AD . . . and slaves enjoyed great popularity in Rome. They were the trusted household servants, teachers, librarians, accountants and estate managers."[92] Because slavery was a form of employment, one could work his or her way out of it in ten to fifteen years. Essentially, what Paul is advising slaves in this passage is that they work hard and respect their superiors. He is not saying that it is good to own another human being or that slavery itself is a good thing.

Let's say we threw the Bible aside because we didn't like what we *thought* it said about slavery. If we did this, we would be rejecting Christianity based on something we didn't understand. A *wrong assumption.* We would be denouncing Jesus out of our own ignorance by assuming the Bible's use of a certain word is the same as how we use it today. I made this mistake a few years ago when I sat down and read the book of Genesis in two sittings for a class I was taking. It was an invigorating experience, but I struggled as I read about the patriarchs Abraham, Isaac, Jacob, and Joseph. I was offended by their treatment of women. They each had multiple wives, and it appeared that they would just trade women and barter over bride prices. Jacob said that he wanted the beautiful Rachel, and her father said that Jacob needed to take his daughter Leah instead because she was ugly (see Genesis 29:15–30). As the father of three daughters, I was horrified. How could these supposedly godly men treat women so poorly?

As I continued to read through Exodus and Leviticus, I began to realize that there's a world of difference between the Bible *explaining* what is happening and God *affirming* and encouraging what is happening. Again, Timothy Keller is helpful here in pointing out the contribution of the celebrated Jewish scholar Robert Alter. Alter says that there are two institutions in the book of Genesis that were universal in the ancient Near East: (1) polygamy, the idea that a man can have as many wives as he wants, and (2) primogeniture, the idea that the oldest son should get everything (including all the inheritance in a family). However, Alter points out that when understood in context, the Bible is actually quite *subversive* about both. Take polygamy. Socially, culturally, and spiritually the lives of these people are a mess. The children born of Abraham's relationships with his wives hate each other (and their descendants still do!). Isaac's children fight, lie, and turn on one another. Jacob deceives. And on and on it goes. There is complete dysfunction in the family. A careful reading of the story leads you to conclude that polygamy doesn't work out so well. Far from endorsing it then, the Bible is actually quite negative about the practice.

Or consider the practice of primogeniture, giving favored position in the family to the older son. This gets challenged again and again. God almost always chooses the *younger* son over the older one: it's Abel, not Cain whom God uses, Isaac not Ishmael, Jacob not Esau. The Bible is telling us that this too is *not* the ideal practice.

Treating women and children like this are not methods that God ordains or commands at all.

Now again, imagine you rejected Christianity because of your shallow reading of the Bible. You would never realize what the narrative itself was working to accomplish, that it was actually in agreement with your concerns, using culturally appropriate methods to challenge the status quo that you simply didn't recognize. Others have rejected the Bible for similarly uninformed reasons. I know that for many years, university professors taught that the Gospel of John could not be trusted because the writer says there is a place called Bethesda that has a pool "by the Sheep Gate" and that there are "five roofed colonnades" (John 5:1–2). Because archaeological work had been done in that area and there was no pool to speak of, much less a gate or roofed colonnades, scholars argued that this was *proof* the Bible couldn't be trusted. Swarms of students took that to heart over the next few decades and abandoned their trust in the Bible. They walked away from Christianity and died.

And then . . .

In the mid–1900s, archaeologists dug a little deeper. With their more advanced technology they found the pool in Bethesda, the Sheep Gate, and the five roofed colonnades exactly as John describes. I've been to the site myself and have touched the colonnades. I nearly cried thinking of all the people who rejected the claims of the Bible unnecessarily. Nelson Glueck, a renowned Jewish archaeologist, has said that "it may be stated categorically that no archeological discovery has ever contradicted a biblical reference."[93] Don't walk away at the first sign of a contradiction or a problem. Sometimes scientific study needs to play catch-up to the Bible.

Over the past two thousand years there have been countless opportunities to disprove the thousands of geographical and historical references in the Bible, verses referring to historical kings and places, texts giving numbers and events, and yet *not one* of them ever has been disproven. What if you had walked away from the Bible based on a misunderstanding? Based on something that hadn't been revealed yet? That would be problematic at best and tragic at worst.

Aside from these archaeological, more historical/objective examples, we sometimes reject the Bible for other problematic reasons, namely, cultural convictions, of which we must be careful. Why? Because, when we reject the Bible for cultural reasons, we are prioritizing one cultural belief over another, not because we have an objective and detached position from which to judge, but because we are a product of our own time and environment. "Every human community shares and cherishes certain assumptions, traditions, expectations, anxieties, and so forth," biblical scholar N. T. Wright says, "which encourage its members to construe reality in particular ways, and which create contexts within which certain kinds of statements are perceived as making sense."[94] There is no such thing as a "neutral" or "objective" observer. There is no such thing as a *detached* viewpoint.[95] Therefore, we have to be careful that we do not allow *our cultural moment* to define truth blindly or keep us from considering new ideas. We can't continue to hold on to an idea simply because our family or our university or the media has told us it's right. Such ideas must be held lightly and, if challenged by the evidence, abandoned— because it's possible that *our* culture's stories, symbols, and acceptable behaviors are the ones that are misguided or just flat-out wrong.

We must be careful not to elevate our cultural moment above something spoken by God that transcends all cultures and time. In a generation or two *our* ideas are going to look outdated and silly, so we can't let them be the paradigm of truth.

PERSONAL TRUST: THE BIBLE IS NOT ABOUT YOU

In addition to cultural misunderstandings, people may reject the Bible because it demands something of them personally that they don't want to do. Many of the people who show up at our church have walked away from Christianity because they went to church as a kid or read the Bible and instead of it being freeing and life giving, it was a burden. The reason being that they read it as if it were all about *them*. About their moral life and what they could do for God. Instead of setting them free, therefore, Christianity crushed them personally. It was about what they had to *do* to please God, and though they tried with all their might not to lie or steal or gossip or sleep around, they inevitably failed. And maybe that's you. The good news is that Jesus challenges this whole way of relating to God and says in essence, "Do you know what the Bible would tell you if you were reading it properly? It would say, 'Of course you failed at these things. Everybody fails at these things. That's why you needed someone to succeed *for* you, and I am that someone.'" The entire Bible, even the stories of the Old Testament, are pointing us to Jesus Christ, to who he is and what he has done for humanity. As a well-known children's Bible reminds us, "Every story whispers his name." As one preacher I heard points out: Jesus is the true and better Adam who passed the test in the garden and whose obedience is given to us. Jesus is the true and better Abraham answering the call of God to go out into the void to create a new people of God. Jesus is the true and better David whose victory becomes his people's victory even though they didn't lift a stone to accomplish it. The point is that the Bible isn't about you. It's not about what we can do so God will love and save us. It's about what *Jesus* has done. You and I are not brave like Moses or David or Samson—so God had to be brave for us. That's why Jesus came. God doesn't save you and use you *because* of you but *in spite of* you. And that's the most liberating news of all. That's what the gospel is all about. "Cursed be everyone who does not abide by all things written in the Book of the Law, and do them," Paul says in Galatians 3:10. Meaning if we fail to follow the law personally, and perfectly, we are cursed. But then the good news: "Christ redeemed us from the curse of the law by *becoming a curse for us*—for it is written, 'Cursed is everyone who is hanged on a tree'" (3:13, emphasis added). This means the rules don't have to crush you, because they crushed him in your place. They don't have to cause you to run away from God and reject him, because Jesus was made distant from God and rejected by the Father in your place.

Where do we learn about this good news? The Bible, the book Augustine said is "the face of God for us for now." What personal power does it have? As a young man I believed in Christ before I ever entered a church, and my encounter with God wasn't primarily with Christians or a church at all, but with the Bible itself. I would sit at the local parks or out in front of my high school, smoking half a pack of cigarettes and devouring the Bible. I read the stories of Jesus and his teachings and took them to heart. Over time, faith grew within me, and I started to believe and change. I moved from stealing cars, throwing rocks through people's windows, and doing drugs to becoming a seventeen-year-old who loved God and was lit on fire to change the world. Why? Because as I took the teachings of Jesus to heart and believed that he died to liberate me from myself so I could live for him, I found myself praying for people as they faced their own difficulties in life. I saw young people around me give their lives to Christ. I was living in a new mode of existence, a different level of perspective, influence, and joy. Not because a church told me to or leaders were discipling me or parents were guiding me; it was the Bible itself, or God through it—the Word behind the word—changing me, completely separately from his people. This is the power of the Scriptures—personally. They speak, and if we will listen and heed them and let them take us over, they will transform us, forever.

CHAPTER 4

The Problem of
THE CHRIST
MYTH

One difference between God's work and man's is,
that, while God's work cannot mean more than
he meant, man's must mean more than he meant.
It is God's things, his embodied thoughts, which
alone a man has to use, modified and adapted to
his own purposes . . . so many the facts hinted in
every symbol. A man may well himself discover
truth in what he wrote; for he was dealing all the
time with things that came from thoughts beyond
his own.

GEORGE MACDONALD, *THE FANTASTIC IMAGINATION*

I was talking to one of my neighbors recently. He knows I'm a pastor, and he said to me, "I really respect what you do, Mark, trying to help people and all, but I think it's all based on a lie. We all know now that Jesus never really existed!" I was a bit surprised to hear him say this, so I asked him to explain what he meant. As if he were reading a script, he unpacked for me what has become known as the Christ Myth: "Jesus is just a made-up person," he said, "a myth modeled after Horus, Dionysus, and a number of other mythological ancient gods whose stories predate Jesus by thousands of years. You Christians ignore it and continue to believe and promote one of the greatest deceptions of all time. Christianity is the greatest story ever *sold!*"

This is an extremely popular view today. My neighbor, and many others, believe the church invented Jesus, modeling him after existing myths about dying and rising gods that heal people, walk on water, feed thousands, have twelve disciples, and then die, get buried for three days, and rise again. I encounter it often when I speak publicly about Christianity or even just walk down the streets of Vancouver. In our city, people have booths and hand out Christ Myth literature. My neighbor cited several books and films produced in the last ten to fifteen years that have popularized this challenge to Christianity, the most popular of which include *The Pagan Christ* by Tom Harpur (Canada's bestselling book in 2004), *The Jesus Mysteries* by Timothy Freke and Peter Gandy, and *The Christ Conspiracy* and *Christ in Egypt* by Acharya S. Films such as *Zeitgeist, Religulous,* and *The God Who Wasn't There* also present the case for the Christ Myth in a creative and convincing way. Maybe the most noteworthy is the film *Zeitgeist,* extremely popular among college students across North America. Written and directed by Peter Joseph, its claims about Jesus, also echoed in Bill Maher's film *Religulous,* are significant and would be devastating to Christianity if they were proven true. So what do we do with this increasingly popular challenge?

As with any conspiracy theory, I find that it helps to slow down, pause the tape, and look at *facts.* Let's start with where this idea originated. The first modern attempt to deny the historical existence of Jesus can be traced back to the late eighteenth century and the work of two French writers, Constantin-François de Chassebœuf, comte de Volney and Charles-François Dupuis. They argued that Christianity is simply an amalgamation of various ancient mythologies and that Jesus

Christ was constructed by the church as another mythical character in the same mold as hundreds of other stories told throughout history in different cultures.[96] These claims have achieved success at the popular level, so how does one respond?

First, we must realize that these claims are not taken seriously by legitimate scholars. Even scholarly skeptics such as Bart D. Ehrman, who do not accept many of the religious claims of Christianity, agree that Jesus of Nazareth was a historical figure who really existed.[97] Historians continue to debate the nature of Jesus, the exact date of his birth, what he did and taught, etc., but they almost unanimously affirm that he *existed*. It's an accepted fact, which is why H. G. Wells famously summarized the consensus this way: "I am a historian, I am not a believer, but I must confess as a historian that the penniless preacher from Nazareth is irrevocably the very center of history. Jesus Christ is easily the most dominant figure in all history." So why are there still doubts? Because the Christ Myth is regularly sold to a susceptible culture by those who would have us believe it.

The Christ Myth Itself

What is the Christ Myth in its entirety? One of its most widely read proponents, Acharya S, summarizes it this way in her book *The Christ Conspiracy*, "Jesus Christ is a mythical character based on . . . various ubiquitous godmen and universal saviors who were part of the ancient world for thousands of years prior to the Christian era."[98] Believers in the idea attempt to demonstrate that Horus, Mithras, Dionysus, and many other figures of ancient mythology have precise *parallels* with Christ, making his claims illegitimate, including the following:

- Twelve disciples
- Being born of a virgin on December 25

- Magi visiting their birthplaces after following a star in the east
- Miracles, walking on water, feeding many
- Disciples beheaded
- Crucified, and after three days, rising again

Brian Flemming, the writer and director of *The God Who Wasn't There*, contends that the early Christians knew Jesus wasn't real. He was just a good idea. The apostle Paul didn't even pretend that Jesus was a historical person but simply established a new "spiritual" (not historical) worldview. This is why Paul focuses on being "in Christ" and "in the Spirit" instead of urging a pattern of discipleship by following the life of Jesus as a historical figure. So how should we respond to these assertions? As I hinted earlier, the Christ Myth falls apart with just a small amount of historical study. First, we'll look at the question of whether Jesus ever existed, and then we'll examine the supposed parallels between Jesus and the pagan gods.

Did Jesus Exist?

At least ten first-century historians and writers *outside of the Bible* mention Jesus of Nazareth by name,[99] some of them Jewish, some Roman, most not friends of the Christian faith at all. Indeed, they frequently had an *anti*-Christian agenda. Here are two examples:

> **Tacitus:** "Nero fastened the guilt . . . on a class hated for their abominations, called Christians by the populace. Christus, from whom the name had its origin, suffered the extreme penalty during the reign of Tiberius at the hands of the procurator Pontius Pilatus." (Tacitus, *Annals*, 15.44)

> **Josephus:** "About this time there lived Jesus, a wise man, if indeed one ought to call him a man. For he . . . wrought surprising feats. . . . He was the Christ. When Pilate . . . condemned

him to be crucified, those who had come to love him did not give up their affection for him. On the third day he appeared . . . restored to life . . . and the tribe of Christians . . . has not disappeared." (Josephus, *Antiquities*, 18.63–64)

Secular writers such as these make some of the same claims about Jesus that the New Testament makes. They say that he was a charismatic leader, that the Jews and the Romans killed him, that his disciples claimed that he was resurrected from the dead after he was crucified by Pontius Pilate, and that his early followers worshiped him as God, resulting in their own torture and death. Which leads us to a second reason the Christ Myth theory lacks credibility.

Under the persecution of both the Jews and the Roman Empire, Christianity grew from a group of twelve disciples to over thirty-three million people in just 350 years, and by 400 AD, 56 percent of the entire population of the Roman Empire were Christians.[100] Why did it grow so fast? Why were men and women, even close family and friends, so willing to die for Christianity? The logical explanation for this runs contrary to the Christ Myth. Jesus' followers died because they claimed that they had *seen Jesus rise from the dead.* They were persecuted and tortured and told to recant this claim, but they never did. They died for it.

They weren't dying for a set of metaphorical religious teachings or principles of life taught them by a dead sage, but for a revolutionary historical claim: what had happened to Jesus *after* he died. In a long section of one of his letters (1 Corinthians 15:3–49), the apostle Paul makes it very clear that Jesus and the resurrection were historical facts ("he was raised," v. 4) and even goes out of his way to make the point that if this claim were just a religious or mythological idea, then Christianity is false, a waste of time, and Christians are to be the most pitied people in the world (v. 19).

The scandalous historical fact is Christians were not afraid to die for their belief in the historical Jesus. They weren't afraid of being tortured: sawn in half, stretched apart, thrown to the lions in gladiatorial arenas, or stoned to death in the street. They never recanted their testimony about Jesus, and that conviction, courage, and hope caused the gospel to spread rapidly. In fact, the rise of the early church is one of the anomalies of history. That the largest religion in the world arose so quickly from a single man and his twelve followers, often at the cost of their own lives, has caused many skeptics to face another reality. Not only did Jesus live, but he really did rise from the dead.[101]

Taking on the Christ Myth

There are also several problems with the myth itself and those who argue for it on a popular and scholarly level. First, the proponents of the myth rarely, if ever, do one of the major things that good historians do, which is interacting with the *primary sources*. For example, if you write a university paper on *Romeo and Juliet* but you don't quote the Shakespearean text itself, only citing secondary sources or papers written about Shakespeare, you will likely get a failing grade. The primary sources that need evaluation in our case are the Gospels themselves and the ancient texts that contain the myths of Horus, Attis, Mithras, and others. Yet when you read books or watch films about the Christ Myth, it is quickly apparent that the authors and filmmakers have not interacted with the primary sources at all. They simply cite modern authors who agree with their conclusions. For instance, Acharya S claims that Horus had twelve disciples long before Jesus did. Her footnote to this claim is not a citation of an ancient scroll or well-known Egyptian narrative, as one might expect, but the writings of a man named Gerald Massey.[102] But if you read Massey's book (*The Historical Jesus and the Mythical Christ*), while he claims that Horus had twelve disciples, he doesn't cite anyone or any text, ancient or modern, that supports his claim. Moreover, there are no recognized Egyptologists who accept this claim. A mention of Horus's twelve disciples is not found in the *Book of the Dead*, nor is it contained within the hieroglyphs of Egypt.

Furthermore, the Christ Myth loses credibility because it gets the facts wrong not only about the ancient myths but about Christianity itself. For instance, *Zeitgeist* makes several claims about the symbolic number twelve that are flatly untrue. The movie says that the Bible borrows the significance of twelve from the pagan twelve-month calendar, which originally was connected to the movement of stars and the zodiac. It also claims that in the Bible "there are twelve tribes of Israel, twelve princes, twelve kings, and twelve judges." The truth of the matter, however, is that though the Bible does use the number twelve, it never mentions twelve princes, twelve kings, or twelve judges. There are far more than twelve of each of these in the Scriptures.

In addition, the Christ Myth advocates make several factual errors when examining the so-called parallels they draw between Jesus and the major mythological persons. Consider the earlier claim that Horus had twelve disciples. The primary sources (in this case Egyptian hieroglyphs) illustrate that Horus only had *four* disciples. In one place, the sources show that he may have had as many as sixteen, but never does the number twelve appear. Tom Harpur, seen as a scholarly representative of the Christ Myth, goes even further and claims that Horus was a fisherman with twelve disciples.[103] But again, he cites no sources for his claim. Who were the four accepted followers or disciples of Horus? The primary sources point to a turtle, a bear, a lion, and a tiger. But to say that this has any connection to Jesus or his discipleship is more than a stretch. These followers of Horus are not in any kind of relationship with Horus, nor do they become emissaries of his message in any way like disciples of Jesus did. Over and over again the facts are misinterpreted and skewed to force parallels with Christianity.

In the end, it comes down to one simple question. Are there any direct parallels between Jesus Christ and these popular ancient gods? And if so, does Christianity crumble under the weight of them? Let's look at the most cited Christ-parallels: Horus, Mithras, Dionysus, Attis, and Krishna.

HORUS

We've already talked about Horus, who is arguably the main character in this debate. Horus was one of the oldest and most significant deities in ancient Egypt, worshiped from early in Egyptian history right up to the Greco-Roman period. Here are the claims of parallels with Christianity:

1. Horus was born of a virgin on December 25.
2. He was born in a manger.
3. Three kings followed a star in the east to his birth.
4. He was a child teacher by the age of twelve.
5. He was baptized in a river by Anup (who was later beheaded).
6. He had twelve disciples; he was a fisherman; he was crucified between two thieves; and he was raised from the dead after three days.

So, was Horus's mother a virgin? If we look at the story of Horus's conception and birth, we learn that his mother's name was Isis and his father was Osiris. Prior to Horus's conception, Osiris was in a fight with another god during which he was killed and chopped into several pieces. In order to conceive Horus, Isis gathered up pieces of Osiris's body and conceived Horus by hovering over his severed phallus. To call this a parallel to the virgin conception and virgin birth of Jesus is a stretch to say the least.

Secondly, Horus does *not* share a birthday with Jesus. While one of the three birth dates on record for Horus is December 25, we must understand that Jesus was not born on December 25! The celebration of Jesus' birth on that day in the modern Western world was started by Pope Julius I in the fourth century AD to challenge the pagan celebration for the Roman god Saturnalia, which was held on December 25. Scholars do not know the exact date of Jesus' birth, but they posit that Jesus was most likely born in September or October. The point is that the early Christians did not craft Jesus to replace Horus by selecting December 25.

In addition, there is no credible historical evidence to suggest that Horus was born in a manger. Acharya S claims this in her book,[104] but there is no source evidence cited to support a manger-birth for Horus. Furthermore, the idea that Horus and Jesus' births were announced by a star in the East and attended by three kings is deceiving. As the story is told, multiple ancient myths speak of three kings who attended a birth of significance. This is a reference to the constellation Orion since there are three main stars that make up Orion's Belt, as well as a lead star, and the three stars are commonly called "the three kings." In other words, these "three kings" follow the lead star to the birth of a cosmic savior. Skeptics argue that the New Testament writers are writing Jesus' story to reflect this astrology, but there is one small problem with this theory. It is now commonly accepted that no one spoke of the typology of three kings following a lead star in astrology until the nineteenth century. It would be impossible for the Gospel writers to have based their story off this idea—because the story hadn't been even invented yet!

In addition, it's worth pointing out that Christianity never claims that there were *three kings* present at the birth of Jesus. This is a common misconception attached to our celebration of Christmas. Instead, the Bible tells us that the men who came to visit Jesus were *magi*, not kings (Matthew 2:1). Magi were Babylonian or Persian astrologers and magicians.[105] And the Bible never claims there were *three* of them.

Matthew, the only Gospel writer who recounts the story of these traveling men who followed a star to find Jesus, only tells us that they brought "gold and frankincense and myrrh" (Matthew 2:11). There were three gifts but no evidence to suggest that there was only one man for each gift. There could have been two, or there could have been twenty!

Furthermore, contrary to popular Christian legend, these men were not at the actual *birth* of Jesus. The story says they arrived at "the house" and saw "the child" (Matthew 2:11). The magi were not at "the inn" (Luke 2:7), as in the account of the shepherds, nor was Jesus a baby (the Greek word for *child* in Matthew 2:11 means "toddler" not "baby"). Given that Matthew tells us that Herod killed all the children "less than two years of age" in his slaughter, it is likely that the magi arrived when Jesus was around two years old, not on the night of his birth (Matthew 2:16). This is nothing new. Christian scholars have pointed this out for years.

There is also no evidence to support the claims that Horus was a child teacher in a temple by the age of twelve or that Anup baptized him and was later beheaded. These claims are, again, found in the writings of Gerald Massey, and when scholars asked Massey about the source of these claims, he said he had read them in *The Book of the Dead*. Egyptologists challenged him on this, pointing out that such claims are *not* made in *The Book of the Dead*, and Massey eventually admitted that he couldn't remember where he had read them.

Finally, Horus was not crucified between two thieves and resurrected from the dead three days later. In most of the Horus stories, he doesn't die at all. There is only one questionable story in which he does die, and in that story he is cut into pieces by an enemy and then thrown into water. The resurrection parallel is similarly flawed, the closest thing to a parallel being that he is fished out of the water by crocodiles.

MITHRAS

Another mythological figure frequently cited as a Christ-parallel is the Roman god Mithras. Most of what is known of Mithras is taken from ancient reliefs and sculptures produced about Mithraism, a mystery religion practiced in the Roman Empire, particularly within the Roman military, from about the first to fourth centuries AD.[106] The parallels between Mithras and Christ are similar to some with Horus:

1. Mithras was born of a virgin on December 25.
2. Shepherds attended his birth.
3. He had twelve disciples.
4. He was buried in a tomb and three days later rose from the dead.

Let's look at each of these claims in order.

While the birth of Mithras may have been celebrated on December 25, he was not born of a virgin. The story is that he was born fully formed out of a rock with a dagger in one hand and a torch in the other. Is that a virgin birth? I don't know. How does one assess the sexual activity of a rock? The Mithras story does tell of shepherds present at his birth who help dig him out of the rock face. Again, however, there is a simple problem with the claim that the early Christians built a Christ Myth from this. The earliest of the Mithras stories that we have are dated two hundred years *after* the Gospels were written.[107] This is why scholars are quick to point out that the most likely scenario is that stories from Greco-Roman mythology borrowed from Christianity in this instance, not the other way around. Early church writers Tertullian (c.160–220 AD) and Justin Martyr (100–165 AD) make this very point when they address the Mithraic cults of their time, arguing that certain practices in the cult, among them baptism and communion, are copying Christian symbols.[108]

Mithras also did not have twelve disciples, as some claim. There are two versions of the Mithras legend. In the Persian version, Mithras has one disciple, and in the Roman version, he has two. Mithras was never buried in a tomb and resurrected three days later. There is, in fact, no record of Mithras dying in any of the mythological material.

DIONYSUS

A third supposed parallel with Jesus is the Greek god Dionysus, the god of wine. It is claimed that Dionysus was, like Horus and Mithras, born of a virgin on December 25 and that he also rose from the dead. As we saw with Horus, the birth date parallel has a simple, historically verifiable explanation—unrelated to supposed parallels with Christ. But what about the claim of a virgin birth? According to scholars, Dionysus was conceived when the Greek god Zeus impregnated his own mother, Semele, by becoming a lighting bolt and striking her. Later, the goddess Hera tricked Semele and caused her to be burnt to a crisp. The prenatal Dionysus was left sitting on the ground. While certainly a spectacular story, this is not a *virgin* birth. And as with the other stories, Dionysus also did not rise from the dead. The story is that when he was an infant, a gang of Titans attacked him and ate him—everything but his heart. This they left sitting on the ground. Zeus later came down, destroyed the Titans, and then restored Dionysus to life from his own heart. Some cite this as a clear parallel with Jesus' crucifixion and resurrection. But the parallels are weak. A man rising again from death after being crucified and a god being restored to life from his own heart aren't exactly the same story. Again, this is stretching facts far beyond what is warranted, all to fit a preconceived narrative.

ATTIS

Another mythological character cited as a Christological figure is Attis, a Greek god of vegetation, whose death and "resurrection" represented the fruits of the earth, which die in winter only to rise again in the spring. Christ Myth proponents claim that Attis was born of a virgin, crucified on a tree to redeem the earth, and resurrected from the dead. Again, when we look at the evidence we find that Attis was *not* born of a virgin. His mother conceived him when a male god put his semen on a piece of fruit, which she ate, leading to conception. While interesting and strange, this isn't a "virgin conception" parallel with Christianity. While Attis's mother may or may not have been a virgin, this is quite different from the virgin conception of Jesus Christ. The Bible never speaks of the semen of God impregnating Mary or anything close.

What of the claim that Attis was crucified on a tree to redeem the earth? There are two recorded versions of his death. In the first, Attis is killed while hunting when another hunter accidentally hits him with a spear. The second, more popular version of the story begins at Attis's wedding when his disapproving father, Agdistis, arrives and causes chaos that results in a stampede of people and the trampling of Attis's bride. Attis, upset with his father, rips off his own genitals, runs from the wedding, and dies under a pine tree. So, yes, a tree is involved. And, yes, there is blood. But that's as far as the parallel goes. There is no talk of redeeming the world or crucifixion. Attis is not resurrected from the dead. After his death, his father pleads with Zeus to raise Attis, but Zeus declares he can't. Instead, Zeus causes Attis's hair to grow perpetually and his pinky finger to move continuously. Call me crazy, but I think it's safe to say that this is not a parallel with the resurrection of Jesus.

KRISHNA

The final parallel we need to consider is Krishna. There is one parallel drawn between the famous Indian god Krishna and Christ, and that is the claim that he was born of a virgin. However, according to legend, Krishna had seven siblings before he was born. Moreover, the claim regarding his miraculous conception is that a white elephant impregnated his mother. Again, while this sounds spectacular, it is not a *virgin* conception at all.

All of this is to show that when we look closely at the so-called parallels with Christianity we find that they are not parallels at all. There are few details that are similar in these pagan religions to Christianity, but those that are somewhat similar are very loose connections. Several actually come later than Christianity and borrow from Christianity rather than the other way around.

JFK vs. Abraham Lincoln

This is not to suggest that there are no parallels between Christianity and the religions that came before it. Christianity does not claim to be the first religion to speak of the concept of gods becoming human, dying, and then being resurrected—in a general sense. There are other religious beliefs rooted in stories that share these themes. So what does a Christian say about parallels that *predate* Christ? First, we need to be careful to avoid what Craig Evans calls "Parallelomania." This is where authors perceive similarities between events or people and then construct parallels without any attention to cultural context or historical awareness.[109] I once heard someone talk about the similarities between the lives and deaths of Abraham Lincoln and John F. Kennedy. He pointed out that:

- Both men were concerned with civil rights.
- Both were elected to congress in '46 (1846 and 1946).
- Lincoln was elected president in 1860, Kennedy in 1960.
- Both were slain on a Friday before a major holiday.
- Both were shot in the presence of their wives and another couple.

- Of the other couple, the man was wounded but neither wife was.
- Both were shot from behind in the head.
- Lincoln was shot in the Ford's Theatre in box 7; Kennedy was shot in car 7 of the Dallas motorcade.
- Both were pronounced dead at a location with the initials P.H. (Petersen House and Parkland Hospital).
- The successors of both men were named Johnson.
- Andrew Johnson was born in 1808, Lyndon B. Johnson in 1908.
- Both assassins were privates in the military.
- John Wilkes Booth was born in 1839; Lee Harvey Oswald was born in 1939.
- Booth fled from a theater to a library, while Oswald fled from a library to a theater.
- Both assassins were taken into custody by a police officer named Baker.
- Lincoln was shot in Ford's Theatre; Kennedy was shot in a Ford car—the model of the Ford was a Lincoln![110]

The parallels are uncanny. But no scholar believes that because of these similarities there is any legitimate connection between the lives and deaths of these two men. And on top of that, nobody questions the *existence* of John F. Kennedy because he came after Abraham Lincoln. In the same way, it's just not reasonable to question the life and death of Jesus—even if there are some parallels with other mythological figures.

And if there *are* parallels, what if there is a far more compelling explanation for why they exist than the explanations offered by skeptics (that Jesus is a myth) or Christians (that Satan weaved himself into pagan thought so that when Christianity arose it looked like a myth)?

What if nothing could be more natural in the plan of God than the existence of such stories?

The True Myth

In Romans 2:14–16 the apostle Paul says that Spirit of God writes his law in the hearts of all people. This explains why people who aren't Christians still possess convictions of right and wrong. Augustine of Hippo writes about this when he speaks directly to the pagan Celsus. Celsus had argued that it seemed as though God took no care of people in past times. Augustine disagreed, saying, "This very thing which is now called the Christian religion existed before. It was not absent from the beginning of the human race, until Christ Himself came in the flesh, [but it was] then the true religion, that already existed, began to be called Christian."[111]

We find within Christian thought a concept of a *pre-Christian* form of Christianity, a cruciform pattern built into the fabric of human history. This is similar to what the apostle Paul suggests in his letter to the Colossians: "Therefore let no one pass judgment on you in questions of food and drink," he says, "or with regard to a festival or a new moon or a Sabbath. These are a *shadow of the things to come*, but the substance belongs to Christ" (Colossians 2:16–17, emphasis added). Religious practices involving food and drink, or the celebration of festivals, were a "shadow," an anticipation of Christ, who later arrives and supplies the shadows with substance. The ancient myths, symbols, and festivals were God-given anticipations of the Christian story that prepared people to respond to the good news of Jesus. God by his grace used culture, myths, and legends to prepare humankind to hear and understand the gospel.

This is exactly the position that the modern novelist J. R. R. Tolkien held and is, interestingly, how he convinced fellow Oxford scholar C. S. Lewis to become a Christian. Lewis was a scholar of medieval literature who loved the elevating and exciting nature of medieval adventure stories. He believed that the myths and legends gave meaning, beauty, and joy to the world. But he also recognized that they were not *true*. History, on the other hand, while true, harbored no inherent meaning or beauty for Lewis. It related facts but did not imply purpose or design. Lewis's problem was that men derived more spiritual meaning from myths they do *not* believe are true than from the religions they professed. As an unbeliever, he feared that if Christianity were true, then the old stories and myths he loved so dearly were wholly false, "lies, breathed through silver" he said, exciting and full of beauty maybe, but ultimately worthless. One of his primary objections to Christianity was that it would steal his joy. Tolkien showed Lewis that the opposite was true, that the Christian understanding of the world gave equal weight to both of Lewis's passions: reason and romanticism.

In his biography on Lewis, Alister McGrath recounts the story of Lewis and Tolkien's fascinating conversation about this very topic in September 1931. Both men were professors at University of Oxford, and they were strolling with their friend Hugo Dyson along the famous Addison's Walk at Magdalen College. All belonged to a group called The Inklings who would meet at a local pub, the Eagle and Child, to drink and share their writings with one another. It was here that some of the most beloved literature of the twentieth century was first read aloud and shared, including *The Lord of the Rings* and *The Lion, the Witch and the Wardrobe*. On that September evening, Lewis relayed to his close friends his acceptance of the idea of God, clarifying that this was a conversion "only to theism, pure and simple, not to Christianity." Yet twelve days later, Lewis wrote to his friend Arthur Greeves saying: "I have just passed on from believing in God to definitely believing in Christ—in Christianity. . . . My long night talk with Dyson and

Tolkien had a good deal to do with it."[112] What happened that night that convinced Lewis to accept Christianity as true? Tolkien pointed out that myth and history are not all that removed from each other, that Lewis's problem lay not in his *rational* failure to understand God (as he had already acknowledged his existence) but in his *imaginative* failure to grasp God's significance; that a worldview that included the story of Christ gave life more meaning, adventure, and romance, not less. "Just as speech is invention about objects and ideas, so myth is invention about truth," he told him. "We have come from God and inevitably the myths woven by us, though they contain error, will also reflect a splintered fragment of the true light, the eternal truth that is with God. . . . Our myths may be misguided, but they steer however shakily towards the true harbor."[113]

In other words, instead of being wholly false or purely satanic distractions, the stories Lewis cherished were shadows—anticipations of the full truth.[114] Lewis wondered if Christianity was just another myth and whether the Gospels were merely fairy-stories. Tolkien explained that, in a way they were with their miraculous births, adventures, heroes, and happy endings. But there was one critical difference: they were *true*. They actually happened. Christianity was the best of both worlds. It was fairy-story incarnate, legend and history meeting as one. Christianity was, Tolkien said, the one and only place where *transcendence*, the joy myths created in us, and the *reality* of history collide. And so, romanticism and rationalism together were the paths on which Lewis came to Christ.

Lewis came to believe this deeply, concluding that at their best the Christ-shaped stories of the pagan world were a real, though unfocused, gleam of divine truth falling on human imagination:

> The old myth of the dying God comes down from the heaven
> of legend and imagination to the earth of history. It happens—at

a particular date, in a particular place. From Osiris, dying—nobody knows when or where—to a historical person crucified (it is all in order) under Pontius Pilate, it says. Christ is more than Osiris, not less. *We must not be ashamed of the parallels . . . they ought to be there, it would be a stumbling block if they weren't!* Those who do not know that this great myth became Fact when the Virgin conceived are, indeed, to be pitied.[115]

When we try to force parallels between Christianity and the pagan stories, we run the danger of minimizing the clear differences. But there is an opposite danger as well. Myths have their place in human history as expressions of a deep yearning in our consciousness—a universal witness to the hunger and hope that God would come into intimate contact with humankind, repair the damages made by our sinfulness, and grant a safety that would last forever. In the gospel we see that this is exactly what God has done. In other words, we told ourselves these stories until they became true.

Conclusion

If we look at the evidence honestly and do not get lost in conspiracy theories, I believe it leads us unwaveringly to confirm the historical existence of Jesus of Nazareth. That he was a real flesh-and-blood Jewish teacher in first-century Israel, and anything but a mythological projection or reappropriation of ancient legends/astrological stories. In this we are in agreement with the majority of historical scholarship and avoid falling into unsupported theories based on unwarranted assumptions and unchallenged agendas.

CHAPTER 5

The Problem of
EVIL AND
SUFFERING

*I sent one boy to the gas chamber at Huntsville. . . .
He'd killed a fourteen-year old girl. The papers
said it was a crime of passion and he told me there
wasn't no passion to it . . . he told me that he had
been plannin' to kill somebody for about as long as
he could remember. Said that if they turned him
out he'd do it again. Said he knew he was goin' to
hell. I don't know what to make of that . . . maybe
he was some new kind. What do you say to a man
that by his own admission has no soul? . . . But he
wasn't nothin' compared to what was comin' down
the pike . . .*

CORMAC MCCARTHY, NO COUNTRY FOR OLD MEN

The late professor, apologist, and author Ronald Nash points out, "Every philosopher believes that the most serious challenge to theism was, and is, and will continue to be the problem of evil."[116] I have found this to be exactly right. This sentiment was confirmed in a recent national poll that asked, "If you could ask God only one question and you knew he would give you an answer, what would you ask?" The most common response was, "Why is there pain and suffering in the world?"[117] Philosopher David Bentley Hart puts the problem well: "One might well conclude that the world contains far too much misery for the pious idea of a good, loving and just God to be taken seriously, and that any alleged creator of the universe in which children suffer and die hardly deserves our devotion."[118] He goes on to say that the problem of evil is "an intelligible one, with a certain sublime moral purity to it, [and] . . . deeply compelling."[119]

I agree. For me it is maybe the most compelling of all the challenges we are exploring.

I recently conducted a funeral for a man named Andrew. Only thirty-five years old, he was healthy and active as a competitive cyclist. More importantly, he was a selfless and great father with two beautiful kids and a loving, caring family. A few months before I met him in his hospital room, they had found a tumor in his brain, and shortly afterward he had gone blind. Andrew had visited our church a few times, where something connected with him, and he decided he wanted to explore God more. I sat on his hospital bed, read the Bible to him, prayed with him, and led him into a relationship with Christ.

During his funeral I looked down at his young children in the front row as they wept. I felt the weight of their suffering. It felt wrong, *evil*, disjointed from the ways things *should* be. And I found myself asking a question many have asked: *How can I believe in a God who says he is all-loving, and yet he allows this?* How could Andrew face the seeming injustice of his sickness, yet embrace God in his hospital bed rather than reject him? And on a larger scale, how can God allow a world with rape, murder, disease, terrorism, and natural disasters that take the lives of hundreds, even thousands of people every day?

As I'm writing this, the headlines are filled with news that a man drove a truck through a crowded area in Nice, France, killing over eighty people, including many little children. There's another about a man in Alberta, Canada, who killed a mother and kidnapped her five-year-old daughter, who was later found dead as well. Eight police officers were killed in two separate shootings in the last ten days in Dallas and Baton Rouge. And even though you are reading this long after these events, I'm betting that the news has not improved. All day. Everywhere. And it's been like that for thousands of years. One of the most popular versions of this problem was set forth by the eighteenth-century Scottish philosopher David Hume: "Is God willing to prevent evil but not able? Then he is impotent. Is he able to but not willing? Then he is malevolent. Is he both able and willing? Why then is there evil?"[120] This is a fair and challenging question. It asks us to consider if there is a connection between evil and God's *non*existence, and it suggests that the existence of evil in some way proves that God does not exist. While there are some problems with Hume's question, we should note that it assumes that evil is real and that if God exists he is loving. And, going one step further, it argues that those two realities are not compatible. So how does one answer that? Why do I cite all these awful things and, at the same time, believe in God and, more than that, trust and love him? How can I do all of those things at the same time? The answer is hinted at with something the philosopher I cited earlier, David Bentley Hart, concludes after citing the problem of evil himself. He says that the problem of evil and suffering is "an affective" but "not strictly logical—position to hold."[121]

And that is what this chapter is about.

It's a Personal Question

The first thing to say is that the challenge of evil and suffering is more than a *theoretical* or *philosophical* problem—it's personal. We *feel* this question. In my work as a pastor, I visit with families that have lost loved ones to disease, to violence, to natural disasters. I get calls in the middle of the night that someone has committed suicide, adultery, or even murder. My own life story is riddled with brokenness and pain at many levels. My aunt had schizophrenia and killed herself by jumping off a building. My dad was an alcoholic who couldn't keep a job and didn't know what to do with two sons. My childhood is filled with memories of an unstable home characterized by fighting, yelling, and slamming doors. My father, more interested in his own life than those of his wife and children, abandoned us. My parents divorced when I was eight. Shortly after that, I developed Tourette syndrome, likely because of the stress of my childhood, and over time this developed into Obsessive Compulsive Disorder, which debilitated me through my high school years. I fell into illogical habits, exhibiting tics and engaging in compulsive behaviors for which I had no explanation. When I was fifteen I got a phone call from a hospital administrator who told me that my dad had died of lung cancer. He had never even called us to tell us he was sick. I stood before his open casket at his funeral and thought: *There is something disjointed about this, something not good.*

I know you've felt the same. You've watched the news or received a late-night phone call, and you've felt sick and lost and abandoned. And there is good reason why we feel this way, a reason, as we will see, that points us toward God's existence, not away from it.

It's a Biblical Question

The second thing to say is that this is a biblical question. The Bible opens with a poetic introduction to God, who creates a world of beauty. He is a God who is good, characterized by justice and love and joy, yet not three chapters in, we find that evil and suffering are already a part of life on earth. The prophets and the psalmists go on to feel and write about this tension, the disconnect between the goodness of God and the evil in this world. They continuously asked the question: "O LORD, how long" until you make the world right again? (Psalm 6:3; Habakkuk 1:2). Remarkably, the Bible tells us that people in heaven are asking the same question: "I saw under the altar," John wrote in the book of Revelation, "the souls of those who had been slain for the word of God. . . . They cried out with a loud voice, 'O Sovereign Lord . . . how long before you will judge and avenge our blood?'" (6:9–10).

The whole Bible cares deeply about injustice and suffering. It's the story of how evil has affected us: Adam and Eve's fall, Cain's murder of Abel, Noah's flood, the tower of Babel, the patriarchs' sins, Egypt's oppression of Israel, David's psalms of lament (around his own adultery and the tragedy of losing his child), Israel's exile, the killing and torture of the prophets and God's people, and the long, lonely wait for the Messiah—it goes on relentlessly.[122]

The Bible does not avoid this question, as some religions do. It faces it head on and provides the most glorious answer in the marketplace of ideas.

Not Just a Christian Problem

Every worldview, even the classic skepticism of atheism and agnosticism, needs to provide an answer to the question of evil and suffering. You can't shrug it away. If you're a skeptic, what's your answer? What's the answer if you're a Hindu, a Muslim, or a Buddhist? This is not just a Christian question; each of us must wrestle it to the ground and see if our worldview holds up under its weight. So let's start with a brief look at how different religions and worldviews address suffering.

NEW AGE

New Age philosophy addresses the problem of suffering and evil with a combination of ideas borrowed from its roots in Eastern religions.

New Age thinking is rooted in pantheism ("all is one and all is God"), and practices of meditation, praying, and positive thinking in New Age thought revolve around reaching a higher or greater state of enlightenment and illumination. The goal is to reach an enlightened state of existence.[123] New Age philosophy teaches that we all have the divine in us—or more accurately, that we are all part of the divine essence in some way, part of a cosmic consciousness. This view, unlike atheism, doesn't suggest that evil and suffering mean that God doesn't exist, but that *evil and suffering* themselves don't exist. It claims that negative events or moral evils are not "real," they are simply *maya*—an illusion.[124]

New Age philosophy *denies* the reality of evil, and sadly this denial and rejection of evil and suffering has infected mainstream Christianity today. Recently, I went to the house of an elderly Christian woman whose husband was in the hospital dying of cancer. She told me, "My best friend, who is a Christian, will not come to the hospital with me to visit my dying husband." When I asked why, she told me her friend believed if she went to the hospital, she would be acknowledging the reality that the man was sick and in doing so would give this false sickness power over him. "So don't go and visit him," the friend had said, "and don't say the word *cancer*. Because if you do, you're creating that reality in his life." This way of thinking denies reality and is thoroughly unbiblical. The Bible clearly teaches that evil and suffering are very real. They can't be ignored or swept under a rug. They are so real that God himself had to come to earth in the person of Jesus to deal with them himself.

HINDUISM

Historically, Hinduism says that evil and suffering result from karma—an impersonal force of justice that operates like the laws of physics, causing good or bad things to happen based on whether a person has been good or bad in this life and in past lives (our *dharma*). "What goes around comes around," we say glibly. "If you're a positive person, good things will happen to you," we say at cocktail parties. But such a philosophy is both naive and dangerous.

Several years ago, as I was traveling in India, I saw hundreds of destitute, poor, sick, and dying people populating the streets and sidewalks. They were looking for food, money, or a drink of water. A woman holding a baby who was close to death scratched at the windows of our van. "Excuse me, sir. Excuse me, sir," she cried with her hand outstretched. Our guide told us, "You can't give them money. If you stop karma from doing its job to this woman and her baby, she'll have to live this suffering again in the next life." In other words, the underlying belief was that this suffering was deserved and there was no point in trying to change it—it's just the way things are, and we must accept that. The religious idea of karma justifies and even legitimizes suffering in this world. If this is the worldview you have chosen, I would humbly submit to you that your beliefs fail to take suffering seriously and perpetuate an acceptance of the status quo. I do not believe this is an adequate answer to the question of suffering. At best it's a form of denial, and at worst it helps continue the vicious cycle.

Christianity confronts the concept of karma, and Jesus spoke directly against it. When once he encountered a blind man, several people asked him *why* the man was born this way: "'Rabbi, who sinned, this man or his parents, that he was born blind?' Jesus answered, 'It was not that this man sinned, or his parents, but that the works of God might be displayed in him'" (John 9:2–3). Then Jesus healed the man. Jesus taught that the man's blindness was not the result of anything the man or his parents had done in this life or in a previous life. Rather, his blindness was an occasion for God's power to be demonstrated before others.

ATHEISM

A third view, one that is popular in the Western world, is the perspective of atheism. Atheists argue that because evil and suffering exist in the universe, God does not. When a tsunami kills hundreds of thousands of people or terrorists fly planes into buildings or people are slaughtered in tribal genocide, they argue that these events are evidence that a loving and gracious God could not possibly exist. The atheistic conclusion is that "bad" things happen because there is no such thing as a good, loving God. The existence of suffering has been called the "rock of atheism"—irrefutable evidence that God cannot exist. But when we really stop to think about such logic, we see that this argument doesn't hold up.

We Need to Prove More

First, simply saying "God *can't* exist if there is evil" does not make it true. The argument itself is built on several assumptions that need to be proven, not simply assumed, and this is a far more difficult task than many atheists and skeptics recognize. Philosopher Alvin Plantinga has pointed out that Christians believe in five basic premises about God and evil:

1. God exists.
2. God is omnipotent (all-powerful).
3. God is omniscient (all-knowing).
4. God is wholly good.
5. Evil exists.

Atheists argue that these assertions can't all be true at the same time. Yet as Plantinga suggests, atheists "must provide some proofs of why." In other words, it's not sufficient to simply say that they can't all be true; additional proofs are required, and "certainly none of them [atheists] has succeeded"[125] at providing those.

Some have at least attempted to provide these additional proofs. Atheist philosopher J. L. Mackie, for instance, argued, "A good thing [i.e., God] always eliminates evil as far as it can, and that there are no limits to what an omnipotent thing can do," ergo God *should* eliminate all evil because he is all-good and all-powerful.[126] This is a valid attempt, but it is not apparent why either of Mackie's points are *necessarily* true. A good thing always eliminates evil as far as it can? Why must we assume that every case of evil is one that God could eliminate without, at the same time, *eliminating a greater good?* Or what if, in order to stop said evil, God had to violate human free will? Or what if stopping an evil act today would set in motion a butterfly effect that would cause a great artist or scientist not to be born in the future (i.e., creating a greater evil, or at least a lesser good in the world)?

So we are reduced from the initial charge down to God "is all good only if he eliminates every evil state of affairs *which is not a logically necessary condition of a good state of affairs that outweighs it.*"[127] In other words, God is still good if he allows evil in order to retain free will in the universe or if it allows a greater good in the future. With this in mind, we must admit that an omnipotent being could permit as much evil as he pleased "so long as for every evil state of affairs he permits, there is a greater good."[128] Mackie's first premise, then, that a good thing always eliminates evil as far as it can, is shown to be a false assumption. Thus, while the idea of God and evil existing together may be difficult for us to accept, the two are *not* actually incompatible. Atheism assumes they are but fails to *prove* the contradiction.

Suffering as Proof of God

The second and more important idea in this context is that the existence of evil and suffering actually points in quite the opposite direction to that of atheism, *revealing God to us* rather than disproving him. In other words, it is a powerful evidence *for* God's existence. Here is what I mean. The skeptic's position assumes there is such a thing as categorical evil. For example, there is near universal agreement that killing innocent people or abusing children is categorically *wrong*. Others might consider cancer or being the victim of a tsunami or an earthquake also to be suffering. The fact that a skeptic acknowledges categories of "evil" and "suffering" presents a problem for them. Where do these categories originate? Where do we get the idea that human beings are important, that human life has value, and that human beings should be protected and loved instead of tortured and disposed of? We sense in ourselves, and in our larger culture, that there is an inherent moral order to the universe. There is a way things are *supposed* to be. And the existence of these convictions points toward God, not away from him. C. S. Lewis states it this way:

> When I was an atheist, my argument against God was that the universe seemed so cruel and unjust. But how had I got this idea of just and unjust? What was I comparing this universe with when I called it unjust? Of course I could have just given up my idea of justice by saying that it was nothing but a private idea of my own. But if I did that, then my argument against God collapsed too, for the argument depended on saying that the world was really unjust, not just simply that it did not happen to please my fancies.[129]

If we take God out of the picture, the problem becomes even bigger, and that's where the atheist finds himself if he is honest. When I stood over my father's casket, there was something within me that knew the reality I was experiencing was disjointed and wrong. In that was an assumption of a way the universe was *supposed* to be, and this was not it. The Bible says this is because God "has put eternity into man's heart" (Ecclesiastes 3:11). We are designed by our Creator to live in a world without sin and death (Genesis 1–2), and this is why we long for beauty, justice, love, and peace. We were made for a different world than the one we live in, and the feeling of disorder is one of nostalgia. We would not have these moral categories unless God had given them to us.

Doesn't Evolution Provide Moral Categories?

Many skeptics believe that we *would* still have these moral categories as a result of unguided evolutionary processes. A short time ago, an atheist friend posted a "letter from God" on Facebook. It attempted to describe where God was during the horrible movie theater shootings in Colorado in 2012 where twelve people were murdered. The letter explained: "I was in the same place I have been in every other horrible event through history: nowhere, because I don't exist." The poster's Facebook friends loved it, commenting on how much they agreed with him. I wrote: "Where did you get the sense that shooting a bunch of people in a movie theater is *wrong*? Doesn't the fact that it bothers you raise the question of where you got the conviction in the first place? Doesn't it suggest that maybe someone gave you an understanding of right and that you are now using it to put him on trial?" The poster responded that he did have a moral category called evil, not from God but the result of evolutionary processes developed in our brain circuitry over hundreds of thousands of years, based on what was best for society and what had helped us survive in a particular harsh environment. "Good" and "evil," in his thinking, are simply artifacts of what our ancestors were forced to believe in order to survive. They are not transcendently true or virtuous in any way, and certainly not because they were given to us by a higher power. What should we make of this objection?

First, if we formed beliefs only because the beliefs helped us *survive* (giving us comfort, for instance), and not because they are somehow true or virtuous in and of themselves, then we should go all the way and acknowledge that *there is no actual truth to any of our beliefs*. There is no such thing as purpose or design. The concept of truth assumes there is a moral order, a standard by which other things can be judged. But if we just believe stuff because it is "advantageous" to do so in a given moment or environment, and our agreed-upon beliefs are nothing more than pragmatic responses to obstacles in life, then we must apply the same logic to evolutionary theory as well. Maybe we only believe in *it* because it helped us survive.

This self-defeating contradiction was not lost on Charles Darwin, who admitted that if his evolution was true, he probably couldn't actually trust it because it was the conclusion of an animal just trying to mate and survive. "Who can trust the convictions of a monkey's mind?"[130] he said. It's a hopeless situation. We draw conclusions because we believe they are rational and correspond to truth, but if evolution is "true," then we are not rational creatures at all, and all truth claims go by the wayside, including the one that evolution is the way we came up with moral categories!

But there is a second problem with the evolutionary argument. Many of our moral values directly *oppose* those we would have developed if evolutionary survival were the factor determining our sense of right and wrong. We see those who hold power forcing their wills on the weak every day, for instance, and yet it pains us. According to evolutionary theory, this is something we should accept as merely part of the inevitable process of human struggle and mutation. It makes little sense for us to think that genocide or the rich exploiting the poor should be something we abhor. Why would we ever conclude that? These are just part of the outworking of nature, aren't they? But what do we do when our moral conclusions directly contradict things that nature by itself would have likely told us were advantageous?

Prom Mom

In 1997, Melissa Drexler was attending her high school prom as an eighteen-year-old senior when she went to the bathroom and gave birth to a baby. She cut the umbilical cord, strangled the baby to death, and threw it into a garbage can. Then she went back out on the dance floor with her friends. After this story became news, Darwinian evolutionary theorist Steven Pinker wrote an article for *The New York Times* called "Why They Kill Their Newborns." In it he reassured everyone that we must "understand" we are all descendants of women who made the difficult decisions that allowed them to become grandmothers in an unforgiving world, and that we inherited the brain circuitry that led to those decisions.[131] He argued that natural selection affects our behavior by endowing us with emotions that coax us toward adaptive choices. "A capacity for neonaticide is built into the biological design of our parental emotions," he said. "If a newborn is sickly or if its survival is not promising, they may cut their losses and favor the healthiest in the litter."[132] Pinker is being honest here about the implications of an evolutionary worldview. If we are the product of evolutionary chance, then killing kids for the emotional good of the parents shouldn't bother us. But it does. And that is the *real* problem of evil.

What do we make of this conviction that is *contrary* to what would have increased our ability to survive at a given time? Why are most people disgusted by Melissa Drexler's actions? Where did these *un-Darwinian* convictions come from? The fact that we call this act "evil," or at least "awful," points us to a transcendent ethic that originates with an authority *outside* nature.[133] In the end, we all end up moving *away* from evolutionary explanations for our morality, not toward them.

But Isn't Evil Pointless?

There is yet another foundational and unproven assumption built into the atheistic challenge surrounding the problem of evil and suffering. Again, philosopher J. L. Mackie presents it when he says that if God exists, he would not allow *pointless* evil. And because there is so much *unjustifiable, pointless* evil in the world, the traditional God cannot exist.[134] Again, there is a flaw in this assumption. How do we prove that evil and suffering are, in fact, pointless? We can't research every incident of suffering to figure out if any good came from it. Moreover, it may be that the opposite is true—that suffering does have a purpose in the world. The evidence provided by history and confirmed by human experience seems to point us in this direction: that suffering frequently leads to some measure of good. Many will attest that some of the greatest lessons we learn in life come through suffering.

My wife, Erin, and I had been married just a few months when we moved from Toronto, where we had grown up, to Vancouver, where I would attend graduate school. We drove across the country to the Pacific coast, a place where we didn't know anyone. After four days of driving, we pulled up to the house we were renting in Vancouver. We weren't even out of the car when Erin started sobbing. She missed home. We were newly married, broke, and lost in the world. I assured her it would all get better as the week went on. But it didn't. It got worse.

The first night, as we crawled onto our blow-up mattress (our stuff was being trucked across Canada), we smelled something weird. I went to a vent and realized the guy below us was smoking weed, A lot of it, and it was hotboxing our bedroom. More tears. "You brought me to B.C.," Erin sobbed. "We have no family here, no friends, and everybody is a tree-hugging, weed-smoking hippie. I want to go home!" The next day the movers called and said it would cost us thousands of dollars more than we had been quoted to get our stuff back. More tears. We were then told that our house formerly had been used as a crack house, and people had overdosed in our bathroom. Yes, more tears. But here's the thing: we had never prayed together more as a couple than in those days. We had never had to count on each other more as a couple than in that season. We took all that pain, loneliness, and doubt and pushed into Jesus and into one another more than we ever had. In other words, *the experience of suffering was good for us.* It strengthened our marriage in ways we never would have imagined.

Writer and journalist Malcolm Muggeridge agreed that not only are arguments such as Mackie's impossible to prove, they are outright wrong. "Indeed I can say with all truthfulness," Muggeridge wrote, "that everything I have learned in my 75 years in this world . . . that has truly enhanced and enlightened my existence has been through affliction and not through happiness. . . . In other words, if it were possible to evaluate affliction from our earthly existence through some drug . . . the result would not be to make life delectable, but to make it too banal and trivial to be endurable."[135] Why does this ring true for so many people? Why is it that we know pain can actually grow us? If an evolutionary process really was how our brains concluded things about the world, we shouldn't conclude this at all.

But we do.

Years ago I was working at a church on the day a funeral was held for a sixteen-year-old boy. I had such angst about the service that I left the building, walked around the town, and cried out to God. I wanted to know why this boy's life had been cut short. I admitted to God that I struggled to understand what good could come from such pain. When I was done, I went to a coffee shop and sat there in a daze. Soon afterward, a man who attended our church came in and sat next to me. I told him about my time of frustration with God and asked him, "What good could possibly come out of such meaningless pain?" He let me vent for a while, and then he prayed for me. As he was getting up to leave, he asked, "By the way, did I ever tell you how I came to know Christ? I was going down the wrong road," he said, "and God completely transformed my life. And it all started at the funeral of a sixteen-year old boy, a friend of mine. It was there that I heard the gospel for the first time, and I gave my life to Jesus." In that moment God peeled back the veil for a second and gave me a glimpse of a bigger story where good in different measure and in different ways *can* come from suffering, even if from our human perspective we don't always understand it because of our limitations.

So, the assumption that there is never a good reason for evil and suffering cannot be supported by philosophy, science, our life experience, or the testimony of history. It is not a defensible philosophical position. And this is consistent with the view of evil and suffering we find in the Bible. All through the Scriptures God uses suffering to make people who they are, to refine them. Moses, Abraham, David, Job, Paul, and, of course, Jesus himself are examples of lives in which the most awful evil and suffering is turned into a greater good. In the case of Jesus, his death and suffering lead to the greatest good—the salvation of humankind itself.

The Advantage of Disadvantage

This understanding not only resonates with Christians but has been recognized by many secular thinkers as well. In his book *David and Goliath*, Malcolm Gladwell documents the lives of many successful leaders and entrepreneurs who succeed not *in spite* of challenges and suffering in life but *because* of them. He calls this phenomenon "the advantage of disadvantage."[136] Gladwell cites a study from City, University of London that notes that a third of highly successful entrepreneurs are dyslexic (e.g., Richard Branson, Charles Schwab, and Paul Orfalea).[137] Sharon Thompson-Schill recalls speaking at a prominent university donors' meeting filled with successful business people, and when she asked how many of them had been diagnosed with a learning disorder, half of the hands went up. Gladwell's insight on this is profound:

There are two possible interpretations for this fact. One is that this remarkable group of people triumphed in spite of their disability: they are so smart and so creative that nothing—not even a lifetime of struggling with reading—could stop them. The second, more intriguing, possibility is that they succeeded, in part, *because* of their disorder—that they learned something in their struggle that proved to be of enormous advantage.[138]

Consider the example of Joseph in the book of Genesis. It is *because* he was enslaved that he went to Egypt, became powerful in government, and later—when his brothers came to Egypt to seek food—was able to take care of them and the rest of his family. At that point, Joseph delivered one of the Bible's most important truths about suffering: "You meant evil against me, but God meant it for good" (Genesis 50:20). Joseph was careful not to assume, as we so often do in modern times, that when it comes to suffering, that the meaning behind it will be obvious. Often, the meaning or purpose of suffering or evil is more akin to a microscopic organism than something blatant and obvious. So small that it is not *visible* to the naked eye but still *very real*.[139]

The reason we struggle with this concept of purposeful suffering today in the Western world is because we see the point and purpose of life as *happiness*. In that paradigm suffering is always a pointless invasion. By contrast, social theorist Max Scheler argues that an "essential part of the teaching and directives of the great religious and philosophical thinkers the world over has been on the meaning of pain and suffering."[140] Throughout history, virtually every society has sought to teach people how to deal with pain and suffering. Sadly, our current culture has largely neglected this task. Why? Because for generations we've embraced a secular worldview that assumes that the material world is all there is, and that, thus, pain has no meaningful part to play in life. And yet we feel the inadequacy of this approach and yearn for an answer beyond it, don't we? Which is why we as a secular society borrow concepts from religion when tragedy strikes. After every terrorist attack or mass shooting, my Facebook news feed fills up with my atheist and agnostic friends offering "prayers" and "thoughts" to the victims and families of these tragedies. They have to borrow language from religious traditions because their own view of the world offers nothing to them. Several of my friends use the language of karma in normal life ("What goes around comes around," etc.). But such words don't make sense in the face of tragedy. Karmic theology, when truly understood, blames the victims for their fate. So people borrow aspects of the Christian worldview when tragedy strikes because "Christianity teaches that, contra fatalism, suffering is overwhelming; contra Buddhism, suffering is real; contra karma, suffering is often unfair; but contra secularism, suffering is *meaningful*."[141]

Underlying this entire discussion is another, deeper question. What is "good"? Far beyond the suffering we experience in our individual lives, philosophers point out that suffering may be a necessary reality for the universe to reach its *greatest good*. They point out that in order to have a maximum joy, the opposite potential must exist as well. While this is not the Christian worldview, there are some affinities. In the Christian worldview, the greatest good is God. God loves, and his love is expressed in acts of creation; when human beings rebel and disrupt the moral justice of the universe, God's response is ultimately one of love, communicated in an act of redemption and salvation. When God was faced with the question of evil and suffering in the Garden of Eden, he could have changed Adam and Eve into robots. He could have destroyed them. But he would have sacrificed a greater good, that of a loving relationship with humanity. Though we may not understand all of the reasons why, it is possible that God allowed evil and suffering so that the greater good could exist.

In Christian theology, the cross of Christ is the moment where the greatest good, glory, and love of God is revealed to the universe. Why was such suffering necessary? Because human sin had disrupted the moral order, spreading evil. God turns human evil into our redemption and salvation, and so the killing of our Creator is transformed into the supreme act of love. "God preferred *on the whole* the global result of the drama of sin and salvation to a world without it," John Stackhouse Jr. writes. Evil "was *necessary* for that drama and thus evil *does* have a place in the great scheme of things."[142] Without it, there would be no such thing as endurance and bravery and sacrifice and courage.[143] In his wisdom God said, "I want the greater good to happen."

Christianity proclaims a God who is not distant or removed from human suffering. In every other religion, God (or the gods) remains aloof and distant, but the Christian God experienced human existence, identified and empathized with us, suffered with us and for us. And why? Why did God humiliate himself, suffer, and die an awful death? Yes, to save us from our sins, but that is only part of the story. Christianity says that the suffering of the cross is something else: it reveals God's very *nature*. Suffering is a reflection of who God *is*, not just something he *did*. This is an underappreciated idea within Christianity but a massively important one. The New Testament writers tell us that, yes, our need of saving was the *occasion* for God's suffering on the cross, but not its only *reason*.[144] God suffers, not as something additional to his identity, as just a rescue mission in response to our mistakes, but because of his identity (Colossians 1:15–20; Philippians 2:5–11). In other words, the cross of Christ is not just about soteriology (salvation) but Christology (the identity of God and Jesus himself).

The End.

The apostle Paul wrote: "We know that for those who love God all things work together for good" (Romans 8:28). *All* things, not just some things or good things, but *all* things. How does that work? I felt a glimpse of it once. My wife was in a car accident when she was eight months pregnant with our first daughter. We thought we had lost the baby for a couple of hours until we got to the hospital and heard a heartbeat. When our daughter was born, I held her in my arms and kissed her with more emotion and intensity *because* at one point I had faced the possibility of living without her. The pain gave way to a greater glory. I think of this often, and I hold on to hope that when the new creation dawns it will put all the awfulness of the world in context.

In the film version of *The Two Towers*, Samwise Gamgee tries to convince Frodo to keep pressing on to Mount Doom despite all the pain and suffering they have been through and seen. "It's like in the great stories, Mr. Frodo," he says, "the ones that really mattered. Full of darkness and danger they were, and sometimes you didn't want to know the end because how could the end be happy? How could the world go back to the way it was when so much bad had happened? But in the end it's only a passing thing, this shadow. Even darkness must pass. A new day will come, *and when the sun shines it'll shine out the clearer.*" This is the great hope that Christianity holds out to all of us. That somehow, when we see the greater glory we'll look back—as crazy as it sounds right now—and we'll say that on the bell curve of experience, evil and suffering made it all the richer. Perhaps the apostle Paul says it best: "For I consider that the sufferings of this present time *are not worth comparing* with the glory that is to be revealed to us" (Romans 8:18, emphasis added).

Such is the hope of Christianity.

CHAPTER 6

The Problem of
HELL

*In eternity this world will be like Troy, I believe,
and all that has passed here will be the epic of the
universe, the ballad they sing in the streets.*

MARILYNNE ROBINSON, *GILEAD*

The concept of hell is one of the greatest stumbling blocks for Western people. For some, it's the deal breaker. Peter Kreeft writes: "Of all the doctrines in Christianity, Hell is probably the most difficult to defend, the most burdensome to believe and the first to be abandoned."[145] Many are appalled by the idea of an eternal place of punishment for those who don't trust Christ. Their reaction is more than just a *doubt*, I think, but a *repulsion*—by the whole concept. I've had many conversations that started something like this: "Hell is a disgusting doctrine that I can't stomach, and Christians say that hell exists and that God created it, so, quite simply, I don't want to be a Christian or believe in the biblical God."

The famous atheist philosopher Bertrand Russell put the objection this way: "I do not myself feel that any person who is really profoundly humane can believe in Everlasting punishment."[146] This sentiment was also shared by Charles Darwin, who pointed to the doctrine of hell as one of the significant reasons for his own abandonment of the Christian faith. Darwin wrote in his autobiography, "I can indeed hardly see how anyone ought to wish Christianity to be true; for if so plain language of the text seems to show that the men who do not believe, and this would include my father, brother and almost all my friends, will be everlastingly punished. And this is a damnable doctrine."[147]

Hell presents multiple obstacles for people and raises several questions, including:

- How can an all-loving God judge people?
- Why does God condemn people eternally for what they do in a finite amount of time?
- Why is it necessary for hell to involve a kind of torture (i.e., eternal fire, brimstone, etc.)?

So how does Christianity respond to this? Is there any explanation or defense for this teaching? I believe there is and that when you examine the Bible you discover a logic and rationale for hell that may not have been clear before. C. S. Lewis was correct when he wrote: "There is no doctrine which I would more willingly remove from Christianity than this, if it lay in my power. But it has the full support of Scripture and, specially, of our Lord's own words; it has always been held by Christendom; and it has the support of reason."[148] Let's explore all of these obstacles and what they say about this admittedly difficult doctrine.

Campfire and Hellfire

I first encountered the idea of hell when I was nine years old. I hadn't grown up in the church, but I attended a Christian summer camp that year. At the start of the week, the nightly messages were light, focused on a personal relationship with God. But as the week progressed, the messages got more and more serious—and dark. Then Friday came. I later learned that this was referred to as "turn-or-burn night." We gathered around a fire pit in the middle of the campground to sing songs and play games before heading to bed. The speaker stood up, threw some gas on the fire, and as the flames shot up into the air he said, "Do you want that to be you?"

Um . . . no.

"Then believe in Jesus!" To which we all said yes of course, not only the kids but the counselors too. Afterward, I recall the conversation we had as nine-year-old boys gathered in that cabin: "*I* don't want to go to hell; do *you* want to go to hell?" "No, I don't want to go to hell." "Well then, I'm glad I said that prayer that got me out of it. Phew." Which makes sense because really, who *wants* to go to hell? And who won't take a route out of hell simply by saying a prayer about this or that? It's a no-brainer.

This is just one of many problems with the way Christians present hell to people. The presentation that night was driven by the idea that *fear* would motivate people toward long-lasting faith in Christ. Which, as we will see, doesn't work. Don't get me wrong; it's not as though fear can't motivate us. We see throughout the Scriptures that a reverent respect for God and his judgment on our sin is one reason why we respond to his mercy and trust in his offer of forgiveness (Proverbs 9:10; Philippians 2:12). But presentations like the one at camp that summer elevate fear as the primary and exclusive reason to trust in Christ. Moreover, when fear is our motive, it will rarely, if ever, translate into a life of discipleship. Mishandling the doctrine of hell and the reality of God's judgment on our sin can even damage a person's faith, as I have witnessed over and over again in my life.

What is hell, then? What is its purpose? Is it a place? Is it forever? Is it real? Should we fear it? And how should Christians talk about it? Let's take a closer look at this very important biblical doctrine.

Jesus: Teacher of Hell

One reason we need to talk about hell is that it is not a peripheral issue. It's connected closely with the person of Jesus and his teaching. I can sympathize with Bertrand Russell when he says: "There is one very serious defect to my mind in Christ's moral character and that is that he believed in hell."[149] And I agree with his understanding that a rejection of hell necessarily entails a rejection of Jesus. If we want to answer the question, "Why hell?" then we need to look at Jesus and what he thought and taught about hell.

I say this because most people in the Western world *like* Jesus. New Age thinkers such as Deepak Chopra write books about Jesus as a mystic and guru of Eastern religion. Some Christians talk about being "Red Letter Christians" because they want to emphasize obedience to the specific teachings of Jesus in the Bible, prioritizing those over the writings of Paul and the rest of the New Testament. People often say that they don't like the Old Testament God who seems angry and full of wrath, always punishing people. People are warmer to the New Testament because of Jesus, who seems to be more about love and grace and teaching helpful spiritual ideas.

The problem with this is that it's not true. We get most of our understanding of hell not from the Old Testament, but from the words of Jesus. All of this talk about eternal punishment is *not* in the Old Testament; it's in the New Testament. We don't get a clear, refined doctrine of hell in the Bible until we get to Jesus, and he is the one who most explicitly and directly taught about its existence and its nature. If you divide the teaching of Jesus into various subjects, about 13 percent of Jesus' teachings and half of his parables are about hell, judgment, punishment, and the wrath of God. Here are a few examples:

- "Then he will say to those on his left, 'Depart from me, you cursed, into the eternal fire prepared for the devil and his angels.' . . . And these will go away into eternal punishment but the righteous into eternal life" (Matthew 25:41, 46)

- "[But some] will be thrown into the outer darkness. In that place there will be weeping and gnashing of teeth" (Matthew 8:12)

- "If your hand causes you to sin, cut it off. It is better for you to enter life crippled than with two hands to go to hell, to the unquenchable fire. . . . 'where their worm does not die and the fire is not quenched'" (Mark 9:43, 48)

If you want to get rid of hell, therefore, you have to get rid of Jesus. And that's the irony: if we're going to say that the *love* of God was emphasized to a greater extent by Jesus in the New Testament, we have to acknowledge that the *wrath* of God also gets ratcheted up in the New Testament.[150] We can't escape the fact that hell, just as much as the love and grace of God, is a central New Testament, Jesus-driven teaching.

Again, Alternate Beliefs

Several modern presuppositions and cultural sensitivities skew our ideas about hell. It's worth thinking about *why* we are repulsed by the idea of hell, why we hold an *alternate belief* (i.e., that there is no hell), and why we tend to believe *our* assumptions and beliefs about God, the world, and what is right and wrong for God to do or not do. Why would our ideas be more correct than the Bible's or what Jesus teaches? Ideas tend to be products of the culture in which they develop. In this case, many of those reading this book are Western, educated, postmodern, democratic people, a cultural context that informs and influences our beliefs about hell. Undoubtedly.

You have beliefs you have been indoctrinated with your whole life. They may or may not come from the Bible, but they are the result of authoritative voices in your life: your education, your upbringing, Grey's Anatomy, Howard Stern perhaps. You have a whole set of beliefs that you bring to the table, which in this case cause you to dislike, or even be repelled by a particular view of the universe. But being *repelled* by hell, or any other Christian doctrine, is not enough to prove that it's not real or that it doesn't rationally make sense. It just means you don't like it. But not liking something is not a sufficient way of discerning what is true or false. We certainly need to examine how we feel, but we need to push deeper. *Why* don't we like it? What alternate beliefs do we hold that we need to examine and question?

To be fully transparent, I'll tell you why I am repulsed by the idea of hell. My father died at the age of forty-seven and never trusted Jesus as his Savior, at least as far as I know; and now, as I write this chapter, I am getting on a plane to go bury *his* father, my grandfather, who just died yesterday at age ninety-eight with no faith in Jesus either. I pray that someone did enter their lives near the end who led them to saving faith. My hope is that I will see them in heaven, but I also believe that if that did not happen, I need to accept the fact that my own father and grandfather are no different than anyone else. That they are likely in hell. My own blood. The people who I see in my kids' eyes when I look at them. This is not easy for me, and I submit it here with trembling. Needless to say, I did not come to this conclusion lightly. When I became a Christian at seventeen I studied the Bible deeply, and I encountered ideas that were very counterintuitive to my views at the time. One was the doctrine of hell. I was shocked by it but recognized that the objections I had were *cultural* ones—born out of sensibilities and ideals I held because I was a twenty-first-century white, middle-class, educated Westerner with all the accompanying perks that I am not even aware of at times. I worried that I was allowing my ethnocentric understandings take priority over the teaching of

Jesus in the Bible, so I forced myself to try to see through the repulsion to understand the Bible's teaching in context. I realized that there is a logic and justification for hell that makes sense of God, humanity, and the universe itself.[151] So before we look at the *what* and *why* of the Bible's teaching on hell, let's look briefly at a few of the most popular objections people have against it.

1. HELL IS REPULSIVE

We've already covered this first one, but it's worth repeating. We must distinguish between liking or disliking something and whether that thing is true or not. It doesn't feel good to fire someone from a job, for instance, but it still might be the *right* thing to do. On the other hand, there are times where something feels good, but it's not right. I was watching a television interview with the founder of www.adultery.com, an entire business given to helping couples cheat on their spouses, who was arguing that people in adulterous relationships report that it is pleasurable and *feels* good. The variety, the thrill, and romance of it all is something, he said, that we all live for and should stop holding ourselves back from.

But the fact that it feels good doesn't make it right. Very few cultures are going to say adultery is acceptable. The point being: just because I don't like something, in this case the doctrine of hell, doesn't change whether it's *true* or not.

2. HELL IS UNJUST

A second objection to hell is that it is *unjust*. The punishment doesn't fit the crime. Hell is too heavy-handed and harsh and goes on for far too long. This objection is strong, and it has even led many Christians to come up with other options that they feel are more compatible with the God of Christianity. They believe that if God extinguishes everyone from existence (a belief called annihilationism) or brings everyone to heaven in the end (univeralism), he is more loving—and easier to live with. But behind this proposal is the assumption that God isn't just if he allows hell to exist or if anyone is there.

The first problem with this kind of thinking is that when you get outside of the Western world, you learn that some people have the exact opposite feelings about hell and God's judgment. They see the evil that people commit and wonder how God could be just if there *isn't* a hell and if there *isn't* extreme, divine judgment. They believe that hell exists *because* God is a God of justice, not in spite of it. In villages in Africa, the Middle East, India, and China, innocent men, women, and children are raped, kidnapped, tortured, or killed on a daily basis. When you witness or are a victim of horrific crimes like these, questions of judgment and punishment are not just philosophical considerations. Miroslav Volf, a Christian theologian who witnessed much death and destruction in his home country of Croatia, writes: It "takes the quiet of a suburban home for the birth of the thesis . . . of God's *refusal* to judge. In a scorched land, soaked in the blood of the innocent, it will invariably die. And as one watched it die, one will do well to reflect about many other pleasant captivities of the liberal mind."[152]

We are hardwired to cry out *for* justice and *against* injustice. We accept that if a person murders somebody, or rapes, they should be held accountable. If someone gets off because of a loophole in the justice system, we cry out "Injustice!" We picket large corporations that knock down trees. We throw paint on people who wear animals for coats and post videos on social media calling for the end of the captivity of whales. Why? Because we have deep yearnings within us that say *injustice is wrong, and it has to be paid for.*

Hell is all about this very justice.

Ask the men and women living in a village in Africa where recently one tribe abducted hundreds of young women from another tribe, some as young as ten years old, and forced them to be sex slaves and suicide bombers. Do you think the parents of these little girls have a problem with the idea of a place where evil men get punished for their crimes by a just judge? Do you think they object to a time when God will pronounce final and deserved judgment on these men? I can assure you they aren't losing any sleep over it. In fact, any concept of God *without* this final expression to them is *less* just, and he may not be worth worshiping at all. When we suggest that "everyone gets into heaven because God is so good," for many people that sounds downright awful. They hear about a god like that and ask: Why would you worship a god who fails to uphold justice by punishing evil? If we are honest, we know that if there is a God and he is perfectly good and just, he must judge impartially and fairly, and there must be consequences for the evils that people commit.

If God is truly just, then there *is* a hell. Does it make us uncomfortable? Yes. But it also makes *sense*.

The doctrines of hell and God's love are not mutually exclusive. They do not contradict each other. Once we understand what love is, they fit together perfectly. But again, we have to be careful and acknowledge our own cultural blind spots. "People today tend to care only for the softer virtues [of God's character] like love and tenderness, while they've forgotten the hard virtues of holiness, righteousness and justice."[153] But both are true about God, and at the same time. It is absolutely true that God is love; he is compassionate, merciful, and long-suffering (1 John 4:8; Psalm 103:8). But he's also just and moral, a purely good being whose decisions are not based on modern sentimentalism. He is good *because* he is just—this is what the Bible means when it says that God is righteous. Because God is a *perfect* judge, his justice is measured and perfect, far different from the punishment that we as human beings are able to give, and far different from what we have experienced often in this life. Again, Miroslav Volf is helpful in exploring a different point of view on this. Volf frequently hears Western people assume that "it is not worthy of God to wield the sword [or judge]. Is God not long-suffering and all-powerful love?" they say. In response, he writes:

> A counter-question could go something like this: Is it not a bit arrogant to presume that our contemporary sensibilities about what is compatible with God's love are so much healthier than those of the people of God throughout the whole history of Judaism and Christianity?[154]

In other words, maybe, just maybe, our cultural moment is not the preeminent decider on what is right and just for the cosmos. It takes humility to admit that this may be true, but is necessary for all of us to do if we are going to hear ideas for what they are outside of our own echo chambers.

3. ISN'T HELL OVERKILL?

A third objection raised by skeptics is that hell is *overkill*, that if it is intended to represent God's justice, it's actually the opposite—a miscarriage of justice. A person sins for eighty years, for instance, and then gets punished for eternity. How is that just? This is a great question, but like most questions in this context there are a number of biblical and philosophical answers to it.

First, the degree to which a person experiences punishment is not typically based on how long it takes them to commit a crime but on the seriousness of the crime—the weight of its moral offense. It could take a person six seconds to murder someone, for instance, but does just punishment demand a six-second punishment? No, we put that person in jail for the rest of their life, and sometimes even take their life because of their actions. The punishment is based on the *weight of the offense* committed. Because a human life has value and worth, we demand a punishment that accounts for what has been taken, or stolen, something of equal value and worth.

Another problem with the way the objection is framed is that we fail to rightly value the moral offense of what the Bible calls "sin." We tend to minimize our offenses, thinking they are small or light, surely not enough to warrant a heavy or eternal sentence. But again, we are not in the best position to make this judgment. The Bible helps us to understand that one of the consequences of rebellion against our infinite Creator is that we, as human beings, have a distorted sense of moral value. We are not as serious about sin as God is. Only he rightly understands his own moral value and what it means to steal what belongs to him and keep it for ourselves. The Bible says that even though deep inside we understand that we are accountable to our Creator for all that we have, we do not end up honoring him as God or giving him the thanks he deserves. Instead, at the fall, we "became futile in [our] thinking, and [our] foolish hearts were darkened. . . . [We] exchanged the glory of the immortal God for images" (Romans 1:21, 23). In other words, we fundamentally don't understand what sin is and how it affects the universe. It is a far worse crime than we realize. Stealing from God is not the same as stealing from another person. Killing God is not the same as taking a human life. This is not a finite being whom we offended *one* time. God is an infinite being of perfect beauty, a person of infinite value and worth. This means that our sin against him is infinite, not something small that can be easily fixed. An offense against God requires a *just* punishment. How do you make up for stealing something of infinite value? What cost must be paid? When we run away from God for our eighty years, it is an infinite, eternal offense, even if we've only done it for a finite time, because the issue is not simply the nature of the sin or the sinner, but the *one being sinned against.*

Let me explain: right now, my daughters are young, but all three of them have started talking back to me. We were eating dinner one night recently when my youngest stood up and walked away from the table. I said to her, "What are you doing?" and she responded, "I'm leaving." I said, "No you're not," and she looked at me strangely— and then ran away. I got up from the table, chased her around our house, and finally caught her. What did I do with her? I brought her up to her bedroom and plopped her down on her Barbie chair and said, "You will sit here for four minutes." I shut the door, and she was crying. I left her cut off from relationship to punish her for what she had done.

Now why did I do that? Because she deserved a punishment to satisfy the offense she had committed. Every parent in the world knows this is necessary or children will not understand justice correctly. My daughter disrespected her father. If she had done the same toward one of her friends or sisters, the punishment would have been different, likely less. But because I am an authority over her, her disobedience carries more severe consequences. This is a finite human relationship between a father and child, but now apply this to an infinite, eternal, holy God. The punishment must be applied accordingly.

People also wrongly assume that after living and committing sin, they die and go to hell and, in doing so, *stop sinning*. But it's not that simple and misunderstands the biblical teaching of ongoing punishment. The sixteenth-century Reformation theologian Martin Luther defined sin as *homo incurvatus*, humankind turned in on himself. Why would we think that that this inverted focus ceases to be a reality for people in hell? Nothing we read in the Bible suggests that people cease from sinful thinking or behavior in hell. G. K. Chesterton once said, "Hell is God's great compliment to the reality of human freedom and the dignity of human choice."[155] The punishment is legitimately *eternal* because sin doesn't stop when people die; it continues. It is ongoing punishment for ongoing sin, going on forever.[156] We should not assume that people who in *this* life did not wish to surrender their lives to Jesus would somehow change their minds in the next life. Jesus tells the story of a man in hell crying out that someone be sent "to my father's house—for I have five brothers—so that he may warn them, lest they also come into this place of torment" (Luke 16:27–28). Scholars debate how far to push this story, but they point out that the man doesn't ask to leave himself, possibly because the one thing it takes *not* to have been there in the first place is the thing he continues not to be able bring himself to do: surrender to Jesus Christ as Savior, Lord, and treasure. In other words, hell is not a place where people are consigned because they were pretty good people who didn't believe the right stuff for their eighty years:

> They're consigned there, first and foremost, because they defy their maker and want to be at the center of the universe. Hell is not filled with people who have already repented, only God isn't gentle enough or good enough to let them out. It's filled with people who, for all eternity, *still* want to be the center of the universe. . . . What is God to do? If he says it doesn't matter to him, then God is no longer a God to be admired. . . . For him to act in any other way in the face of such blatant defiance would be to reduce God himself.[157]

Still, some wonder how God could give the same punishment to the Hitlers of the world as to the regular Joe who never received Christ into his life but lived a decent life otherwise. How is it fair that their end is the same? The Bible addresses this question multiple times, teaching that the experience of hell (and heaven for that matter) will *not* be the same for every person. Jesus indicates that there will be degrees of suffering and punishment. For instance, in Matthew 11, he says:

"Woe to you, Chorazin! Woe to you, Bethsaida! . . . I tell you,
it will be *more bearable* on the day of judgment for Tyre and
Sidon than for you. And you, Capernaum, will you be exalted to
heaven? You will be brought down to Hades. . . . I tell you that
it will be *more tolerable* on the day of judgment for the land of
Sodom than for you."

(MATTHEW 11:21–24, EMPHASIS ADDED)

Jesus refers to several cities, and presumably the people in those cities,
that will receive less punishment than others. He speaks of servants
who sin ignorantly and will receive lighter punishment than those
who sin with greater knowledge of God and what he expected of a
person (Luke 12:47–48). As theologian John Frame points out: "The
chief variable [in judgment] appears to be knowledge."[158] In fact,
almost every time the Bible describes final judgment, it says that a
measure of punishment (or reward) will be exercised based on what a
person has done in his or her life based on what they knew. Here are
a few examples:

- "Do not marvel at this, for an hour is coming when all who are
  in the tombs will hear his voice and come out, those who have
  done good to the resurrection of life, and those who have *done
  evil* to the resurrection of judgment" (John 5:28–29, emphasis
  added).

- "Before him will be gathered all the nations, and he will
  separate people one from another as a shepherd separates the
  sheep from the goats. . . . For I was hungry and you gave me
  food, I was thirsty and you gave me drink, I was a stranger and
  you welcomed me, I was naked and you clothed me, I was
  sick and you visited me, I was in prison and you came to me"
  (Matthew 25:32–36).

- "Then another book was opened, which is the book of life. And the dead were judged by what was written in the books, according to *what they had done*" (Revelation 20:12, emphasis added).

The reason these judgment passages focus so clearly on the whole context of a person's life, and not just what he or she believes about some doctrines, is because our life and what we do with it will directly equal the measure of glory or judgment we experience for all eternity, and it will be distributed perfectly so to each one of us, even those in hell. The Bible teaches that there is not a one-size-fits-all judgment in the end but a judgment (and blessing) that is proportional to individual lives and the choices we make every day.

Such is the justice of God.

4. ISN'T HELL A TORTURE CHAMBER?

A fourth concern raised by sincere skeptics is whether hell is a "torture chamber." The Christian evangelist-turned-atheist Charles Templeton once said, "I couldn't hold someone's hand to a fire for a moment. . . . How could a loving God, just because you don't obey him and do what he wants, torture you forever—not allowing you to die, but to continue in that pain for eternity? There is no *criminal* who would do this!"[159] This question gets at the heart of our repulsion toward the notion of eternal punishment.

Let's start by challenging some of the assumptions built into this charge, assumptions that simply aren't reflected in what the Bible teaches. The image of God holding bodies over flames and burning them forever is an example of how easy it is for modern readers to *misread* the Bible without taking into account cultural, historical, and literary backgrounds. For example, when Jesus says there's going to be fire, utter darkness, weeping and gnashing of teeth (Matthew

13:42, 50; 22:13; 25:30), we have to understand that as a first-century prophet—similar to Old Testament prophets such as Elijah, Ezekiel, and Isaiah—Jesus is using *apocalyptic language and imagery* to make a theological point. Fire was a common *image* for judgment (see Genesis 19:23–28; 2 Kings 1:12; Ezekiel 38:22), but it is largely figurative, symbolic language that teaches us something about the nature of hell while not necessarily reflecting the actual, literal experience of it. In the passages where Jesus uses this apocalyptic imagery, he is warning Israel, and by extension all of humanity, of the implications of rejecting his message. Those reading and listening to him would have recognized the apocalyptic genre, a genre that should not be pressed for stark literalism because it is filled with metaphor, pointing to something beyond itself. New Testament scholar N. T. Wright describes the genre this way:

> The different layers of meaning in vision-literature of this type . . . demand to be heard in their full polyphony, not flattened out into a single level of meaning. If this had been noted a century ago, biblical scholarship could have been spared many false trails. Apocalyptic language uses complex and highly colored metaphors in order to describe one event in terms of another. . . . Indeed, it is not easy to see what better language-system could have been chosen. . . . the metaphorical language of apocalyptic invests history with theological meaning.[160]

Knowing this helps us understand the *way* the New Testament, and Jesus himself, taught about hell. Rather than pushing an exact parallel to the imagery, we need to understand it in accord with the literary genre. If one were trying to read J. R. R. Tolkien's *The Lord of the Rings* in the same way one reads the evening newspaper, for instance, *meaning* itself would be lost and confused. Again, for example, we note that in his commentary on the book of Revelation, renowned scholar G. K. Beale points out that the "lake of fire" into which Satan and his angels are thrown (Revelation 20:10), "is not literal since Satan (along with his angels) is a spiritual being. The 'fire' is a punishment that is not physical but spiritual in nature."[161] The Bible often uses imagery when speaking of spiritual realities. The book of Hebrews, for instance, tells us that God is a "consuming fire" (Hebrews 12:29), but this does not mean that God is a *literal* fireball. The writers of Scripture are simply trying to convey something true about God's character. In this case, fire is a powerful, purifying, and deadly force of nature—and that corresponds with the nature and character of God. Or consider Revelation 19, where we read that Jesus will return with a sword coming out of his mouth (verse 15). This does not mean that Jesus will have a literal sword between his teeth, preventing him from speaking. The sword is a symbol for the Word of God. Elsewhere, Jesus is pictured as a lamb (Revelation 5:6), but when the Bible says Jesus is the Lamb of God we should not imagine that when we arrive in heaven we will see Jesus with four legs, woolly coat, and hooves.

All of these images are pointers to something true and real. They are attempts to invest a person, place, or experience with theological and spiritual meaning and significance. At the same time, I'm not suggesting that the way to solve every hard text is to say it's "just a symbol" so it has no meaning in real life. On the contrary, the goal is to be faithful and accurate to what the original context demands, which is always a description, however cloaked, of reality in the real world. In this context then, hell is almost always spoken of in some kind of apocalyptic, symbolic form. Which raises legitimate questions. If Jesus isn't really going to be a lamb, are there going to be people in actual flames of fire in hell? The answer, once you have immersed yourself in the genre and the relevant texts, is that it's not outside the realm of possibility (God can do whatever he wants), but given the context of the passages, it is doubtful. The references to fire throughout the Bible almost always are a pointer to the spiritual experience of living under the judgment of God forever. Timothy Keller summarizes:

> All descriptions and depictions of heaven and hell in the Bible are symbolic and metaphorical. Each metaphor suggests one aspect of the experience of hell. (For example, "fire" tells us of the disintegration, while "darkness" tells us of the isolation.) Having said that does not at all imply that heaven or hell *themselves* are "metaphors." They are very much realities . . . [but] all language about them is allusive, metaphorical and partial.[162]

More Than, Not Less Than

Some people hear this and are relieved because they take this to mean that hell will not be all that bad after all. "If it's *just* a symbol," they say, "there is no need for me to worry about it." But this is a misunderstanding of how the Bible communicates. Most of the pictures we find in the Bible are pictures of a reality not *less* but *more* real than the picture itself. If you were walking through a mall, for instance, and the custodian was mopping and beside him was a bright yellow sign with a picture of a man mid-slip, falling, you might say, "Wow, that experience looks harsh." But if you personally hit a wet patch and fell, smacking your head, you would likely agree that while the *picture* looked awful, the *experience* was far worse. This is how this all works. Yes, the image of "fire and utter darkness" is a symbol. But symbols are powerful things, pointing us toward a reality deeper than what an image can capture. My wedding ring is a symbol, but is the beauty of living in my marriage relationship *less* than the ring? No. It's far greater. The reality behind the symbol is greater than the symbol itself.

So while I would argue that hell is not necessarily a *physical* torture chamber (though there are images in the literature that are about being in physical locations of torture, etc.), it *is* a place of emotional, psychological, and relational suffering and anguish. That's what the images of darkness, weeping, gnashing of teeth, and a "lake of fire" (Revelation 20:15) are trying to convey. It is an awful, hopeless, and lonely existence. It's a place none of us would desire our worst enemy to go. "Those who die in their sins do not pass into nothingness. There is indeed a time beyond death for the damned,"[163] a time that is the opposite of pleasure, joy, grace, and love. And this is a reality the Bible does not take lightly. It serves as a stark warning to all of us to take seriously the consequences of rejecting God.

Good Infection

As C. S. Lewis once said, responding to the question of hell: "It is not about your wife or son, nor about Nero or Judas Iscariot; it is about you and me."[164] So we must all face it head on if we are honest. And in that vein there is one last question that pokes at us about hell, though it's one that is rarely explored: *Why* is hell the way it is? Why the anguish? Why the pain? Why the suffering and isolation? The answer to this question is eternally important to each one of us.

Why is hell the way it is? Because if God is the life-giving source of everything in the universe, of everything good that we experience in life (all joy and pleasure, all laughter, art, music, food, sex, water, etc.), and if these things are given to us because of the common grace of God, wherein he "makes his sun rise on the evil and on the good" (Matthew 5:45), what are we left with if his presence, and this kind of grace, is removed? In one sense, hell can be understood as the outworking of our choice to experience total autonomy from God. We are allowed to be our own god and are allowed to sustain and provide for ourselves. The problem is that this is impossible, and we are thus left with nothing, because everything came from his hand.

In Jesus' story from Luke 16 mentioned earlier, the man in hell calls out to Abraham, asking him to "send Lazarus to dip the end of his finger in water and cool my tongue, for I am in anguish in this flame" (v. 24). But here is the haunting part: there is no water. In other words, hell is the place where the common grace of God, the blessings and comforts that he provides to all of us, no longer exist. All the stuff we enjoy, that we think we possess because we worked so hard for it, is no longer there. God's grace is absent. It can no longer "pass from here to you" he says (v. 26). There is a chasm, and it is fixed. In hell people can't create the feelings or provide the resources they thought they could. Hell exposes the lie we have told ourselves since the garden, the lie that *we don't need God*. Those who draw away from the source of all that is good are left with only bad things. As C. S. Lewis says:

> There is no other way to the happiness for which we were made. Good things as well as bad ... are caught by a kind of infection, if you want to get warm you must stand near the fire: if you want to be wet you must get into the water. If you want joy, power, peace, eternal life, you must get close to, or even into, the thing that has them. They are not a sort of prize which God ... just hand[s] out to anyone. They are a great fountain of energy and beauty spurting up at the very center of reality. If you are close to it, the spray will wet you: if you are not, you will remain dry. Once a man is united to God, how could he not live forever? Once a man is separated from God, what can he do but wither and die?[165]

A Tragedy for God

Another thing skeptics dislike about the doctrine of hell is that it seems to give the impression that God is happy about punishing people in hell. That he is excited about it all. But the story Jesus tells in Luke 16 of the man in hell gives us an altogether different picture . The story is a tragedy. And we must not forget that it's a tragedy for God above all. Jesus tells us: "But Abraham said, '*Child*, remember that you in your lifetime received your good things'" (v. 25, emphasis added). Here is a guy, consigned to hell forever, whose life was filled with "good things" but not ultimate things. Not eternal things. And what does God say to him when he is in hell? Does he yell at him and call him a "sinner" and an "evildoer"? No. He calls him *child*. The Greek word is *teknon*. It's a beautiful word parents would call their children.

Every one of us, even all those who end up eternally separated from God, is loved, and this final state is a pain and agony to his heart as a parent. That's why in the famous judgment passage of the sheep and the goats Jesus tells us that hell itself was "prepared for the devil and his angels" (Matthew 25:41). Did you catch what he's saying? God did not create hell *for people*. It was created for Satan and his followers. But when people choose to follow the devil in his kind of rebellion, they end up where that rebellion ends up. Traditional religious art and modern pictures of hell often present it as Satan's headquarters, a place where demons run around torturing human souls, but nothing could be further from the truth. Hell is a place where *Satan* is punished. It is the culmination of his defeat by God, and God is sovereign over it, not Satan. It is a place where final justice—originally designed for Satan, not people—is meted out.

Thy Will Be Done

This raises the final objection skeptics have about hell: that it is forced on *unwilling* people who are sent there against their will. But is this the image the Bible presents? No. Philosopher J. P. Moreland contends that hell is a place for people who, given what is needed to belong in heaven (submission to Jesus), do not *want* to go to heaven. Thus, hell is the natural consequence of the choices people make. It is a monument to human freedom.

So are people given a test that says, "Hell or heaven, choose one"? No. It's actually far more gracious than that. The apostle Peter, writing to a church he loves, observes that they are surrounded by scoffers who say, "Where is this 'coming' [God] promised? Ever since our ancestors died, everything goes on as it has since the beginning of creation" (2 Peter 3:4 NIV). How does Peter respond to these mockers? "The Lord is not slow in keeping his promise, as some understand slowness. Instead he is patient with you, not wanting anyone to perish" (v. 9 NIV). In other words, every day that we wake up, our feet hit the floor, and we see the sun rise is another day to receive the salvation God offers as a gift. Or it's another day to choose to reject it. Every day awards us an opportunity. We each choose our eternal destiny every day, every moment of our lives, even in the small stuff.

> God will judge, not because God gives people what they deserve, but because some people refuse to receive what no one deserves; if evildoers experience God's terror, it will not be because they have done evil, but because they have resisted to the end the powerful lure of the open arms of the crucified Messiah. . . . Should not a loving God be patient and keep luring the perpetrator into goodness? . . . But how patient should God be? The day of reckoning must come, not because God is too eager to pull the trigger, but because every day of patience in a world of violence means more violence and every postponement of vindication means letting insult accompany injury.[166]

So, one day God must come in judgment. And mete out judgment and salvation based on the thousand choices we made every day, because people are not defined by one decision they make in their lifetime, something separate and distinct from everything else that leads them to a place called hell. They are formed by the thousands of choices they make every day. We choose to value the things God values, or choose not to, and those choices have a trajectory. They echo out into eternity. Every decision that we make is either moving us toward God or away from him every day and in every way.

Each of those directions is an answer to a larger question: Whose will is sovereign in your life? Is it God's will or your will? Lewis soberly concludes his famous essay on hell this way: "There are only two kinds of people: Those who say, 'Thy will be done,' to God or those to whom God in the end says, 'Thy will be done.' All those who are in hell choose it. No soul that seriously and constantly desires joy will ever miss it. I believe that the damned are successful rebels until the end. They enjoy the horrible freedom, which they have demanded."[167]

So I ask you, what kind of old man or woman do you want to be? In each one of us something is growing that will result in hell if it is not curbed. If it is not dealt with and defeated, it will turn us into the kind of person who is defined by selfishness and rebellion in this life and echo out into the next. What is a fit place for such a person? A place where you're separated and isolated from the one person in the universe whom you've rejected and who could save you. You've decided that you don't want him, so that rejection has fully and completely come to define you.

The Expulsive Power of a New Affection

As I told you at the beginning of this chapter, I was first introduced to God as a way out of hell, an escape from eternal punishment. But it didn't result in deep-rooted discipleship born from a love for God and his grace because a fear-based presentation of salvation does not change the fundamental desires of a person's heart. Only love can do that. Maybe you have read this chapter and are still thinking about the logic of hell. I hope you see why it is an important doctrine within Christianity and how the existence of it is tied to justice. Perhaps this discussion has opened you up to the Christian faith, or maybe you have become even more closed off to God. Talking about hell can do that. That's because you need something else. It's not enough to run *from* something. Salvation is about running *toward* something— indeed someone. It is not enough to build your life on hating or being afraid of an idea, a place, or a consequence (hell) and loving its opposite (heaven). Fear doesn't create true obedience, only outward compliance, and only for a season. Fear was what motivated the rich man in Jesus' parable who wanted to save his family. "I beg you, father [Abraham]," he said, "send [Lazarus] to my father's house—for I have five brothers—so that he may warn them, lest they also come into this place of torment" (Luke 16:27–28). "Send someone from the dead," he is saying, "to scare my brothers into not coming here. Go, and tell them about hell and my anguish." His logic seems sound. "If someone goes to them from the dead, they will repent" (v. 30). This has been the strategy of many who have claimed to represent Jesus over the centuries. Just give them the flames. "Turn or burn," "fire and brim-stone," and they will convert. But what is Abraham's response?

No, they won't, he says.

"They have Moses and the Prophets. Let them hear them. . . . If they do not hear Moses and the Prophets, *neither will they be convinced* if someone should rise from the dead" (vv. 29, 31, emphasis added). Why? Because you can't just tell people what they should run *from*. You have to explain what they're running *to*. At the end of Luke's Gospel, Jesus makes it clear what Moses and the Prophets were really all about: himself (24:44). The end of the law is not about following the rules—it's about God becoming human, dying for sin, and rising again to redeem sinners from death and punishment, including the punishment of hell itself. Jesus saves us by dislodging our addiction to the things we love that land us in hell. But he doesn't use fear to do this. His love for us leads us to love something—or rather, Someone—more than those things. It's a *positive affection* that changes us, not a negative one.

The eighteenth-century Scottish preacher Thomas Chalmers wrote a sermon on 1 John 2:15 ("do not love the world") in which he said that simply *not* loving the world is by itself impossible because "it is seldom that any of our tastes are made to disappear by mere force of reasoning or determination." So what must one do? "What cannot be destroyed," he says, must "be dispossessed. The heart is not so constituted; and the only way to dispossess it of an old affection is by the expulsive power of a new one . . . the youth ceases to idolize pleasure, but it is because the idol of wealth has become stronger and gotten the ascendancy . . . even the love of money ceases to have mastery over the heart of many a thriving citizen, but it is drawn into the whirl of city policies . . .and he is now lorded over by a love of power. There is not one of these transformations in which the heart is left without an object."[168] The way to disengage the heart from the positive love of one great object (sin, ourselves, etc.) is to "fasten it in positive love to another, then it is not about exposing the worthlessness of the former, but by addressing to the mental eye the worth and excellence of the latter."[169]

The only way to truly walk away from sin and the things of this world, which ends with us in hell, is by finding something you love *more* than those things. A new love that trumps the old is the only thing with enough power to unhinge you from the sin that so easily entangles. It's the only solution.

This is the climactic point in Jesus' story, in essence: Fear will not save them. They need a new heart, a new affection. Let them be stirred to love God with all their heart, soul, mind, and strength. "We know of no other way by which to keep the love of the world out of our heart, than to keep in our hearts the love of God."[170]

Conclusion

In the end, what are we to do? The Bible claims hell is real, whatever its nature and specifics. Our reason says that the idea of hell makes sense, even while making us uncomfortable. But, as we have seen, being uncomfortable with an idea is not the same as having a rational reason to doubt it. The better thing is to let the *evidence* and the *angst* lead us somewhere that retains both. Nowhere is this truer than when wrestling with the idea of hell. As George MacDonald warned, "When there are wild beasts about, it is better to feel afraid than to feel secure."

Hell is real. And scary. But in that there is a seriousness that can give way to security if we trust in the one who took hell on himself for us. God worked through his Son, driven by love and a desire for none to perish, to save us from hell to something glorious and wonderful. So,

> In the long run, the answer to all of those who object to the doctrine of hell is itself a question. What are you asking God to do? To wipe out the past sins of the damned and at all cost to give them a fresh start, smoothing every difficulty and offering every miraculous help. He has done so in Jesus. Are you asking God to forgive him? They do not want to be forgiven. Are you asking God to leave them alone?
>
> Alas, I am afraid that is what he does.[171]

CHAPTER 7

The Problem of
SEX

If one wanted to depict the whole thing
graphically, every episode, with its climax . . .
every experience is unrepeatable. What makes
lovemaking and reading resemble each other most
is that within both of them times and spaces open,
different from measurable time and space.

ITALO CALVINO, *IF ON A WINTER'S NIGHT A TRAVELER*

M any people reject Christianity because of its teachings on certain ethical issues, especially the Christian teachings on sex
and human sexuality. Bertrand Russell, a famous twentieth-century
atheist philosopher once said, "The worst feature of the Christian
religion is its attitude towards sex."[172] Christianity's teachings about
sex have been deemed oppressive and antiquated in the modern
world. Many believe the Bible's teachings on it should be abandoned
altogether. Margaret Sanger, the founder of Planned Parenthood,
argued that Christians are "moralists" who promote self-denial and
suppression[173] because of their teaching on abstinence before marriage.
And Christopher Hitchens suggests that any religious view should be
banned from the modern discourse about sexuality in general.[174] In
other words, if we wish to have a constructive discussion about sex as

a culture, and if we wish to be truly free as individuals, the Christian perspective on sex has no place in the discussion.

The Priority of the Autonomous Self

From where does the animosity toward Christian ethical teaching on this issue come? Why is there such strong opposition against biblical ideas of sexuality? The first thing that must be said is that many of the objections have arisen as a by-product of the already established *ideals of the Western world*, a society built around "the priority of the autonomous self."[175] From the Enlightenment period of the seventeenth and eighteenth century to today, the highest good has been seen as "freely choosing, autonomous individuals, deciding out of rational self-interest to construct a progressive society."[176] Because we hold this to be true about everything in our lives (money, business, marriage, etc.), it feels limiting and unnatural to embrace restrictions on our sexual lives in any way. Any limit on our behavior is seen as a violation of our basic human rights as individuals. We believe we have the right to use our bodies in whatever way *we* want, and this is the ultimate expression of our freedom and our autonomy. We want options, and we are content as long "as the moral world, like the material world, is supremely represented as a shopping mall."[177] In other words, we are good capitalists when it comes to sex.

Another reason people reject Christianity is their assumption that *God and the Bible are antisex*. Sex is one of the great joys of our lives as human beings, and the average person doesn't equate God with joy or pleasure. Instead, God is commonly seen as the one who restricts us, limiting what we can and cannot do. It's not difficult to see why people believe that God does not like or encourage sexual activity, so they reject him. But, as we will see, this couldn't be further from the truth.

The Bible teaches that God created us as sexual beings. Sex is

God's idea, and God's purpose for sex is multifaceted, countering both of the errors mentioned above. Sex is much *more* than just a personal, autonomous experience. It is two people taking pleasure in God's creation in a myriad of fun and exciting ways. The biblical perspective on sex is robust and stands contrary to the three alternative views that have been popular throughout history: sex-is-*bad*, sex-is-*god*, and sex-is-*appetite*.[178] Christianity offers a healthy and balanced alternative to all of these perspectives, an alternative that provides joy and freedom and has the power to transform an entire culture like ours. It teaches that sex is a *God-given gift.*

Sex Is Bad

One common view about sex challenged by true Christianity is that *sex is bad*. Growing up outside the church, I was convinced that this was the Christian view. I thought God was against sex because everything I had heard about it from church leaders was negative. As a nine-year-old at Christian summer camp it was pretty clear, as one preacher put it, that "sex is dirty, nasty, vile, and wrong . . . so save it for the one you love!"[179] And when I was a teenager I learned that some churches prayed to Mary because she was a *virgin*—the very opposite of what I wanted to be![180] This was enough for me—my body filled with hormones and a head full of music videos—to keep Christianity at arm's length. Maybe some of you reading this feel the same way.

In my late teens I started reading the Bible for myself, however, and I discovered that my ideas about Christianity were not biblical at all. Along with many in our Western culture, I had simply picked up these marginal Christian attitudes toward sex without really exploring the biblical teaching. In fact, what I found in the Bible was almost the *opposite* of what I had heard. I learned that God was the one who created sex and that he celebrated and encouraged it among human beings.

THE CHRISTIAN FAILURE REGARDING SEX

Sadly, there are historical reasons why my first encounter with the Christian teaching about sex did not match what the Bible said. Throughout history Christians have often taught a *sex-is-bad* theology. Clement of Alexandria (AD 150–215), for instance, taught that sexual intercourse is sin unless it was done to beget children. Origen (AD 185–254) was so convinced of the evils of sexual pleasure that he castrated himself. And Chrysostom (AD 349–407) taught that Adam and Eve could not have sex before the fall. So there is a reason for the bad rap Christians get in this area. But the Bible says that God created the physical world and called it "good" (Genesis 1:25), and the climax of his work was the making of our *naked, physical bodies*, which he declared as "very good" (v. 31). This biblical picture then, rather than later Christian misrepresentations, should be our starting point for understanding a Christian view of sex.

Unfortunately, such misunderstandings and confusion continue to exist today. I was talking to a friend recently who grew up attending a private Christian school, and the school's approach to sex education was to just not talk about it. *If the public school talks about sex, and all those kids are having it,* they apparently thought, *then the solution must be to not talk about it at all!* In other words, if we don't talk about it, maybe the kids won't figure it out. I suppose the thinking was that a student would grow up blissfully naive about sex until he turns twenty-five, meets a girl, and asks her to marry him, only to learn on his wedding day about the secret of sex. "You're married. Praise God. Here's what happens tonight. . . ." Of course, this is an epic fail.

THE CONDOM INCIDENT

In the book of 1 Corinthians, the apostle Paul is trying to counter a number of sexual perversions that have made their way into the church in Corinth. He's dealing with people having "Christian" sex orgies, others sleeping with their stepparents—in other words, not ideal. One of the teachings that had infiltrated the church was a *sex-is-bad* theology, which would have been tempting for Paul to tap into. Stop being perverse. Stop having sex. But this isn't how Paul responds. He does not avoid the issue, neither does he tell them to live a "good conservative life," but he takes on the error directly. He says: "The husband should give to his wife her conjugal rights, and likewise the wife to her husband" (7:3). In other words, don't run from sex but toward it. But in its right context, between a husband and wife. The Corinthians had wrongly begun to believe that it pleased God to completely avoid all sexual activity. But Paul encourages the exact opposite, arguing the best way to counter sex-is-bad theology is a healthy and robust sex life!

Many Christian parents, leaders, and pastors talk in almost exclusively negative terms when speaking about sex today to all ages, including youth and young adults. But this is a mistake. Beyond the fact that it's not biblical, it can be psychologically damaging. You can't suddenly transition from an entire lifetime of "sex is disgusting and wrong" as a teen and young adult to "now you're married, go and enjoy it!" As a pastor, I've counseled couples who have been traumatized by sex on their wedding night largely due to negative teaching about it. Some went two or three years after they got married without engaging in sex and needed significant counseling to get through the trauma of the experience. I also meet with lots of young, newly married couples who entered marriage as virgins and who are in my office several months later saying they don't know what to do because there is no passion or sexual vitality in their marriage at all. They assumed that by being married it would turn on the passion switch and they would automatically spend the first years of their marriage having sex like rabbits.

These experiences took place partly because the church in many ways has become a sheltered place when it comes to sex. Let me explain:

I didn't grow up attending church, and when I finally started attending I met a beautiful girl named Erin (who later became my wife). She was the golden girl of the youth group: on the youth committee, part of the worship team; she invited every person she knew to church. The pastors loved her! Then I showed up, started hanging out with her, and everyone took notice. My baggy pants didn't fit in; I was a chain-smoker who swore more than Will Hunting. One time we were having a youth worship night at church and I had brought along my friend's backpack for some reason. Now this friend was a bit of a womanizer during our teen years. Erin and I were standing in the front row, singing and chatting with our friends between songs. Before the pastor got up to speak, I reached back into the backpack, unzipped one of the pockets, and grabbed a pen to write some notes. A few minutes later one of the youth leaders walked up to me and tapped me on the shoulder. Her face was white as a ghost. I turned around and looked down at my feet. The floor was littered with condoms! I slowly looked up from the floor, not sure what to say. *They're not mine?* She wasn't impressed. Erin and I were dragged into the pastor's office and reprimanded, and of course, the word around the church was that I was coming to church just to sleep with all the girls in the youth group.

Of course, it wasn't wrong for them to follow up with me about the condoms, but the thing that stood out most to me was that there was only the investigation. There was no counsel given, nothing said about sex or what Christians believe about sex. I was a new Christian who had no idea what the Bible taught about sex, and no one attempted to help me understand. You see, sex, while not the most important thing in life, is not bad or something to be avoided. It is beautiful, God-given, and should be *enjoyed* in the context of marriage. That's Paul's whole point when he writes to the Corinthian church. But he isn't finished. Paul not only says we should be having sex with our spouse, he says it needs to be *frequent.*

HOW OFTEN SHOULD YOU BE HAVING SEX?

When I do marriage counseling, couples often ask: How regularly should we be having sex? I share with them what Paul says to the Corinthians: "Do not deprive one another, except perhaps by agreement *for a limited time* . . . but then come together again, so that Satan may not tempt you because of your lack of self-control" (1 Corinthians 7:5, emphasis added). Skeptics sometimes argue that the Bible restricts sex to the purpose of procreation. But that isn't true. Here Paul says that sex is a gift to be enjoyed frequently! And he argues for the importance of frequency, not to have children, but because it will help couples feel connected and protect their marriage from sexual temptation. Paul doesn't exactly answer the question of frequency, but he does encourage it. So what is a healthy sex life? Statistics give us some clue as to an answer:

- Couples under the age of 24 have sex an average of 132 times per year (every 2–3 days).
- Married couples under 30 have sex about 111 times per year (2–3 times per week).
- Married couples in general have sex with their spouse 58 times per year, or a little more than once a week on average.
- About 15 percent of married couples have not had sex with their spouse in the last six months to one year.[181]

I recently met with a couple who had been married five years and asked them about their sex life. "How often are you guys having sex?" She didn't hesitate. "Once a week," she said. I looked over at him and asked him if this was true. "Once a month—maybe," he said. Obviously, there is a large gap between a couple having sex fifty-two times a year and twelve times a year! For most men, if they are only having sex with their spouse twelve times a year, they are likely finding it elsewhere. Some men will seek outlets through pornography, habitual masturbation, or partners outside their marriage. The point of Paul's exhortation is to make sure married couples are giving each other their "conjugal *rights*." And his word to couples is a positive challenge to the sad state of sex in many marriages today. God knows how he made us. What I have said to couples in counseling over the years is that given a generally healthy marriage, if you are going weeks or months without having sex with your spouse, you are not fulfilling your conjugal duties (and delights!). Unfortunately, as others have pointed out, among Christians there are consequences for going *too far* (adultery, premarital sex, etc.), but none for *not going far enough* (abstaining for too long or punishing a spouse by withholding sex).[182] In reality, not going far enough is just as unbiblical. Even the Puritans, who are known as some of the most conservative Christians ever to have lived, recognized the dangers of infrequency. In one case, a man was excommunicated from the church and put under church discipline because he refused to have sex with his wife for two years.[183] God takes sex seriously, and he wants married couples (when they are able) to engage in it frequently.

While no Bible verse tells us how often to have sex, I have found Martin Luther's goal to be helpful and practical: "Twice a week seems to be enough to stave off the Tempter," he said. For most people, that's a goal worth shooting for. Of course, there are seasons that don't allow for this, including pregnancy, sickness, disability, separation, conflict, or travel. But the point is that God wants us to have sex, and there is no reason why we should refrain from it for long periods of time when we are married. To make that happen, both spouses must put in the effort.

Contrary to the romanticism of our modern culture, this does not mean that both spouses have to be "in the mood." If couples always waited for the right mood, sex would be pretty rare. Usually, one of them has to work at it a little. There is nothing wrong with this; it's perfectly normal and part of a healthy and selfless sex life. This is why in the same argument against a sex-is-bad theology Paul says that neither spouse owns their own body once they are married (1 Corinthians 7:4). Instead they give a shared authority to their spouse and need to serve the other selflessly. As Dr. Emerson Eggerich says, a husband is called to "minister" to his wife's *spirit*, being present emotionally, serving her, etc., which is one of her deepest needs, even though he may not "feel" like it at a given moment. Likewise, the wife is called to "minister" to her husband's *body* with frequency in the same spirit. This is a healthy cycle. Sex is not a math equation. Serving our spouse's needs should be our priority over our own. This is what the Bible lays out as a goal, and statistically it works.

SEX IN MARRIAGE

Contrary to popular opinion, married couples statistically don't have worse sex than singles, but *better*. In their groundbreaking study, *The Case for Marriage*, Linda J. Waite and Maggie Gallagher point out that 40 percent of married people have sex twice a week, compared to 20 percent of single and cohabitating men and women. Over 40 percent of married women said their sex life was emotionally and physically satisfying, compared to about 30 percent of single women. Fifty percent of married men are physically and emotionally content versus 38 percent of cohabitating men.[184] A survey of sexuality conducted jointly by researchers at State University of New York at Stony Brook and the University of Chicago—called the "most authoritative ever" by *U. S. News & World Report*—found that of all sexually active people the most physically pleased and emotionally satisfied were *married couples*.[185] The myth of our culture is that the single life is a life of great sex and the height of pleasure, but this is a lie. Waite and Gallagher conclude: "Promoting marriage . . . will make for a lot more happy men and women. *Sex in America* reported that married sex beats all else. . . . Married women had much higher rates of usually or always having orgasms, 75 percent, as compared to women who were never married, 62 percent."

The reason for this is simple: good sex is hard work and we need time to get it right. Maximum pleasure takes the amazing and exclusive relationship of marriage. Recently, I sat with a young newly married couple who were struggling with communication and conflict. After working through several issues with them, I asked how their sex life was. They both went red. He admitted that while he wanted to be more sexually attracted to his wife, he wasn't, and thus they didn't have sex very often, about once a month or so. She, on the other hand, was always ready and willing to have sex, but his lack of enthusiasm discouraged her. I asked a few more questions and learned that she was not experiencing a great amount of pleasure when they had sex, which subconsciously discouraged him, because the reality is men are even more attracted to giving pleasure to a woman than receiving it themselves. So his pride was taking a hit, causing him to be less and less attracted to her. A vicious cycle for sure.

They had settled for this unhealthy pattern. I shared with them some statistics, that about 10 percent of women never experience certain levels of pleasure and more than 50 percent struggle to consistently have great pleasure during sex.[186] Most importantly, I helped them to understand that the main reason for this is that experiencing the next level of pleasure and joy for a woman is a *learned* skill. It necessitates that a woman becomes very aware of her own personal sexual response so she can communicate that to her husband. Because of the nature of the female anatomy, which is far more complex than the male anatomy, women need to take some responsibility for their own pleasure and be an active participant.[187] It was God, after all, who created the clitoris, the part of a woman's anatomy that is packed with nerve endings and wired directly to the pleasure center of her brain. It's a part of her body made purely for pleasure, having no reproductive value at all. As best we can understand, its purpose is to motivate a woman to have more sex, and that's exactly what happens when it is engaged properly!

TAKE PLEASURE

So let's return to our original question: Is the Bible *antisex*? We have seen that Paul encourages sex, but from where does he get this idea? As a Pharisee, Paul knew his Hebrew Bible (the Old Testament), throughout whose pages God encourages sex in amazing and sometimes explicit ways. Yes, sex serves the purpose of procreation, but another primary purpose is *pleasure* itself. Marriage is where God intends that one's erotic desires should be fulfilled. God wants us to "rejoice in the wife of your youth" (Proverbs 5:18). It was so important for a newly married couple to be united together in this relationship that when a soldier got married in ancient Israel, he was commanded to stay home for one year to enjoy his wife (Deuteronomy 24:5). This joy is God's design, and he comes back to it again and again in the Scriptures when he speaks about sex: "Drink water from your own cistern, flowing water from your own well. . . . Let your fountain be blessed, and rejoice in the wife of your youth, a lovely deer, and a graceful doe. Let her breasts fill you at all times with delight; be intoxicated always in her love," the writer of Proverbs says (Proverbs 5:15, 18–19). Rather than being antisex, God encourages sexual pleasure.

If you still have doubts, take time to read the book Song of Solomon (also referred to as the Song of Songs in some translations). Speaking of a married couple's sex life in poetic language, this book is so explicit that Jewish boys were not allowed to read it until they were of the proper age:

- "Your breasts [are] like clusters of fruit," Solomon says. "I will climb the palm tree; I will take hold of its fruit" (Song 7:7–8

NIV). He goes on to describe the woman's body in graphic poetic detail. "Your belly is a heap of wheat" (Song 7:2), he says—which I don't recommend men repeat to their wives.

- "Your navel is a rounded goblet that never lacks blended wine. . . . Your breasts are like two fawns, like twins of a gazelle. Your neck is like an ivory tower. Your eyes are the pools of Heshbon" (Song 7:2–4 NIV).

- "I came to my garden . . . my bride, I gathered my myrrh with my spice, I ate my honeycomb with my honey, I drank my wine with my milk" (Song 5:1).

All of this is sexual metaphor and erotic poetry.

So how does God feel about all this explicit language? He's not saying, "Don't talk like that, you dirty kids!" Instead, he says: "Eat, friends, drink, and be drunk with love!" (Song 5:1). In other words, "I want you to enjoy yourself." Far from being a killjoy, God rejoices in our sexual pleasure. God says sex is an adventure for a husband and wife, committed to each other in love, where we explore different ways of enjoying his gift. Instead of being prudes, we are to be pleasure seekers and pleasure givers.

And in case you assume that all of this talk about sexual desire is just for *men*, consider what Old Testament scholars Dan Allender and Tremper Longman III say in their commentary on Song of Solomon:

> The role of the *woman* throughout the Song of Solomon is truly astounding, especially in light of its ancient origins. It is the woman, not the man, who is the dominant voice throughout the poems that make up the Song. She is the one who seeks, pursues, initiates. She boldly exclaims her physical attraction ["His abdomen is like a polished ivory tusk, decorated with sapphires . . ."] Most English translations hesitate in this verse. The Hebrew is quite erotic, and most translators cannot bring themselves to bring

out the obvious meaning. . . . This is a prelude to their lovemaking. There is no shy, shamed, mechanical movement under the sheets. Rather, the two stand before each other, aroused, feeling no shame, but only joy in each other's sexuality.[188]

The Bible is clear: sex was not just made for procreation but for pleasure. To *redeem* sex from all the dysfunctional ways it is abused and used means that we celebrate it as a gift given to us for our enjoyment to the glory of God. To equate sex with Satan or evil or sin is to miss one of the greatest expressions of God's love toward humankind. C. S. Lewis captures this idea poetically in his novel *The Screwtape Letters*, wherein an uncle demon writes to his nephew saying of God (the enemy):

He's a hedonist at heart. All those fasts and vigils and stakes and crosses are only a facade. Or only like foam on the seashore. Out at sea, out on His sea, there is pleasure and more pleasure. He makes no secret of it; at His right hand are "pleasures forevermore" as he writes in that blasted book of his. . . . He's vulgar, Wormwood. He has filled the world full of pleasures. . . . Never forget that when we are dealing with any pleasure in its healthy and normal and satisfying form, we are, in a sense, on the Enemy's ground. I know we have won many a soul through pleasure. All the same, it is His invention, not ours. He made the pleasures; all our research so far has not enabled us to produce a one. All we can do is to encourage the humans to take the pleasures, which our Enemy has produced, at times, or in ways, or in degrees which He has forbidden.[189]

Sex isn't bad. It's good. But as with any good thing, we need to make sure that we don't fall into the other extreme and make a good thing a god. Sex is a good thing, but it cannot replace God. To this we now turn.

Sex Is God

While a *sex-is-bad* philosophy is wrong and unbiblical, so is the opposite extreme: *sex-is-god*. In this perspective, sex is seen not merely as a good but as an *ultimate* good. A defining good. It becomes the central component to our identity as human beings, and thus freely satisfying our sexual appetites in whatever way we want is essential to our emotional health and development. "Sexual liberation is the only method to finding inner peace and security and beauty," Margaret Sanger says. "Remove the constraints and prohibitions, which now hinder the release of inner energies and, most of the larger evils of society will perish. Through sex, mankind will attain the great spiritual illumination, which will transform the world and light up the only path to an earthly paradise."[190] Sex becomes our religion, our salvation. We think it can set us free, bringing peace on earth and good will toward men.

At this point, some of you reading this might be thinking: What is wrong with a worldview like that? Isn't sex the defining factor of our humanness? What's wrong is Christians trying to *restrict* our freedom, including sexual freedom, and not letting us just be who we are. This is why biologist Alfred Kinsey opened his study, *Sexual Behavior in the Human Male,* by critiquing scientists who divide sexual behavior into categories of "normal" and "abnormal," instead urging us to view all forms of human behavior without ethical comment. Kinsey repeatedly taught that sex is "a biological function, acceptable in whatever form it is manifested."[191] This understanding of sex and the subsequent pursuit of sexual liberation has become a moral crusade for our culture, and the Christian vision of sexuality (that the only legitimate expression of sex is between a male and female in the context of marriage) is viewed as the enemy of that crusade.[192]

This sex-is-god worldview is, of course, nothing new. Throughout history, people have oriented their lives around the pursuit of sexual pleasure. The Bible was written to people living in cultures of extreme sexual perversion wherein people regularly engaged in premarital sex, extramarital sex, sexual slavery, temple prostitution, orgies, homosexuality, and various forms of promiscuity. Sex-is-god thinking was as normal in the first century as it is today. The form and accessibility of these things, however, has evolved, of course. We in the twenty-first century face unique challenges arising from the sexual revolution of the 1960s, internet-distributed pornography, the development of accessible and effective birth control, and easy access to abortion, among many others.

Skeptics often contend that premarital sex has not really increased among us as a culture since the 1940s and '50s but rather is simply talked about more openly. Scholars, however, have evidence to the contrary. In their book *SuperFreakonomics*, University of Chicago professor of economics Steven D. Levitt and coauthor Stephen J. Dubner point out the dramatic change prostitution has undergone in the last century. Prostitution has always existed based on a simple fact of economics: *men have always wanted more sex than they could get for free.* So, in more traditional cultures unmarried men would have to pay for sex outside of marriage. It is estimated that at least 20 percent of American men born between 1933 and 1942 had their first sexual intercourse with a prostitute.[193] In fact, in the 1910s, 1 of every 50 American women in their twenties was a prostitute.[194] Now, what does this have to do with anything?

Well, how is the prostitution business today? Levitt and Dubner point out that their "wage premium" today pales in comparison to the one enjoyed by even the low-rent prostitutes from a hundred years ago because "demand has fallen dramatically." Not the demand for sex. But prostitution, like any industry, is vulnerable to competition. Who poses as competition to a prostitute? Simple; "any woman who is willing to have sex with a man for free."[195] And of course, it is precisely this market that has taken off in the last century. "It is no secret," Levitt and Dubner say, that sexual mores have "changed substantially in recent decades. . . . The shift in sexual mores has given [us] a much greater supply of unpaid sex."[196] In their book *The Demise of Guys*, Philip Zimbardo and Nikita Duncan address the impact of a more liberal sexual ethic on men in particular in Western culture:

> This is the first time in U.S. history that our sons are having *less* education than their fathers. When confronted with an abundance of women, men become promiscuous and unwilling to commit to a monogamous relationship. Today's well-educated, empowered, successful women don't want lame, slacker husbands, and most men don't want to feel inferior to their wives. Will this push us into becoming more of an individual, rather than a family-based, society? . . . [E]asy access to sex affects men's motivation to achieve other life goals. Given the choice between masturbating over online pornography and going out on a date with a real girl—that is to say, a girl who doesn't look like a porn star and isn't wearing lingerie—more and more young men [say] that they prefer online porn.[197]

Today, sexual exchanges, whether real or virtual, are viewed more flippantly than any other point in Western history, and it is affecting us all, especially men. We have a whole generation of men who haven't been called to anything in their lives and are defined by what psychologists call "prolonged adolescence"—or what others have called "Peter Pan syndrome"—doing little else than masturbating and playing an unequaled-through-history amount of videos games and other passive activities while living at home with their parents and being unemployable. All of this, along with a number of other factors, results in a lack of commitment on the part of men to women and children (10 million American children live with unmarried partners), among other problems.

THE TROUBLE WITH TRIBBLES

Many pop commentators, politicians, and even modern educators suggest that "sexual liberation" is just an innocent move away from our traditional past, one that will make us more emotionally and spiritually healthy. But the modern form of sexual liberation—where sex is all about self-realization and personal, private behavior—is far more threatening than that because it naively *isolates sexuality* from the whole picture of what it means to be human in society. Such compartmentalization is not how individuals or societies work in reality. Everything is far more intimately connected. As one writer has said when discussing sex and spirituality, for instance, "*this* [sex] is always about *that* [spirituality]."[198]

I once heard Timothy Keller use an illustration that is helpful here. In the original *Star Trek* series, on an episode called "The Trouble with Tribbles," one of the characters, Nilz Baris, wanted his grain guarded by a starship, so he put out a priority-one distress signal. The problem was that this particular signal was only to be used in the most serious of circumstances. All of the starships in the galaxy came to his rescue, only to find out that he simply wanted them to guard his grain. The officers were furious. Why? Not only for this one mistake (of using the signal when he didn't really need it) but also for the larger consequences. As Keller points out, *if you begin to use a nonverbal signal that means one thing to mean something else, you destroy its ability to be used.* It becomes useless because who will know what it means?

The implications of this hit me as I began to think about how our culture uses sex. The biblical story is that God gives sex as a gift and stitches it into history as the greatest and most powerful nonverbal signal of unity, love, covenant, and commitment—even a picture of the gospel message itself (Ephesians 5:31–32). The meshing of two souls takes place and the unspoken message in that act is, "I belong completely, totally, and exclusively to you." Our separate souls and personhoods create an entity and unity that did not exist before the act took place. Two become one. But what happens when we use this signal to mean something else? We destroy it. It would be bad enough if that were the only implication, and I wish it were, but it's actually so much more. In his celebrated book *The New Testament and the People of God*, N. T. Wright contends that every worldview: (1) provides the *stories* through which we view reality, (2) informs the fundamental *questions* that determine human existence, (3) expresses itself in cultural *symbols*, which then (4) leads to a *praxis*—a way of being in the world.

He says that all four of these elements are connected, interacting with one another like an ecosystem:

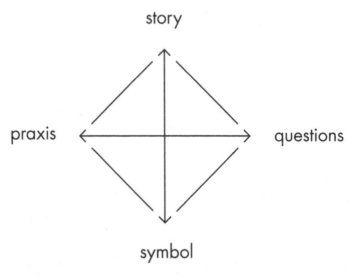

Wright's point is that if a culture experiences the loss of meaning in *one* of its central symbols, *everything* else in that culture is affected, including its stories, its questions, its other symbols, and most importantly, its praxis—its very way of being in the world—precisely because of how the elements work together and play off one another.[199] This, I propose, is precisely what has happened in the misuse of sex in Western culture. Turn on the television, search the internet, look at billboards, and read magazines. Our stories, questions, and praxis have changed. We misused and destroyed one of the central symbols God gave us to *define meaning* in the world and, in turn, have called into question and confused not just sexuality or personhood or marriage, but *meaning* itself.

This is why the New Testament speaks sixty-plus times about the dangers of sexual immorality. What is at stake is not just "personal godliness," or whatever we shrink being sexually moral into, but our cultural and societal flourishing. The problem with sex-is-god cultures is that people think being more open and accepting about sexual options will liberate us and make us healthier as a species. But the facts seem to indicate precisely the opposite. Years ago, writing about unwed, teenage mothers, Peggy Noonan captured this very tension:

> We have all had a moment when all of a sudden we looked around and thought: The world is changing. . . . This is for me the moment when the new America began: I was at a graduation ceremony at a public high school in New Jersey. It was 1971 . . . One by one a stream of black-robed students walked across the stage and received their diplomas. And a pretty young girl with red hair, big under her graduation gown, walked up to receive hers. The auditorium stood up and applauded. . . . The girl was eight months pregnant and had had the courage to go through with her pregnancy and take her finals and finish school despite society's disapproval. But Society wasn't disapproving. It was applauding. Applause is a right and generous response for a young girl with grit and heart. And yet, in the sound of that applause I heard a wall falling. . . . The old America had a delicate sense of the difference between the general ("We disapprove") and the particular ("Let's go help her"). We had the

moral self-confidence to sustain the paradox, to sustain the difference between "official" disapproval and "unofficial" [help]. The old America would not have applauded the girl in the big graduation gown, *but some of its individuals would have helped her* not only materially but also with some measure of emotional support. We don't so much anymore. For all our tolerance and talk *we don't show much love* to what used to be called girls in trouble. As we've gotten more open-minded we've gotten more closed-hearted.[200]

In other words, celebration is often too simplistic a solution and leaves many of the questions and needs of real people untouched. As a pastor I see this pain every week in the lives of people wrestling with the reality of marriages ending in divorce, sexually transmitted infections, rape, unfaithfulness, pornography, and gender confusion. This is one place the church's role can be clearly felt. While we can't agree with everyone's lifestyle, we can do what others have moved on from doing for these people, namely *be there*. Long after the ticker-tape parade is over and the community has been used to push a political agenda one way or the other. Be present. Love and listen after others have moved on, patting themselves on the back.

SEX IS NOT ULTIMATE

Maybe the most important thing that can be said to a sex-is-god culture is that while sex is amazing—maybe the best pleasure this life has to offer—there is a greater joy that will one day retire it. Take the analogy of marriage in the Bible. People often ask me why Jesus' standards are so absurdly high for it, giving only a few reasons to ever legitimately divorce (adultery, abandonment, etc.). The reason is because marriage is just a pointer to an eternal reality but is itself not that reality. It is not forever. "In the resurrection they neither marry nor are given in marriage," Jesus says (Matthew 22:30). In other words, in heaven *we will not marry*. Marriage is thus momentary, "a brief blessing. A great one, but not an ultimate one. A precious one, but not a permanent one."[201] This explains why Jesus can be so radical. "Never to have married is not a tragedy. Otherwise Jesus' life is a tragedy. Tragedy is craving the perfect marriage so much that we make a god out of being married. Jesus' standards are high because marriage does not and should not meet all our needs. It should not be an idol. It should not take the place of Jesus himself. Marriage is but for a moment. Jesus is for eternity. How we live in our marriages and our singleness will show if Jesus is our supreme treasure."[202]

The same must be said about sex. It is a great gift but a temporal one. A pleasure that can't be seen as the highest of priorities because it is not *ultimate*. It will be eclipsed by an even greater pleasure. The joy of getting God himself. A pleasure that sex is just a small pointer to. This is why Christians are to be sexually subversive and challenge the dominant ideologies of the world, whether single or married, by living in such a way that shows others that Jesus, not sex or any temporary physical pleasure, is our ultimate satisfaction.

Sex Is Appetite

The third perspective, popular at the time the New Testament was written and still very popular today, is that sex is nothing more than a *natural appetite*. When we get hungry, we eat whatever is around. When we get thirsty, we drink what we can find. When we are sexually aroused, we should have sex with whomever is around so we can satisfy that need. In the animal kingdom there is little concept of marriage or fidelity; there is simply mating. Like eating a meal, there is *no moral value connected to sexuality*. We are animals, and the same behavior should be the norm for us.

The apostle Paul critiques this view in a powerful and fascinating way. He begins by stating the view of those teaching it: "Food is meant for the stomach and the stomach for food" (1 Corinthians 6:13). Greeks taught that the body was bad and the spirit was good, and that what you do with your body didn't matter as long as you kept your spirit pure; in fact, it's basically the same philosophy as the modern, naturalist, Darwinian view of sex. We are told that "our ancestors were not monogamous" but were instead "harem builders (like seals and walruses), where any male who monopolized power and wealth could also monopolize females, thus ensuring the survival of his genes."[203] In such a construct, adultery and polygamy are simply a remnant or fossil from our genetic past. This being the case, Richard Dawkins, recognizing where his philosophy leads him, claims that his own monogamous marriage to his wife is an "un-Darwinian personal decision."[204] But, of course this is ridiculous, because if we are really programmed by our genes through Darwinian selection, how *could* anyone make an "un-Darwinian" decision?

HEAVY PETTING AND SEXUAL IMMORALITY

A Darwinian model of life allows for a variety of ways this can go. In an article entitled "Heavy Petting," for instance, popular Princeton University professor Peter Singer argues for the legitimacy of sexual relations between humans and animals based on Darwinian theory, saying that "sex *across the species barrier* ceases to be an offense to our status and dignity as human being."[205] Similarly, in an article called "Why Men Rape" in *The New York Academy of Sciences*, Randy Thornhill and Craig Palmer argue that rape itself is not a pathology but instead "an evolutionary adaptation for maximizing reproductive success," a natural phenomenon that is a by-product of human evolutionary heritage, similar to "the leopard's spots and the giraffe's elongated neck."[206] In other words, rape is natural. Such examples may seem extreme, but these are mainline naturalistic thinkers simply applying their logic to the realm of human sexuality, and they are just being honest. A naturalistic approach that sanctions our biological appetites removes all moral culpability from our sexual choices.

Of course, the apostle Paul strongly disagrees with this perspective, arguing instead that "The body is not meant for sexual immorality, but for the Lord, and the Lord is for the body" (1 Corinthians 6:13). In other words, and contrary to Greek thought, because we are made by God our bodies are not disconnected from our souls. So, "Do you not know that he who is joined to a prostitute becomes one body with her? For, as it is written, 'The two will become one flesh'" (vv. 15–16). Paul is pointing out "the monstrosity of physical oneness without all the other kinds of oneness that every sex act should mirror"[207] and "denies that [sex is] . . . no more than an appropriate exercise of the genital organs. On the contrary he insists that it is an act which . . . engages and expresses the whole personality in such a way as to constitute a unique mode of self-disclosure and self-commitment."[208] In other words, we never just have sex with a body, and we can't just act on our feelings. Sex is not less than appetite but so much more.

My point here is not to convince you that what the Bible teaches is true. But I would ask you to honestly consider which view rings true to human experience and to your own. Could our naturalistic assumptions be too simplistic? Many cultures and religions have recognized the existence of a spiritual dimension that transcends the physical, even if they could not explain it. What we do know is that in our modern Western world, the sex-is-appetite approach translates into sex as *self*-gratification, *self*-pleasure, and *self*-actualization. When all that matters is our animal appetites, sex becomes a selfish endeavor. However, the Bible teaches something quite different and radical: that sex is *other*-centered, a selfless expression where one joins oneself to another person's soul—his or her life, experiences, failures, and faults.

That through this act we somehow transcend a mere physical unity and experience something deeper, something wonderful and mysterious. Christianity teaches that sex is holistic. We should never get naked and vulnerable with a person only physically without getting naked and vulnerable with them in every other way: socially, economically, geographically, spiritually, and emotionally. To do anything else will always end in catastrophe. In a culture of hookups, swinging, sexting, pornography, and one-night stands, the Bible says to have sex with someone is to *know* each other in every way.

Sex isn't just about animals feeding an appetite. Ask someone who has been sexually assaulted if the pain stops when the sex stops. It does not, because we're more than just physical creatures, but spiritual, emotional, and psychological creatures too. God created sex so that we would experience maximum pleasure, security, unity, and joy when a male and female leave the covenant relationship with their mother and father for a covenant relationship with their spouse. The two become one in every way. This is God's plan for human joy and flourishing. Anything outside of this falls short.

While this can feel restrictive, we need to remember that many of the best things in life require disciplined focus and commitment. The greater yes is only possible when we say no to other things. Contrary to modern thinking about freedom, for which restrictions are seen as oppressive and we should fight to be liberated from them, the wisdom of the Bible, and of most of human experience, is that restrictions are the secret to deeper truth, flourishing, and joy. Fish are restricted to water, but *only in water are they free to flourish.* If a fish tries to live outside of those restrictions, it finds itself dying a slow death. In the same way, when we accept who we are as human beings and learn to live within God's sexual restrictions, we begin to experience life as it was originally designed for us. At first, it may feel like a kind of death, but that is because we have grown addicted to junk food when a healthy feast awaits us.

The restrictions around sex do not exist because God is mean or limiting or a killjoy. God loves sex, and he wants us to maximize our pleasure and joy in his gift, used in the right way in the right context. They are the water given graciously for our adventure.

Yet any sexual restrictions are considered antiquated and the reason why many skeptics are convinced that Christianity should not have a role in the cultural discourse or a say in public policy today. Faith informing public policy is considered dangerous, they say. This, of course, is a naive way of thinking, because as we have seen, the most secular of humanists have a faith-position whether they admit it or not; it certainly informs their policies, yet those convictions are not dismissed because of that fact. This is one of the many contradictions of secularization in the West. Whether a particular Christian ethic is welcomed or dismissed seems more of a reflection of the *host culture* and what it already likes or doesn't like, rather than whether the teaching itself is sound or of any value. As D. A. Carson points out, "If Christians weigh in on, say, abortion, homosexuality, or stem cell research, they are inevitably charged with smuggling Christianity into the public arena, where it does not belong . . . [but] if they weigh in, as Christians, on, say, the homeless, the poor, public welfare, and consumerism, then they are widely . . . thought to have a prophetic voice."[209] This means that cultural convictions of a particular place and time have become the arbiter of truth and the most important filter for values as a society. This is backward. The cart before the horse. The Christian position, in contrast to this ever-changing target model, is that the biblical definition of sexuality should not be redefined or challenged by a cultural ethos, no matter what culture it exists within, and no matter how much a culture "progresses," because if the Bible is, in fact, trustworthy and true, it transcends any one culture or time, and all the sentiments of that place and moment.

It is when we understand this that we see why the church has continued to preach and practice a biblically informed sexual ethic in the world, and why it must continue to do so. It is not because the church likes to "judge" people or infringe on rights or proselytize. It is about holding fast to the one expression of sex that God designed for our ultimate joy, pleasure, and flourishing, trusting that he knows better than us, and then holding that out to the world around us and offering it gladly.

SUBVERTING THE EMPIRE

The rationale is also to prevent sex from being usurped by the myriad of different constructs offered by the empires throughout history, including the empire of the modern Western world. Ever since Israel was in Egypt, the call to God's people was to "be holy" or set apart (Leviticus 11:44) and not swept up in the trends of the collective consciousness in which they lived. God's people were to challenge and overthrow key pathologies of their time. Because "empires maintain their sovereignty . . . by *monopolizing the imagination of their subjects*,"[210] the church must see its call to push back. For in what way are we as a species more captive subjects than when it comes to our sexual ethic? We read the prompter as a culture and accept whatever definitions are thrown at us. What is the Christian community to do in the face of this reality? Live and think in a way that subverts the world around it and the definitions that have come to be absorbed uncritically.

It is here that we see the skeptic accuse the Christian of exactly the opposite of what the Christian truly seeks: *freedom* for people, not restriction. People say, "I am not enslaved! I am free! All of my sexual choices are *my* choices!" But as the Danish philosopher Søren Kierkegaard made clear time and time again, *feeling* free is not necessarily real freedom. It may actually be bondage, because in those moments when we feel this or feel that, we are being defined by our aesthetic life—our emotions and not something that transcends them.

This in the end, he said, may be the ultimate prison. The aesthetical life winning out over anything else, including the rational life, because feelings are more powerful than reason.

This was the warning of the much celebrated book *Amusing Ourselves to Death* by Neil Postman, who argued the same point, comparing the visions of the future presented by George Orwell (in *1984*) and Aldous Huxley (in *Brave New World*). "What Orwell feared," Postman says,

> [W]ere those who would ban books. What Huxley feared was that there would be no reason to ban a book, for there would be no one who wanted to read one. Orwell feared those who would deprive us of information. Huxley feared those who would give us so much that we would be reduced to passivity and egoism. Orwell feared that the truth would be concealed from us. Huxley feared the truth would be drowned in a sea of irrelevance. Orwell feared we would become a captive culture. Huxley feared we would become a trivial culture, preoccupied with some equivalent of the feelies, the orgy porgy, and the centrifugal bumblepuppy. In *1984* people are controlled by inflicting pain. In *Brave New World* they are controlled by inflicting pleasure. In short, Orwell feared that what we hate will ruin us. Huxley feared that what we love will ruin us. This book is about the possibility that Huxley, not Orwell, was right.[211]

Postman astutely discerned that the real problem is not that we are captive to *outside* totalitarian forces but to the power of *internal* forces— our addictions to our own pleasures. What we love enslaves us. And Christianity teaches that our desires, created good, have become disordered. We don't *naturally* hate that which God hates. Even worse, we love it, and it feels good. It brings us a form of pleasure. But, and this is part of the Christian prophetic critique of Western culture, simply loving something and taking pleasure in it *does not make it right* by default.

The Christian understanding of our human condition would say that Huxley was correct. We are *captive* to our pleasure, not freed by it. What we love has ruined us. And Christianity seeks to wake us up from this very slavery. It calls us to harbor dreams of both a *personal* and a *social* reality, which are alternative to the empires that surround us. And so Christian proclamation and cultural practice should "seek to demythologize the empire and devalue its currency. Such proclamation . . . will always be a subversion of the dominant version of reality."[212]

This means that when atheists such as Richard Dawkins and Sam Harris accuse Christians of "brainwashing" our children with Christian sexual ideals, I wholeheartedly agree. You're darned right I do! Because if I don't, *Grey's Anatomy* and Rihanna and Beyoncé will. They will tell my daughters what sex and power and womanhood are! But it is my job as a parent who believes that *Jesus* is the center of all things, rather than one's sexuality, to help my kids think through their worldview informed by the Christian story in contrast to the other stories that surround them ubiquitously. And it has not stopped being the church's prophetic role to offer an alternative vision to the world's in regard to sex: a truly radical vision but the most fulfilling of all. As Richard Hays says, Christians need "to stop seeing themselves as participants in the 'normal' social and economic structures of their city and to imagine themselves instead as members of the eschatological people of God, acting corporately in a way that will prefigure and proclaim the kingdom of God. . . . [Paul] is seeking to *resocialize* them into a new way of doing business, a new community consciousness."[213]

Sex as a Pointer to Heaven

Finally, we must come to see that all pleasure is a grace given to us by God. Sex—like love or any of a myriad of "good and perfect" things we enjoy in this life—is a gift "from above, coming down from the Father of lights" (James 1:17). And while we can enjoy these gifts in themselves, they are also pointers to a pleasure that will be experienced only in heaven when sin and its deadening effect on our senses is removed forever. We will experience a joy to which the pleasures of this world are just the tip of the iceberg.

Sex is glorious indeed, but one of its glories is that it is not ultimate but instead points away from itself "to the eternal delight of soul that we will have in heaven . . . [it] point[s] to the deep, infinitely fulfilling, and final union we will have with Christ . . . it's the most ecstatic, breathtaking, daring, scarcely-to-be-imagined look at the glory that is our future."[214] Again, Jesus taught that people won't marry in heaven, not because marriage is bad, but because it is temporary. It is good, and for the present time it has a good purpose. But there will come a time when it will be surpassed by something far better. In the midst of everyday life, this isn't always easy to remember. C. S. Lewis makes an apt observation that captures it perfectly:

> I think our present outlook might be like that of a small boy who, on being told that the sexual act was the highest bodily pleasure should immediately ask whether you ate chocolates at the same time. On receiving the answer "No," he might regard absence of chocolates as the chief characteristic of sexuality. In vain would you tell him that the reason why lovers in their carnal raptures don't bother about chocolates is that they have something better. The boy knows chocolate: he does not know the positive thing that excludes it. We are in the same position. We know the sexual life; we do not know, except in glimpses, the other thing which, in Heaven, will leave no room for it.[215]

We do not know the other thing, but we have pointers to it—to him. Instead of keeping people away from God, sex should draw us all closer to him. And that, in the end, may be the most radical idea of all.

CHAPTER 8

The Problem of
HYPOCRISY

The greatest Liar has his Believers; and it often
happens, that if a Lie be believ'd only for an
Hour, it has done its Work, and there is no further
occasion for it. Falsehood flies, and the Truth
comes limping after it; so that when Men come to
be undeceiv'd, it is too late; the Jest is over, and
the Tale has had its Effect.

JONATHAN SWIFT, *THE EXAMINER*

In 2007, the Barna Group did an extensive research project in which they asked non-Christian people why they rejected Christianity. Many Christian leaders were surprised to learn that none of the top six answers were *evidential* reasons. They rejected Christianity for *moralistic* reasons. The *top three* problems people had with Christianity were that it was viewed as (1) anti-homosexual (91 percent of responders), (2) judgmental (87 percent), and (3) hypocritical (85 percent).[216] Modern people contend that the greatest proof that God does not exist is the behavior of Christians themselves! In short, the way Christians live and act is solid proof in their minds that what Christians believe is not true. Besides the view that we are mean-spirited and judgmental, as cited above, skeptics also point out the atrocities throughout history the Christian church has carried out, including killing and torturing those who disagree with them, the Crusades, etc. These realities and perceptions are enough to keep many people from believing in Christ.

For some, it is the *Christian* faith in particular that is the problem; for others, it is a broader objection to religion in general. "Good people will do good things," Steven Weinberg cynically quips, "bad people will do bad things, but for good people to do bad things—that takes religion."[217] Some believe that religious people are dangerous because their beliefs are not reasonable. The beliefs are informed by and originate with *God* and cannot be opposed, thus leading to the demonization of others and frequent violence. Religion has fueled wars, oppression, witch hunts, murder, homophobia, crusades, inquisitions, *jihads*, and *fatwas* all through history and ongoing. More recently, one can point to 9/11, ISIS, the Orlando shootings, and the bombing of abortion clinics by Christian extremists.[218]

A common challenge I often hear when talking with skeptics is the more specific historical record as well. "The Crusades slaughtered millions in the name of Jesus. The Inquisition brought about the torture and murder of millions more," as Robert Kuttner says.[219] During the witch trials, the church in Europe killed "more than five million women," skeptics popularly claim, informed by Dan Brown's *The Da Vinci Code*,[220] not to mention all of the social judgment, exclusion, and slavery the church has supported throughout history. Why would anyone want to align themselves with a faith like this? How does one respond?

The First Step Is Admitting It

The first thing is to admit that some of these charges are absolutely true, of course. Many who call themselves Christians throughout history and today have done, and are doing, horrible things in the name of Christ. This is especially true when religion becomes a systematized, institutionalized, and politicized organization that wields political and military power over others (all of which, as we will see, Jesus was against). Horrific acts have been committed in the name of Christ, and Christians should not take the challenge of these injustices naively. We must approach them humbly, admitting that people have hurt others in the name of Christianity, and we should apologize for and repent of those actions.

In his book *Blue Like Jazz*, Donald Miller tells the story of how he and his friends built a confessional booth on the campus of their liberal university. When people entered to confess their sins, Miller would instead confess to them the sins of the church, apologizing for the pain it has caused throughout history—its mistreatment of homosexuals and women, burning people at the stake, etc. Among the students on campus, this helped Christianity gain credibility and a hearing. That's where our response to these charges needs to begin, and the model for this is Jesus. Jesus began his ministry with a call to "repent" (Mark 1:15), but as historians point out, he was not talking to irreligious people. He was speaking to many of the most religious people of the day. Every person needs to start with a humble admission of his or her mistakes and sins, starting with us as followers of Jesus. As Christians we need to take responsibility for institutions that carry the name of Jesus. But we also need to clarify that these institutions do not always represent Jesus or reflect what he taught.

Fake Disciples and Hypocrisy

There are two major reasons for the existence of hypocritical, judgmental, and mean-spirited people in the church, both throughout history and in modern times. The first reason is because the church is filled with people who *aren't actually Christians*. I know this seems like an obvious point, but it needs to be understood by armchair critics of the church who hold Christians responsible for every act done by any crazy person who has a Jesus bumper sticker on their car. Jesus clearly taught that there are not only false *teachers* in the world who lead people astray into false doctrine and behavior (Matthew 7:15–20), but false *disciples* in the world who lead themselves astray into false beliefs and false lives (vv. 21–23). This is why Jesus warns people not to judge Christianity by the morality of the people who try to follow it, but to focus attention on Jesus himself—on his life, teachings, and actions. Christianity is not good advice to help good people lead moral lives. It's good news about Jesus—who he was and what he did.

Churches are filled with people who attend every Sunday service, don't say bad words, don't watch bad movies, and make sure to give their offering every week. However, they don't actually *know, love, or walk* with God at all. They have simply adopted a cultural Christianity, an exoskeleton of religious trappings. They are people whom Jesus called "lukewarm" (Revelation 3:16) and "hypocrites" (Matthew 23:13), who say one thing but behave contrary to the ways of Christ. Jesus reserved his most scathing critique for these people (Matthew 23:1–39). Jesus warns us that at the end of days, a group of religious people will say to him, "Lord, Lord," but he will cast them out and say, "I never knew you" (Matthew 7:22–23). It is a scary thing to think about, but nonetheless true: there will always be those who deceive others, sure, but there are also those who deceive *themselves*. My point is the atrocities done in the name of Christianity are often (most often?) not done because the teachings of Christianity are bad but because some people who claim to follow Christ don't actually know him or follow him. They do not produce the fruit of the Holy Spirit, the virtues of "love, joy, peace, patience, kindness, goodness, faithfulness, gentleness, [and] self-control" (Galatians 5:22–23).

It is often those who have adopted this *cultural form* of Christianity who create the image problem for Christianity. For instance, several years ago a poll was taken that showed that the lifestyle activities of Christians were statistically the same as those of people claiming not to be Christians when it came to the following list: gambling, visiting pornographic websites, taking something that didn't belong to them, saying mean things behind someone's back, consulting a medium or a psychic, having a physical fight or abusing someone, using illegal or nonprescription drugs, saying something to someone that's not true, getting back at someone for something they did, and consuming enough alcohol to be considered legally drunk.[221]

There was *no statistical difference* between a Christian and a non-Christian in these ten areas of their lives. The only activity that was less common for Christians (and this is not a joke) was recycling (68 percent vs. 79 percent)![222] This exemplifies what people mean when they say Christians are hypocrites. They see people who *claim* to be morally upright yet look, sound, act, and live no different than anyone else in the world. According to the Bible, though, if there is no outward change in behavior, allegiances, loves, and passions, Jesus would question whether these people are actually Christians at all. The problem, though, is that their lives misrepresent Christianity to the world.

If this objection is a strong one for you, I would encourage you to assess the Christian worldview based on its central teachings and not on the people who try to follow it. Our first questions need to be: What did *Jesus* teach? How did *Jesus* live? The essence of Christianity is Jesus, not how people have attempted to follow him and fumbled the ball. Leo Tolstoy once said, "Attack me rather than the path I follow and which I point out to anyone who asks me where I think it lies. If I know the way home and am walking along it drunkenly, is it any less the right way because I am staggering from side to side?" The church is full of people who come from different backgrounds, have different experiences, and are at different stages of growth. If a person claims to love Jesus but never actually tries to learn from him or live the way he taught, it's hard to take that claim seriously. The writer of James says that even demons know God exists—they have *faith*, but that faith doesn't save them (James 2:19). Why? Because "faith by itself, if it does not have works, is dead" (v. 17). It is a scary thought, but there is such a thing as faith in God that doesn't save. This is a warning to all those who claim to be Christians: *our beliefs must be coupled with lives that are God-honoring.* True Christians can't be separated from the evidence of the fruit of their lives.

The Church: A Place for Sinners, Not Perfect People

I've already hinted at a second reason why hypocrisy and the church are often bedfellows, but it needs to be understood. It's because people misunderstand *the message* of Christianity—as if it's about making bad people into good people. Many people assume that being a Christian means you follow all the rules and have your life together. They assume that "Christian" equals "good person"—when the opposite is true. The gospel is not about what *we* can do for God (good advice), but what *God has done for us* (good news). Jesus lived a perfect life precisely *because* we can't. That's why we live in humble dependence on God's grace (Ephesians 2:8–10), his favor shown to people who don't deserve it. If this is the core of the Christian faith, then what *should* we expect the church to look like? Certainly not a country club of perfect people sipping lemonades waiting for the first tee, but a *hospital*, a gathering of broken, messed-up people who admit they are sinners (who have disregarded God's ways and tried to live for themselves) seeking the love and grace of a saving God. Heads low in reverence, and appreciative if God would forgive them this one last time. Not proud and entitled people. If that's the case, rather than condemning Christianity because

Christians aren't instantly good after attending a church service, we should recognize that people are at different places in their lives in the process of becoming like Christ. And be more willing to live in the place where grace and sin meet. Just because someone attends church doesn't mean he or she is a mature follower of Jesus.

When we started Village Church in 2010, we met in a small elementary school gym located on a quiet suburban cul-de-sac. When the church began to grow, people would park wherever they could find a spot—in front of driveways, fire hydrants, on people's lawns. I got a phone call one Monday morning that a guy had parked his tires on a person's lawn the day before. The homeowner came out, yelled at him, and told him to move it. The guy was in a hurry to get to our church with his young family, so he turned around and gave the guy the finger, shouting, "Screw you; I'm late for church!" We could easily accuse this man of being a hypocrite and making a mockery of Christianity, but before we do that we should learn more about his story. In this case, as with thousands of people at Village Church, he and his family were just starting to explore Christianity. They came from a very un-Christian background and had not come to a point in their walk with God where their talk was kind and respectful, or as the Bible says, "seasoned with salt" (Colossians 4:6). Their lives were a mess, but they were coming to be under the grace they so desperately needed.

When I started to attend a church near the end of high school, I didn't look or sound like the other Christians there. It was a nice, conservative Baptist church with orange carpet, and the pastors wore suits and ties. One day the pastor preached on not being "unequally yoked," which is a Christian-ese way of saying that Christians should not date or marry non-Christians. A man came up to Erin (now my wife) and said, "You need to stop dating Mark because he's not a Christian." She said, "What are you talking about? Why do you say that?" He said, "I saw him smoking the other day. You need to break up with him." Erin paused for a moment and then asked: "What was he smoking?" He looked at her, puzzled. "Um . . . he was smoking cigarettes." To which Erin responded: "Praise God! That's better than what he used to smoke!"

That day this man learned something about the church: Instead of judging someone on the basis of what we immediately see, we need to ask a deeper question. Instead of asking, "Where is a person, at this moment, spiritually, or morally?" we should be asking, "From where did this person *start?*" The church is comprised of people who have come to realize they are imperfect and messed up. And that doesn't change overnight. It can look hypocritical from the outside.

And it's the same with the checkered history of Christianity, including the crusaders and those burning witches, as we will address next. We have to conclude that at some level these people didn't know the first thing about Christianity because either they weren't actually Christians or they were naive about true Christianity altogether. As we read the New Testament and look to the men and women throughout history who really followed Jesus, there is no model of discipleship into which these atrocities fit. Christianity is about Jesus dying at the hands of his enemies and refusing to pick up a sword. And this is not some abstract secondary doctrine but the center of Christianity! The call to either the self-deceived or those who are just starting out in their journey with Jesus Christ is the same: *repent* of these awful actions and become more like Jesus, who laid down his life for those he disagreed with and never killed them or even threatened to.

Christianity's Violent Past: Conspiracies and Witch Hunts

Still, even if we accept the two points above, we are still left with an awful list of atrocities to explain and answer for. How should Christians respond to these? I believe we need a second level of discourse with an eye toward uncovering facts and avoiding conspiracy theories and half-truths that are common in the portrayal of Christian history by skeptics. In personal conversations with several skeptics, I've encountered exaggerations, historical revisionism, and a plain misunderstanding of actual historical events, so much so that one must agree with Oxford historian Alister McGrath that one of the greatest tasks confronting the church today is "to rescue Christianity from misunderstandings."[223]

We must look at facts versus mythology.

For instance, I once had a conversation with a university-educated young man who was convinced that the moon landing in 1969 was a conspiracy. He argued that it didn't really happen and that NASA had set up a sound stage and hired Stanley Kubrick to direct the landing (which then led to a hidden confession through symbolism in Kubrick's film *The Shining*). He argued that the film footage of the moon landing exposed the conspiracy because the American flag planted on the moon remained stiff and this would never have occurred in a gravity-free environment. I pointed out the fact that NASA has enough bright people on staff to realize that it would be necessary to put a stick behind the flag so it would remain stiff on the moon before they ever took off. He stared at me like *I* was crazy.

Admittedly, the world of facts is sometimes less interesting than myth, but it is the necessary world we must inhabit. It takes work to keep up with all the charges people throw at the church. Since mythologies are built over time, if we fail to face them head-on, sooner or later they are simply absorbed into our cultural consciousness, and it becomes more difficult to challenge them. But, alas, we must. Let's explore some of the most popular examples.

THE CRUSADES AND THE INQUISITION

Consider the Crusades and the Inquisition. I've frequently heard skeptics refer to the Crusades as "religious wars" where "the church" slaughtered tens of thousands of innocent Muslims. But we must understand that at the time of the Crusades and the Inquisition, Western Europe was fighting complex *geopolitical* wars while being culturally Christian. Catholicism as a religious institution held great places of power in Europe at the time. Church and state were not separate. Europe would wage its wars under a Catholic banner, and because of this people conclude that the Crusades are an example of Christianity trying to expand by way of the sword. But this was simply not the case. Many of these fights were political and *nationalistic* battles, not religious ones. This was not about the advancement of the kingdom of God and the heartfelt conversion of people to Jesus, but the expansion of European rule, draped in a vaguely Christian exoskeleton. And in many cases they were fought defensively, to protect Christians from invading Muslim attacks or to reclaim land that had been lost to Muslim invaders.

The Roman Empire officially became Christian under Constantine in the fourth century AD because he converted to Christianity, yet Rome continued to expand its nationalistic rule through conquest and violence. Christianity was absorbed and hijacked by the agenda of the Roman Empire at times as Rome continued to do what it had always done—fight battles to expand its worldly kingdom and hegemony. Throughout history, Christians have been critical of this and have sought to distinguish between the kingdom of God and the state—a kingdom rule by worldly means and with a worldly agenda. But Jesus made clear, "My kingdom is not of this world" (John 18:36). Jesus' intent was not to set up empires of worldly power. In other words, no matter what religion or god the Roman Empire served, the outcome would have been the same.

Timothy Keller gives some helpful illustrations of this point. Take a modern example like Northern Ireland, he suggests. It is often argued that the Protestants and Catholics in Northern Ireland are fighting a religious war. But they are not. They aren't fighting over matters of *doctrine* (transubstantiation, baptism, the doctrine of justification by faith, etc.). Their fight is for autonomy, retribution, and ultimately who gets to run the country. The fight is not between committed followers of Jesus who want to ensure that people have pure doctrine and believe the truth that Jesus taught. These are political freedom fighters. Throughout history, we observe *political* wars with which Christianity is associated. And while we may find Christianity having influence on a culture, a country, and its leaders, we rarely find the church itself taking up arms to wage war against others.

In fact, when we study the Bible and Christian doctrine we find that Christians are *prohibited* from using coercive action toward others in the name of Jesus (Matthew 5:44; 26:52). Harm to others is antithetical to the spirit of Christianity, which has always worked better on the margins of culture rather than in the seats of power. Christianity has always had its greatest appeal among the poor, oppressed, and persecuted. This is evident in how Christianity's epicenter has continually moved over the last two thousand years. The hub of every religion on the planet has tended to stay in their culture of origin: Islam is primarily still Middle Eastern, Buddhism is primarily Eastern, Hinduism is primarily Indian. But Christianity is different. It began as a breakaway Jewish sect, moved throughout the Mediterranean, then to Europe, the Americas, and now is growing primarily in Asia, Latin America, and Africa. Why? Because in every case when Christianity assumed a seat of power, it fell asleep. It stopped being subversive, and it died. So, it moved. The teachings of Jesus are embraced most powerfully where Christians live underground and are persecuted.

Jesus Christ rejects power as a means of hurting or coercing others. He warns us of the temptation to be in power over others politically and militarily. It's almost as if he predicted the Crusades and the rise of cultural Christianity and wanted to be clear that they have nothing to do with following him. For instance, when James and John, two of his disciples, came to him and asked to sit at his right and left in the kingdom, Jesus said, "You know that those who are considered rulers of the Gentiles lord it over them, and their great ones exercise authority over them. But it shall not be so among you. But whoever would be great among you must be your servant, and whoever would be first among you must be slave of all. For even the Son of Man came not to be served but to serve, and to give his life as a ransom for many" (Mark 10:42–45). In other words, Christianity is fundamentally not about possessing political or military power and authority over people, but about *serving* them. "Love your enemies," Jesus taught, and "pray for those who persecute you" (Matthew 5:44). Jesus never led a revolt. He went to the cross to absorb sin, and he prayed for God to forgive his killers. That's what's amazing about Christianity. It has a self-correcting ethic built into it that continually realigns us with God's ways when we are inevitably tempted toward power.

So, it cannot be denied that Christians have carried out violence and injustice throughout history, but saying these were conflicts fought *for* the Christian faith is dubious, because they certainly fall outside the intention of Christianity's founder. Anything that hurts or marginalizes people in the name of Christ is a rejection of everything Jesus himself was about.

THE WITCH HUNTS

In his bestselling book, *The Da Vinci Code*, Dan Brown claims that the church in Europe killed an astounding "five million women" during the witch trials, which spanned over four centuries. Carl Sagan makes a similar claim, saying, "No one knows how many [supposed witches, the church] killed altogether—perhaps hundreds of thousands, perhaps millions."[224] But that's a big *perhaps*. Sagan cites no sources here because he has no idea how many were killed. Most scholars today put the estimate at 40,000–60,000 people (20 percent of whom were men).[225] Granted, this is still a substantial number and a horrible mark on the church's record. But factually it is a far cry from Sagan's and Brown's bloated and exaggerated "millions."

The American version of the hunting and killing of witches by the church is popularly associated with the Salem (Mass.) witch trials. Here we find it similarly exaggerated by skeptics who claim there were *thousands* of women sentenced to death. But the reality, historians tell us, is that there were actually "fewer than twenty-five. Nineteen were sentenced to death, and a few others died in captivity."[226] In fact, if one adds up all the deaths during the Crusades, the Inquisition, and the witch trials across both Europe and the Americas we find that "Christians" killed between 200,000–250,000 people over the course of 500 years. Again, these are lives of real people, so it's a tragic number, but we should clarify that these are not the numbers that have worked their way into modern mythology. And we must recognize that many of these were killed in the context of warring armies between nations.

Does Religion Poison Everything?

In his book *God Is Not Great*, atheist Christopher Hitchens contends, as his subtitle says, "religion poisons everything." The violence and hatred in our world, he says, arise almost exclusively from religion, which "is not unlike racism," but "is an enormous multiplier of tribal suspicion and hatred."[227] His solution to this "poison" is atheism, which he claims will remove all the divisive reasons humankind kills and oppresses. This is an argument I hear quite often, but there are several problems with it that are well documented among historians and scholars.

First, *religious* worldviews are not the only systems of belief that result in violence, demonization, and destruction in the world. If we look at the past hundred years, the most violent and horrific regimes humankind has seen have been atheistic, not religious. Joseph Stalin's Russia, Mao's China, the Khmer Rouge in Cambodia, and of course Adolf Hitler's "final solution" in Europe were all driven by communist, Marxist, and *atheistic* philosophies that rejected organized religion and God as a central tenet of their system of belief. In other words, secular, nonreligious worldviews created the context for some of the most horrific violence the world has ever seen. As Alister McGrath points out, the twentieth century "gave rise to one of the greatest and most distressing paradoxes of human history, that the greatest intolerance and violence of that century were practiced by those who believed that religion causes intolerance and violence."[228] Such is the irony of the atheistic solution to violence and the "poison" that kills us.

But why would this happen? Just because a group of people decides they don't believe in God doesn't mean they will oppress others with their belief system. It's more complicated than that. When God is removed from a society, deity as organizing principle doesn't just disappear but gets *replaced* with other ideas that drive behavior, because humankind is relentlessly religious. Adam Smith made the market the driver of history. Freud replaced God with sex as the answer. Marx replaced God with the state. And Nazi Germany deified and mythologized race and the motherland to a quasi-divine state. And here is what these replacements of God did as *atheistic* regimes over the last one hundred years:

- Hitler killed 6 million Jews, gypsies, homosexuals, etc.
- The Khmer Rouge killed 2 million of their own people.
- Stalin killed 20 million through mass slayings and labor camps.
- Mao exterminated an estimated 50 to 70 million of his own people.

Altogether these *nonreligious* convictions killed one hundred million people in one hundred years. Contrast this with the so-called

Christian conflicts throughout history that, as noted previously, killed 200,000 people over the course of 500 years.[229] History has proven that adopting a philosophy wherein the answer to violence and oppression is *less* religion is a failure. In light of this, it is ironic that people will sometimes seek to lay modern atrocities committed by Christians on the table and claim that all Christians take responsibility for them. Daniel Dennett, for instance, says that all Christians must bear the responsibility for abortion clinic bombings.[230] By the same criteria, atheists, including Dennett, have to bear the responsibility for *all* the above atheistic atrocities. I think we would all agree this is not reasonable or fair.

What is fair, however, is to contrast the worldviews of Christianity and atheism to see which best avoids the injustices we all abhor. And on this count Christianity succeeds where atheism fails. A central and foundational tenet of secular atheism, informed by naturalistic Darwinism, is the idea that only the fittest of a species survives, resulting in the killing and exclusion of weaker groups. "Survival of the fittest," it is commonly called. But Christianity holds that *all* people are made in the image of God (Genesis 1:26–28). People have worth and value no matter how weak or strong, able or disabled, they happen to be. Christianity teaches that we are to "love [our] neighbor as [ourselves]" (Mark 12:31), care for the "orphans and widows" (James 1:27), and fight for the weakest and most vulnerable among us (Isaiah 1:17). In this way Christianity pushes back against nature, against what comes naturally. It pushes against hate, oppression, exclusion, and our enslavement to our passions.

Not only does it push against these, it gives us a paradigm for *fighting against* them. For instance, a majority of cultures throughout history have had slaves. It was Christianity that came along and called it out as wrong and said every human being is made in the image of God; that slavery, whether good for the market or not, should be abolished.

It was not a secular Darwinist who fought against slavery in the British Empire, but a Christian, William Wilberforce (1759–1833). Wilberforce worked tirelessly his entire adult life calling his fellow countrymen to stand against this evil, not by becoming *less* religious but *more*—to stand against the status quo and the tide of history in the spirit, not of Nietzsche, but of the Old Testament prophets and Jesus himself.

What about Christians who *literally* fight back, however? Those who have used torture and violence throughout history against enemies? What does one make of this? Some argue they are simply working under Jesus as the bringer of judgment in the present age, friends of the Rider on the white horse who spills the blood of his enemies (Revelation 19:11–21). This is to misunderstand the text and actually accomplish the opposite to what it means for us. As Miroslav Volf, writing from firsthand experience as a native Croatian living through the war in the former Yugoslavia, points out:

> Christians are not to take up their sword and gather under the banner of the Rider on the white horse, but to take up their crosses and follow the crucified Messiah. . . . The close association between human nonviolence and the affirmation of *God's* vengeance in the New Testament is telling. The suffering Messiah and the Rider on the white horse do indeed belong together . . . not as accomplices in spilling blood, but partners in promoting nonviolence. Without entrusting oneself to the God who judges justly, it will hardly be possible to refuse to retaliate when abused. The certainty of God's judgment at the end of history is the presupposition for the renunciation of violence in the middle of it.[231]

Volf is arguing that the only way to achieve a peaceful response in this world is to embrace the idea that we don't have to pay back evil for evil *because* there will be judgment on every act of evil under heaven by God himself, whether we ever see it in our lifetimes or not. "Never avenge yourselves, but leave it to the wrath of God," Paul says, "for it is written, 'Vengeance is mine, I will repay, says the Lord'" (Romans 12:19). Without the foundation Christianity provides, human beings don't have a good reason to return evil with good. Why not seek revenge? Why not destroy one's enemies? Survival of the fittest makes sense as a superior way of life—as the only way to live—if one abandons a Christian worldview.

Truth Claims and Power Grabs

The popular perception is that being a *dogmatic* person is dangerous. People who believe in absolute doctrines will inevitably want to lord those over others, resulting in control and oppression. The proposed solution is to abolish absolute truth claims altogether. This is what Michel Foucault, Friedrich Nietzsche, and many other thinkers have proposed. This movement has been especially popular in the West, where postmodern relativism is now assumed. Westerners are especially careful to avoid "imposing" their beliefs on others. We have made a way of life around the phrase "true for you but not for me." But such a view poses problems to a consistent way of living because the very idea that all truth claims should be abandoned is itself a truth claim! In his book *The Abolition of Man*, C. S. Lewis points out the contradiction of those who claim to abandon truth claims:

> [Y]ou cannot go on "explaining away" forever: you will find that you have explained your own explanation itself away. You cannot go on "seeing through" things forever. The whole point of seeing through something is to see something else through it. It is good that the window should be transparent, because the street or garden beyond it is opaque. How if you saw through the

garden too? . . . If you see through everything, then everything is transparent, but a wholly transparent world is an invisible world. To "see through" all things is the same as not to see.[232]

Sigmund Freud argued that all truth claims are a result of guilt and insecurity, and that any statement or belief about God therefore needs to be abandoned. But as many have pointed out, if Freud is right, then we must not listen to Freud either, since by his own definition, his truth—that God doesn't exist—must arise from Freud's *own* guilt and insecurity. Denying truth claims by saying that they are power grabs is itself the *ultimate* power grab. In trying to deconstruct power, saying nobody can tell you what to do, you are attempting to define reality by asserting what is true for all in an attempt to become the one in control.

Jesus challenges our modern beliefs about truth when he says, "I am the way, and the truth, and the life" (John 14:6). Christians believe that there is absolute truth, but with a twist. Truth, in its essence, is not an ideology, a principle, or a religion, but a *person*—Jesus. Can the concept of truth lead to oppression, as postmodernism fears? Of course. But so can the postmodern version of truth. Christianity is different because it is the truth of a person who came humbly to die for his enemies. It is truth that has inspired hearts with justice and fairness throughout human history, from the abolition of slavery to the promotion of third-world education and the building of hospitals among the poorest of the poor. I have personally witnessed the acts of Christians who love and provide for the poor and the widows in India, Mexico, Turkey, and San Francisco, and who save sex-trade workers enslaved in Vancouver. They do this because they are motivated by their *Christian* convictions, rooted in Christ as their example.

Christians live as those whose vision of reality is based on the beatitudes of Jesus (Matthew 5:1–11), an upside-down kingdom opposed to this world:

- Blessed are the *merciful*. Christians are people defined by mercy for others. Dietrich Bonhoeffer says, "As if their own needs and their own distress were not enough, they take upon themselves the distress and humiliation and sin of others."[233]
- Blessed are the *peacemakers*. Christians "not only *have* peace but *make* it . . . they renounce all violence and tumult. In the cause of Christ nothing is to be gained by such methods . . . choosing to endure suffering themselves rather than inflict it on others."[234]

These are the claims of Christianity. And while many have done evil while claiming the name of Christ, we have seen far more examples of Christians who put themselves in the path of contagious disease, who devote their time and energy and make great personal sacrifice to give to those whom Jesus called "the least of these" (Matthew 25:40). Why? Because the gospel is true, and it's worth that cost. This is a cost Dietrich Bonhoeffer (among countless others throughout history) didn't just write about but lived out, to the point of being killed while opposing the Nazis in the name of Christianity. Bonhoeffer recognized that rejection, not recognition, is most often the reward of a true disciple (Matthew 5:10–12).

Skeptics will still argue that people who believe in heaven only care about getting there and are content to let the world go to pot. But again, this is a false assumption, and the opposite seems true. If the only life I get is this one, why not live it up? If there is nothing after this life and what I do will not be remembered in the course of eons of time and space, why should I sacrifice my time and resources for others? I am not saying atheists are worse people than Christians, and in fact, some of those I know are among the nicest people I've ever met. I am simply saying their own worldview doesn't give a rational explanation for why they *should* care for others or sacrifice their own time and energy.

On the other hand, if I know that this life matters, not just for this life but for the quality of my life in eternity, my actions will reflect that belief. If that experience will be defined by how I live my life here on earth, as virtually every judgment passage in the New Testament makes clear, I will be far more likely to serve others and live for eternal values that reflect the nature and character of God, sacrificing myself for those ends. I will seek to love the stranger and find time for those who need mercy. Benjamin Fernando from Sri Lanka makes this point when he writes:

> There is no such thing as a separate individual gospel and a separate social gospel. . . . Social problems assume a greater importance in Christianity than in Buddhism or Hinduism [for instance]. The theory of Karma and rebirth gives a fairly reasonable explanation for social inequalities of this life which on the one hand are consequences of the previous life and on the other hand can be compensated for in the next life. But to a Christian there is only one earthly life and so social problems have to be dealt with now or never.[235]

Trivial Objections

Before concluding I want to make sure we are self-aware when making the claim against Christianity we have explored in this chapter. What is actually happening when a person refuses to believe in God based on the actions of another person or group throughout history? It's what scholars call a *trivial objection*—"focusing critical attention on a point less significant than the main point or basic thrust of an argument."[236] Basically, it's using inconsequential data as a roadblock. In this case, past Christian action is brought to bear on the question of whether Christianity is *true* or not. While I understand why skeptics do this, I think ultimately their effort is misguided.

Let's say next month a science journal exposes Albert Einstein as a kleptomaniac. Would that impact the *truth* of his work? Would anyone decide to throw out Einstein's mathematics because he was a thief? No. That would be a category mistake, a trivial objection. In the same way, evaluating whether Christianity, or any other idea/hypothesis, is *true* must be based on research and data, not whether particular adherents succeed or fail at living it out. The reality is, "If there is a God, you are, in a sense, alone with him. You cannot put him off with speculations about your next door neighbors or memories of what you've read in books."[237] In the end, when you are standing before God, the question will be, "What did you do about the offer of salvation in and through the finished work of Jesus?" The question will not be, "What did *other people* do with it?"

Conclusion

If you believe the church is filled with hypocrites, I agree with you. But that doesn't mean Christianity isn't true or that it doesn't work. On the contrary, it may actually mean that it *is* working. That it is exposing the very sin Jesus came to set us free from in the end, bringing it to the center of the lives of those gathered.

For instance, I spoke at a retreat for a private Christian high school a short time ago. Each time I spoke I was approached by a crowd of students afterward asking for prayer: "I don't believe any of this," one confessed. "I only go to this school because my parents ask me to and I want them to think I'm a Christian." "I smoke a lot of weed, and nobody knows about it." "I'm looking at a lot of porn, and I don't know what to do about it." And so on. In the face of such responses, we could call these students *hypocrites*. "How did they get into a good Christian school if they live these immoral lives?" we might ask. Or we can recognize that when the kingdom of God comes into a person's life, it causes an upheaval. Sin starts coming to the surface, and things in the church get messy. The gospel goes out and people feel the weight of it and their sin is exposed. God confronts people and shakes them, and they either run away from him or they push into him and, in so doing, start to live in the tension he brings. Remember, the church is comprised of people who have come to a place where they are trusting Jesus to save them not because they are perfect already but because they are not. History reflects this, and at times the church must simply admit it—that we have often failed.

Thanks be to God that our faith is not about us but about him.

None of this is an excuse for hypocrisy in the church or for times Christians have hated others or sought power at the expense of love. No one puts a higher moral demand on people than Jesus. To live as new creations in the world, fighting injustice and absorbing violence at every turn, was the vision Jesus laid down for his people. *True* Christianity does not drown witches or burn people at the stake. It does not tear down or destroy enemies; it gives them a glass of water and washes their feet. True Christianity, rather than being the enemy of humankind, is its only hope. The Bible calls us to judge the truth of Christianity by the life of its founder, Jesus Christ himself, not by the lives of those attempting to follow him, because in him and him alone will you find someone worthy of trust and imitation.

CHAPTER 9

The Problem of
EXCLUSIVITY

*Maybe ever'body in the whole damn world is
scared of each other.*

JOHN STEINBECK, *OF MICE AND MEN*

The central claim of Christianity is maybe its most controversial in modern times. It's the claim that Jesus Christ *alone* connects humankind back to God. That he is the exclusive means of salvation— the *only* way to heaven, peace, and ultimate joy in life, and that no other religion or worldview can provide these things.

Many find it extremely offensive to claim there is only *one way* to God. A recent article in Canada's *Maclean's* magazine entitled "How Canadian Are You?" claimed, for instance, that "more than 30% of Canadians were 'most uncomfortable' around evangelical Christians, a similar percentage as other top 'untouchables' like drug addicts and child abusers."[238] The reason? Primarily because Christians are viewed as *narrow-minded* bigots who believe that their way is the only right way when it comes to salvation. Similar to our examination of the concept of hell, we want to see if there is any truth behind this view of things, because, as we have already noted, it is not enough for us to write off an idea simply because it leaves a bad taste in our mouths.

The truth is that even many Christians wrestle with the notion of exclusivity. This is especially true when they travel or interact intimately with people of other cultures and are regularly exposed to the religions of the wider world. They ask themselves, "How could God say all these people are *wrong* and are going to an eternity without him just because they belong to a different religion?" As someone who has traveled around the world doing global missions, I wrestle with the exclusivity of Jesus every day. I wrestle with it as well as a pastor in Vancouver, a city that's filled with diverse cultures and religions at every turn and that leads the world in the three most significant global trends of the twenty-first century—Asianization, globalization, and urbanization. Canada itself is a cultural mosaic, not a melting pot, where traditions and cultural expressions are *retained* by immigrants rather than swallowed up by the host culture. So day in and day out, I see beautiful people of different faiths and convictions, yet must acknowledge that if Christianity is true, they are wrong about God and need to be saved from their sin by Jesus, and by him alone. This unsettles many people. It unsettled me when I first considered Christianity, but over time I came to see it is the most logically consistent and honest position of all—and it has shaped my life ever since.

The Heresy of Ricky Bobby

If you walk past people sitting in a Starbucks in most urban centers of the Western world, you'll see many of them reading books by thinkers such as Deepak Chopra, Eckhart Tolle, and Rhonda Byrne, all bestselling self-help, new age spirituality authors. The category happens to be the most popular section of any bookstore in North America. One tenet of this philosophy is something called "inclusivism"—the idea that no one has a lock on the truth, indeed, that all religions have some measure of the truth, merely being different paths to the same

"God," or whatever transcendent reality exists. So while atheism says that *all religions are false*, inclusivism says that *all religions are true*.

If you want to understand inclusivism, consider a scene from the comedy movie *Talladega Nights: The Ballad of Ricky Bobby*. If you haven't seen it, Ricky is a professional race car driver whose car crashes during a race. Thinking he's on fire, he runs around the track in his underwear crying out, "Help me, Jesus! Help me, Jewish God! Help me, Allah! Help me, Tom Cruise! Use your witchcraft on me to get the fire off of me! Help me, Oprah Winfrey!" In other words, when it comes to god, you'd best hedge your bets. One god doesn't necessarily exclude the other gods, so don't limit yourself to just one when you can believe in all of them at once! This concept has its roots in Hindu and eastern philosophy, and has largely been adopted in Western culture. It can be found in several popular versions:

> *I am absolutely against any religion that says one faith is Superior to another. I don't see how that is anything different than spiritual racism.*

> —RABBI SHMULEY BOTEACH

> *My position is that all great religions are fundamentally equal.*

> —MAHATMA GANDHI

> *One of the biggest mistakes humans make is to believe there's only one way. Actually, there are many diverse paths leading to God.*

> —OPRAH WINFREY

Inclusivism's basic premise is that all religions are true, or at least partially true, and have value. And in our culture it is considered narrow-minded and judgmental to believe anything else. So how do we respond to the theology of Ricky Bobby?

That Time I Had to Go Back to High School

The first thing Christianity would say in response is that the philosophy of inclusivism generally comes from a place of good intentions. We live in a pluralistic culture of people from diverse backgrounds, religions, and countries, and we want to live at peace with our neighbors, friends, and coworkers. This means that Christians need be in dialogue with people of different faiths, even partnering where opportunities arise, fighting for the right of others to practice their religion and to hold their own convictions and beliefs.

For instance, during my last year of college, the administrator informed me I had missed a high school credit required for graduation, and I would have to go back to high school if I wanted to get my degree. So, in disbelief, I signed up for summer school at a local high school. It was a memorable experience, to say the least. After writing a few essays and completing a few assignments, my teacher (who did not know my age or circumstances) thought I was a genius. Eventually, he called me to his desk and asked me what the deal was. The gig was up. I wasn't brilliant, just almost done with college! As the days and weeks went on, I noticed he was very anti-Christian in his teaching. He and I would spar over philosophy in front of the class. He would criticize Christianity. I would push back, trying to clear up misrepresentations. Back and forth it would go.

During that summer I spent time with various classmates, telling them about Jesus and teaching them how to improve their essay writing. I became friends with one of the Muslim girls, and we would talk about our faith and compare worldviews, challenging each other and even arguing about whose faith was more historically accurate. One day I showed up late for class, and as I was walking through the hall, this girl ran to me crying. I asked her what was wrong, and she shared: "The teacher made fun of my faith in front of the whole class. He said he knows more about the Qur'an than I do. I didn't know what to say!" I gave her a hug and told her I would speak to him. As she walked to the restroom, she called my name, and as I turned around, she wiped tears from her face and asked, "How do you do it? How do you take it and have the energy to always be defending yourself all the time?" It was a good question. And I can't remember my answer.

After class, I confronted the teacher for calling out a young Muslim girl's knowledge of the Qur'an in front of her peers. I said that it was a hurtful thing to do. While I had indicated *I* didn't mind public debate as a person of faith, I told him that it wasn't fair to criticize someone so unfairly who didn't welcome it. Thankfully, he agreed, and at the beginning of the next class he apologized to her in front of the whole class. She later thanked me for standing up for her, saying that I was the only one among the class who understood. The reality is that not only can we coexist with those with whom we disagree, but we can *defend* their right to believe what they believe and work with them toward similar goals in the world.

God has given common grace to people, and there are values and desires that we universally share, and we as Christians need to work with others to bring about those things in the world, what the Bible calls *shalom* (peace and justice). Philosopher John Stackhouse Jr. says that we fail at times to bring about peace and justice in the world because we do not see "that, at least for *this* issue and on *this* occasion, Muslims or Mormons or Marxists might share the same goals and support the same plan [as Christians]."[239] Stackhouse goes on to cite Jesus' parable of the talents, wherein the master gives his servants differing amounts of money and later returns to see how well they multiplied what they were given (Matthew 25:14–30). To those who doubled their money, the master said, "Well done, good and faithful servant. You have been faithful over a little" (vv. 21, 23). To the servant who did not multiply the money, he said, "You wicked and slothful servant!"

(v. 26). "The definition of faithfulness here is *results*," Stackhouse says. "It is effectiveness—and not just effort, either, as some would prefer to view the story."[240]

Christianity involves working toward certain goals, and at times, we should be working in secular settings to accomplish them. If we do these things in the service of Jesus, it is sacred work. But cooperation does not mean *agreement* in everything, and this is where Christians depart from some in our current cultural ethos. Soon after I became a Christian, I became really good friends with a Wiccan witch. You'd have been a bit surprised to see us together because she was always dressed in her black garb and dark makeup, and I was just a typical, white, skater-boy teenager. We would sit outside of our school and she would smoke dope and read her Wiccan books while I smoked half a pack of cigarettes and read her the Bible. We would argue about life and God and salvation, and she would say to me, "Hey, tonight I'm going to a fire down at the beach with my friends, and we're going to offer sacrifices to Satan and have an orgy. Wanna come?" Needless to say, I always turned down her offer.

I would talk to her about how God calls us to worship him, that there is no need for sacrifices any longer because Jesus made the final sacrifice, that Jesus now calls us to use our minds, hearts, and bodies to honor him. We talked about heaven. I would tell her that Jesus was the only way to God. She rejected Jesus and believed that she was going to a place called Summerland when she died. It was a bizarre friendship, but a good one. And here is the thing: we would *never* have concluded that we were both right about God. Yet we did not feel that our differences and disagreements necessitated ending our friendship. We held on to both of those things at the same time. And that is what people today have a difficult time accepting.

Our culture assumes if my beliefs are different or critical of something you do or believe then we cannot tolerate one another. We mistake cultural pluralism—acceptance and celebration of different cultures, peoples, races, and religions—with *metaphysical* pluralism, accepting *as true* all the ideas, convictions, and worldviews of those peoples and religions. Cultural pluralism is good and necessary, but metaphysical pluralism is a disaster. Why? Because all beliefs cannot be *true* without fundamentally changing what they are. And in the end, if you don't land in the watered-down muddle of acceptable beliefs, you are no longer welcome. While we can certainly exist within a cultural pluralism, metaphysical pluralism is a bridge to nowhere. It requires us to say, "Not only do I respect your right to hold your beliefs, but also I adopt them to be *true*."

While we can fight for people's rights to say what they believe, we do not have to conclude that what they believe is true. "Christian civility does not commit us to a *relativistic* perspective," and "civility doesn't require us to approve of what other people believe and do. It is one thing to insist that other people have the right to express their basic convictions. It is another thing to say that they are *right* in doing so."[241] The present day leap to metaphysical pluralism has proven devastating to the current state of religious and cultural discourse. It is rooted more in emotional sentiment than in reason or logic.

Christianity Is Not Alone

Christianity is not alone in being exclusive in its truth claims. Islam is exclusivist. It teaches that there is one God (Allah), and Muhammad is his prophet. In Islam, heaven is a paradise of sensual pleasure for some, and hell is for those who oppose Allah and reject the teachings of Muhammad. The only way to go to heaven is to convert to Islam, which includes believing the six main doctrines and practicing the five duties of Islam. The six doctrines involve specific, exclusive beliefs regarding God, angels, scripture, Muhammad, the end times, and predestination. The five duties involve a statement of belief, prayer five times a day, the giving of alms, fasting during Ramadan, and a pilgrimage to Mecca at least once in a lifetime if at all possible (called the *Hajj*).

Buddhism is another example of an exclusive religion, though many do not immediately see it that way. Buddhism began when Siddhārtha Gautama, who was born a Hindu (c. 560 BC), rebelled against Hinduism, going against many of its major tenets, including the authority of the Vedas (the Hindu sacred scriptures), the caste system, the idea of the human soul, and the entire Hindu sacrificial system. He believed all these to be unnecessary for people to experience nirvana.[242] Sikhism later rebelled against both Hinduism and Buddhism. And atheism, of course, rejects all of these beliefs and anybody who believes in God or anything beyond the material world altogether. It's impossible to find a worldview that *isn't* exclusive in some way. In fact, by trying to be inclusive, one actually becomes exclusivist. Take the "Western Nicety" religion many Westerners have adopted. This is the civic religion we live every day where everyone's views are true and right as long as we avoid conflict. The people who tend to be most vocal about this are the same people who are highly critical of the "narrow-minded judgmentalism" of Christianity. They're happy to argue that all worldviews should be accepted as true. And the reality is, that stance is exclusivist itself for two reasons: first, in trying to be inclusive, ironically, the view ends up excluding the exclusivist! And second, its premise is exclusivist in that it says "I have a particular/exclusive/true/right way of thinking about *all* religions, namely, that they're all true."[243]

Christianity, on the other hand, asserts that there is, in fact, truth. Jesus says, "I am the way, and *the truth*, and the life. No one comes to the Father except through me" (John 14:6, emphasis added). The apostle Peter preaches, "There is salvation in no one else, for there is no other name under heaven given among men by which we must be saved" (Acts 4:12). These confessions form the cornerstone of Christianity and are the driving force behind the mission of the church. Christians respond to the needs of the world with love and grace because they believe people need to hear about Jesus or they can't know God in this life or the next.

Inclusivism pushes back against the claims of Jesus and the apostles by arguing that there is no one truth. And in doing so, it cuts off the branch on which it sits, because saying "there is no absolute truth" is itself a truth statement! Thus it is a worldview built on a contradicting system of thought, and therefore needs to be abandoned.

... But If You Weren't Born in Canada

At this point, some people will tell me that the only reason I'm a Christian is because I happen to have been born in Canada (and not Saudi Arabia or India, for instance), implying that if I had been born elsewhere I likely wouldn't be a Christian, but maybe a Muslim or a Hindu. They believe I'm a product of ethnocentricity, a narrow-minded individual created by my own culture. But in its purest form this is simply a sociological observation (where one lives) and has nothing to do with an evaluation of the validity of one idea over another, or anything else in regard to the subject of religion. There is no reason to reject the truth of Christianity based on this observation alone.

In addition, we must say that *everyone's* worldviews are informed by where they were born and the culture in which they were raised. This doesn't mean that their ideas are less reasonable. The skeptic is raising a question that rises directly out of a worldview they adopted because they were born in the West! So, Alvin Plantinga says: "Suppose we concede that if I had been born of Muslim parents rather than Christian parents, my beliefs would have been quite different . . . the same goes for the pluralist [inclusivist]. If the pluralist had been born in Morocco, he probably wouldn't be a pluralist. Does it follow that his pluralist beliefs are produced in him by an unreliable process?"[244] Plantinga's point being that even though the pluralist's views are a direct product of where he was born, he would deny that his beliefs are unreliable because of these factors, and the same is true for the Christian. The debate needs to move beyond this observation to what is most true and logical.

Logical Impossibility

Another reason religious inclusivism must be rejected is because it proposes that *multiple religions are true* at the same time even though they contradict each other. The pluralist will say that this doesn't matter, because "your truth is your truth and mine is mine." But they should at least admit that they aren't being logical or reasonable in holding this opinion, but are instead building a worldview on what philosophers call the "principle of noncontradiction," which states that if something is true, its opposite cannot be true at the same time and in the same way. If my wife says I am wearing socks and my daughter says I am not, it is no use saying they're both right in order not to offend one of them. Either I am wearing socks or I am not. Similarly, the idea that religions are basically the same is informed by the idea that "all religions basically teach the same thing." This view, though popular, is naive and ill informed. Basic research will show that not only do most religions present very different teachings on God and salvation, but they actually contradict one another on multiple levels (e.g., what they say about heaven, hell, Jesus, sacred writings, etc.).

The problem is, we want to ignore these differences as a culture and pretend they don't exist. Timothy Keller tells the story of a time he was invited to be the Christian representative in a panel discussion with a Jewish rabbi and a Muslim imam in New York City. "We all agreed on the statement," he says, that "if Christians are right about Jesus being God, the Muslims and Jews fail in a serious way to love God as God really is, but if Muslims and Jews are right that Jesus is not God but rather a teacher or a prophet, then Christians fail in a serious way to love God as God really is."[245] The religious leaders recognized that they couldn't *all* be right. "Several of the students were quite disturbed by this," Keller says, because "to insist that one faith has a better grasp on truth than others was [seen as] intolerant."[246] And herein lies the great irony of the modern position. While it's born out of a desire to *not* be judgmental or offensive, it may be the most offensive view of all because it says that every exclusivist worldview is wrong and, in doing so, excludes all the exclusivists!

Furthermore, to deepen the offense, this "tolerant" position implies to Muslims and Jews that they will both be in heaven together; they are just taking different routes there. It tells Palestinians and Israelis, died-in-the-wool enemies of each other, that they'll worship together in a great final cosmic embrace. Keep in mind that in many cases these are people whose loved ones have fought and died, and continue to fight and die, for ideas that they believe are true in an absolute sense (regarding holy land, sacred practices, beliefs about God, etc.).

Doesn't it seem both condescending and judgmental to tell adherents of these religions that the blood that's been spilled is really all worthless because "everybody's views are right, and everybody is going to the same place"?

It seems to me that it's more rational and respectful to say *one religion is true* than to say *all* religions are true. To face the hard reality that if Muslims are right, Christians are going to hell. We worship the wrong God. And if we're wrong, we're wrong. There's no point in comforting ourselves by thinking that Allah will accept us anyway, because he won't. The nature of truth claims is that if something is true, its opposite has to be false.

All Ideas Are Not Equal

To take this one step further, however, we can say that some world-views are simply *better* or more coherent than others when judged by the standard assessments of history, science, reason, and experience. All views are not *equally* acceptable or convincing. Think about some of the arguments we have already explored. Christianity answers the question of *origins* in a comprehensive and holistic way, for instance, while Buddhism and atheism do not do as well. When it comes to *morality*, again, the Judeo-Christian explanation that God gave us a moral law because we are made in his image makes logical sense of our reason and desire, more so than the evolutionary story that we come to moral conclusions that are only *helpful* in a given moment for survival and reproduction but are not necessarily *true*.

Or reconsider the question of evil and suffering. Many in our modern world find pantheism appealing as a worldview—the idea that there is divinity in everything. Proponents put forth the notion that God is everything and everything is God. A culture that loves to celebrate itself of course applauds this. Yet this worldview crumbles under the weight of evil and suffering: "You really have to try hard to believe that there's divinity in *everything*, including wasps, mosquitoes, cancer cells, tsunamis, and hurricanes," N. T. Wright points out. "It can't cope with evil when everything (including yourself) shares in, or lives within, divinity; there's no higher court of appeal when something bad happens. Nobody can come and rescue you."[247]

In contrast, Christianity makes coherent sense of evil and suffering and offers a hopeful response and resource in the midst of it. It presents us with *a suffering God* who enters into our pain to rescue us. When we consider views of God in other religions, suffering has to be excluded from the divine nature because the two are seen as contradictory. The God of deism is aloof and distant. Hinduism and

Buddhism reject evil as an illusion. Greek thought says that the divine substance is incapable of suffering. But Christianity says the opposite. Throughout Israel's history God identifies with their pain and suffering and comes down to deliver them (Exodus 3:7–8). The Bible speaks constantly of God's *self-humiliation* and identification with his people's pain. This entire idea is then brought to its fullest expression in Jesus—the Son of God becoming a human being—who feels and hungers and cries and dies, and who takes evil on himself in order to end death forever.

In other words, some ideas are just *better* than others. And it's important for the sake of debate that we admit this as we explore worldviews. Countless times I've heard people say "all religions are equally valid." But many espousing this view have in mind modern Western or sentimentalized versions of religion. They forget that the ancient Ammonites worshiped a god named Moloch who demanded children be burned alive while drums were beaten to drown out their screams. Is that a valid religion? Years ago a man named Jim Jones led a group of people to believe very strange things about the world, God, and himself, eventually convincing more than nine hundred followers of his deranged ideas to kill themselves. How do we feel about *his* doctrine? Many people will admit they don't like *those* religions. But the question is, why not? Which religions are deemed acceptable to a postmodern, tolerant mind? And for what reasons, if all are equally valid? Or is it that we just accept the *popular* or mainstream religions of the world? Or the domesticated ones, or the middle-class ones?

The better route forward is to weigh facts and ideas against one another in order to find the view of life that is consistently true, makes sense of the world, and produces measurable improvement in the lives of those who believe and practice it, as well as those of society as a whole.

Four Blind Men and an Elephant

Instead of that, though, popular thinkers continue to propagate an inclusive, pluralist view of God and truth by proposing that different religions are simply different paths to the same place. To support this idea, people use the story of Four Blind Men and an Elephant. Lesslie Newbigin, a missionary in India for thirty years, said that he would often get this rebuttal when presenting the gospel. The story is that four blind men were walking along the road and came upon an elephant. One man grabbed the elephant's tail, another grabbed his leg, another his ear, and one his trunk. The one who held the tail said, "We have stumbled upon a snake!" The one who grabbed the leg said, "No, it's too thick and solid to be a snake; it's a tree!" The one who held the ear said, "What are you guys thinking? It's thin and dry: it's a piece of paper!" And the one who held the trunk said, "No, it's a hose."

The assertion of the story, of course, is that the different religions of the world are like these men, each having a small glimpse of total truth but not a comprehensive understanding of reality. We do our best to interpret data, but in the end, we are all talking about the same thing. This presents a powerful picture of the normative conviction of many people in the post-Christian Western world. But as Newbigin points out, the story backfires because it is being told from the vantage point of *someone who can actually see*, someone who is not blind, someone who *does* have a comprehensive vision and understanding of reality, which the story claims nobody has. So Newbigin says:

> The story is constantly told in order to neutralize the affirmation of the great religions, to suggest that they learn humility and recognize that none of them can have more than one aspect of the truth. But, of course, the real point of the story is the exact opposite. . . . The story is told by someone who can see and is the immensely arrogant claim of one who sees the full truth all the

world's religions are only groping after. It embodies the claim to
know the full reality [which it claims that religions can't].[248]

To put it another way, by saying there's no such thing as a comprehensive vision of truth, a person is claiming to *have* a comprehensive
understanding of truth—all the while not allowing anyone else to have
it. And this implies that there really *is* a comprehensive vision of truth
somewhere. The question behind the story, then, is not *if* truth exists,
but *what is it?*

Did you know that there's a Flat Earth Society in America? Who
among us would say that their perception of the earth is just as valid
and acceptable as the other views of the earth? We may fight for their
right to believe this, but we won't mistake that with a confirmation
of its truth-value. If someone says something absurd, we challenge it.
We mine for truth, even if it threatens civility. Settling for untruths in
the name of getting along is negligent in every other sphere of life. No
one on a search for the cure for AIDS or the beginning of the universe
or the nature of certain chemical compounds would be freed up to
embrace contradiction in the name of fellowship. So neither should
this be the case when it comes to the most important questions of
our lives, those of God and salvation. Unfortunately, these very truth
questions are the ones we tend to sacrifice in order to get along with
one another as a society. We sacrifice answers to eternally significant
questions in the pursuit of a less strained social order, and we do so
without questioning: Is this a good trade-off in the long run? I have
come to be convinced that it is not.

Because It's Comforting?

Some skeptics see Christianity as a *crutch*, something weak-minded
people lean on and believe in. Growing up, I assumed this about

religious people. I thought to myself, *Religious people must use God to find comfort during difficult times. But that doesn't make him real.* But now having been a Christian for a number of years I must say, looking back, I did not come to believe in Christianity because it was comforting. That said, I do believe that Christianity is the most comforting, hopeful, and beautiful worldview among the marketplace of ideas on offer to us in the great debate of life. But that's not the reason I believe it. No, I believe historical, philosophical, and scientific conclusions confirm the legitimacy of Christian faith.

Beyond not believing that people are Christians because it's comforting, I in fact believe that Christianity is *not* all that comforting at times, because it is a belief with consequences. Was Christianity comforting to the hundred million Christians who have been killed for their faith over the past two thousand years or so? Was it *a crutch* for them? Was it the *easier* way? I think the opposite is true. Today, holding to a pluralist, relativist, postmodern worldview costs you nothing. You fit right in with the rest. It's easy, comforting, and allows you to put off asking the really hard questions of life.

Every day Christians have to defend what they believe. They have to defend the Bible, the resurrection, and questions about suffering. Is this the *easier* of the options? Ask a Christian kid in high school or university how comforting, easy, and crutch-like Christianity is.

Having said this, we must understand that nothing in Christianity is about truth *for truth's sake.* Truth has power, and as Jesus himself said: "The truth will set you free" (John 8:32). I believe in Christianity not just because it's true but because it *works.* It sets people free. It liberates us from the pains and restrictions of the broken world around us. It gives us hope in the midst of despair and a transcendent perspective in the direst of circumstances.

I've spent years looking out at people in my own church as they sing worship songs to God, take notes during my sermons, cry in joy or repentance, and laugh as they greet people at the door of the auditorium. And then I look into their sunken eyes, hold their bony hands, and watch as their bodies waste away on a hospital bed. All while they smile and say, "I'm not scared, Mark. Jesus really rose, and I know where I'm going." In those moments I realize that Christianity brings great comfort, but this comfort doesn't negate its truth. It is not the *reason* to believe—it is the *fruit* of believing. Jesus' point is that truth sets us free (from fear or insecurity or death itself) *because* it's true. This means that if we abandon the search for the latter (truth), as many in our culture have done, we will never really experience the beauty of the former (freedom). And that would be the greatest tragedy of all.

CHAPTER 10

The Problem of
JESUS

There was just such a man when I was young—an Austrian who invented a new way of life and . . . tried to impose his reformation by the sword, and plunged the civilized world into misery and chaos. But the thing which this fellow had overlooked, my friend, was that he had a predecessor in the reformation business, called Jesus Christ. Perhaps we may assume that Jesus knew as much as the Austrian did about saving people. But the odd thing is that Jesus did not turn the disciples into storm troopers, burn down the Temple at Jerusalem, and fix the blame on Pontius Pilate. On the contrary, he made it clear that the business of the philosopher was to make ideas available, and not to impose them on people.

T. H. WHITE, *THE ONCE AND FUTURE KING*

Years ago, broadcaster Larry King was asked if he could interview one person in all of history, who it would be. Without hesitating he said, "Jesus Christ." The follow-up was this: "If you could only ask him one question, what would it be, and why?" Again King did not hesitate. "I would ask him if he was really born of a virgin, because the answer to that question changes *everything*." In other words, everything hinges on what you believe about Jesus Christ.

The question of Jesus' virgin birth is one of many aspects of his person, work, and message that are considered essential Christian doctrines. The question of his being God is another, and the two are directly connected. If Jesus was not conceived by a human father but by the power of the Holy Spirit, it confirms his claim to be the Son of God. Larry King asks the question because he understands: If Jesus is God, I need to reorient my whole life around him and his claim. And the same is true for you and me. The answer to the question, "Who is Jesus?" changes the way we live our lives, the way we raise our kids, even what we do when we go to the grocery store. Everything changes if Jesus is God, the maker and creator of the universe.

The Book of Mormon, Kinda

Several years ago, some Mormon missionaries stopped by my house. I invited them inside, and we talked for hours about God, the Bible, and Jesus. They explained to me what they believed about Jesus, and I explained what the Bible said about him. They didn't seem too bothered. In fact, they told me: "Yeah, we are saying the same thing. We are in the same ballpark." I was surprised. I said to them, "Guys, I'm saying the one true God of the universe—Creator, Redeemer, God Almighty—became a human being in the person of Jesus of Nazareth, lived a sinless life, never married, went to the cross to die for our sins and was resurrected three days later victorious over Satan, sin, and death in order to save people not by what *they* do, but by what he has done *for* them. You are saying that Jesus was a demigod, a polygamist, and the half-brother of Lucifer. Not only are we not in the same ballpark, we aren't even playing the same sport." They promised they would bring back one of the higher level "elders" in the coming weeks to discuss these discrepancies, but I never heard back from them.

The identity of Jesus is the central question of our lives. It is the question around which all others orbit. If Jesus is God, and he taught his followers that he is God, and it can be demonstrated that he is God in some way, we should follow him and give our lives to him. "But," one might say, "I haven't been convinced that he did claim this or that he demonstrated it, so until then, I don't have to do anything." I meet many people who think this way. They like Jesus and respect him as a teacher or a leader or a revolutionary, but they don't worship him or follow him because they aren't convinced he really is God. Fair enough. So let's start there—with some foundational questions about Jesus—and then determine the implications for how we are to live. Did Jesus really claim to be God? If so, what did he ask people to do with that claim? And where does this claim fit as it relates to other religions?

Did Jesus Claim to Be God?

You will sometimes hear people say, "Jesus never claimed to be God." And what they mean is that Jesus never said the words, "I am God." Which technically is true; we do not have a written record of Jesus putting those three exact words together in that precise sequential order. But that is a far cry from saying he never claimed to be God, because he had many other ways to do it, and he made the most of those ways every chance he had. In other words, in every way that *mattered*, in speaking to his own culture and, as we will see, to our own as well, Jesus claimed clearly and directly to be God, utilizing the stories, questions, symbols, and activities that were recognized in the world in which he lived and taught.[249] That's what often gets missed. We need to first see Jesus in *his* historical-cultural context to understand what he is claiming about himself. If we don't, we will likely misunderstand, twist, or relativize what he was saying.

For example, consider the above desire for Jesus to say "I am God" in those three words, and now consider the context of Eastern

Eastern

religions of his time. In these religious worldviews, Jesus' claim to be God in that way would not seem all that scandalous. Why? Because they believed that *all* human beings are, to some degree, divine. As C. S. Lewis points out, "Among Pantheists like [Eastern] Indians anyone might say that he was a part of God, or one with God: there would be nothing very odd about it."[250] This is why Jesus goes further than claiming to be "god" in this generic, Eastern sense in his life and ministry. He speaks as a devout Jewish man in a culturally Jewish context to monotheistic Jews and identifies himself not as *a* god, as part of God, or even "God" as commonly understood by many in the modern Western world, but claims to be *Israel's* God—the Creator, the God of the entire cosmos, the *one and only* God of the whole world. He is the God who called Abraham and Moses, the One who made all things, who is sovereign, who alone forgives sin and deserves our worship. Jesus gets more specific than saying "I am God" in a generic sense. He identifies the precise God he claims to be, and once we understand this, the scandal starts to unfold.

Claiming to be Israel's God in first-century Judaism guaranteed that you would be killed. The Jews were *monotheists* (those who believe there is only one God), a clear contrast to every other religious system of that time. Every other religion had a pantheon of diverse gods they worshiped in different ways for different reasons, but Judaism never wavered from its affirmation that there is one God and only one God—YHWH. And to claim to be him was to blaspheme, the consequence of which was death.

The scandal is not someone claiming to be God—that was pretty normal—but as Lewis notes, "*among these Jews* there . . . turns up a man who goes about talking as if He was God. And when you have grasped that, you will see that what this man said was, quite simply, the most shocking thing that has ever been uttered by human lips."[251] In other words, you can claim to be God in a polytheistic framework (many gods) or a pantheistic framework (everything is god); it's not all that outrageous because you would just be one example of divinity among others.[252] But Jesus claimed there is only one God in the whole universe (note his prayer to the Father: "This is eternal life, that they know you, the only true God, and Jesus Christ whom you have sent," in John 17:3), and that he was it. Such a claim, made within the Jewish worldview, was absurd. The Old Testament made it clear that "God is not man" (Numbers 23:19). Such a claim was reason enough for the Jewish elders to request capital punishment under the charge of blasphemy when they brought Jesus to trial (Leviticus 24:10–23; Numbers 15:30–31). Jesus claimed that he would come on the clouds one day, bringing judgment on the world, and the response of the religious leaders reveals they understood exactly what he was saying: "What further witnesses do we need? You have heard his blasphemy" (Mark 14:61–64; Matthew 26:65–66). Blasphemy means "the act of claiming for oneself the attributes and rights of God."[253] So why did the Jews come to see Jesus' life and teachings as *blasphemous*? The Gospels make the case that they did so because Jesus himself made it clear that he was God in both "deed and word" (Luke 24:19).

Jesus and World Religions

Most people are at least willing to admit that Jesus existed, that he was a good teacher, and that he *did amazing things*. What many call "miracles" or "mighty deeds." Historian N. T. Wright points out that "Jesus' contemporaries, both those who became his followers and those who were determined not to become his followers, certainly regarded him as possessed of remarkable powers. The church did not invent the charge that Jesus was in league with Beelzebub; but charges like that are not advanced unless they are needed as an explanation for some quite remarkable phenomena."[254] All of this—teacher, miracle worker—is pretty standard fare that people accept for the most part, but when it comes to the idea that Jesus is God, many hesitate. This is why theologian J. I. Packer says, "The real difficulty, the supreme mystery with which the gospel confronts us, lies not in the Good Friday message of atonement, nor in the Easter message of resurrection, but in the Christmas message of incarnation. . . . This is the real stumbling-block of Christianity."[255] There are typically two reasons for this stumbling: either people already have an idea of who God is and can't fit Jesus into that, or they already have an idea of who Jesus is and can't fit God into that. When we study the life and teachings of Jesus, we see that he challenges both of these stumbling blocks and redefines both his own identity and the identity of God himself.

Before we explore Jesus' claim to be God, it is helpful to understand what other worldviews and religions believe and claim about him. In other words, who is Jesus among other gods?

- Buddhism teaches that Jesus was not God but an enlightened man like Buddha.
- Hinduism teaches that Jesus is *an* incarnation of god, like Krishna.
- Islam teaches that Jesus was a man and a prophet but was inferior to Muhammad.
- Jehovah's Witnesses say that Jesus was merely the archangel Michael, a created being that became a man.
- Mormonism teaches that Jesus was only a man who became one of many gods, and that he was a polygamist and a half-brother of Lucifer.
- New Age guru Deepak Chopra says Jesus is a state of consciousness we can all aspire to.
- Scientology (the religion of Tom Cruise, John Travolta, and others) teaches that Jesus was an implant forced on Thetan about a million years ago.[256]

None of these portraits of Jesus have any basis in history or fact. They are attempts to fit Jesus into an existing belief system or religious view that rejects him as the central character in redemptive history but still recognizes his historical existence and impact.

Recently, I went on a walk with a friend who is a new believer in Jesus and starting to explore the details of Christianity more deeply. He had a lot of questions about what other religions and cults taught about heaven, hell, salvation, and God, and was struggling to figure out how to defend Christianity against these other ideologies. After listening to him for a while, I said to him, "If you want to get to the root of the issue, there is one question you can come back to every time: *Is Jesus Christ God?*" In other words, ask the representatives of these other religions or cults to *explain who Jesus is* and this will help you understand the differences, the main one being the issue of his deity. Jesus is where Christianity parts ways with the rest of the world, because it says that he is and always has been God himself and should be followed and worshiped as such.

Jesus Claims to Be God

Come back to the popular critique that Jesus never claimed to be God. Here is why Christianity holds so firmly to the idea that he most certainly did. Jesus said things that those in his culture interpreted as clear claims to divinity. For instance, in a heated debate with his fellow Jews recorded in John 8, where they ask Jesus, "Who do you think you are?" Jesus' response is culturally and religiously scandalous at the highest level:

> "Your father Abraham rejoiced that he would see my day. He
> saw it and was glad." So the Jews said to him, "You are not yet
> fifty years old, and have you seen Abraham?" Jesus said to them,

"Truly, truly, I say to you, before Abraham was, I am." So they picked up stones to throw at him, but Jesus hid himself and went out of the temple."

(JOHN 8:56–59, EMPHASIS ADDED)

First, Jesus affirms what theologians call the doctrine of *pre-existence*: that he existed as God *before* he was born in Bethlehem, and even "before Abraham" himself (v. 58). Abraham had lived over two thousand years before Jesus of Nazareth was born, and yet Jesus claims to have existed *before* him. Note that he is not saying that he was previously a human being who lived before Abraham (a form of reincarnation); he is affirming the fact that he had a prior existence to becoming human. This is what the apostle John alludes to when he says, "Every spirit that confesses that Jesus Christ *has come* in the flesh is from God" (1 John 4:2, emphasis added). John's emphasis is not simply that Jesus was born, but that he already existed and has now "come" into the world. Later in John's Gospel Jesus refers to his preexistence while praying: "Father, glorify me in your own presence with the glory that I had with you before the world existed" (John 17:5). Here he speaks of his existence prior to the creation of the world.

Jesus repeatedly speaks of himself as *coming from and originating in heaven* several times throughout his ministry: "No one has ascended into heaven except he who descended from heaven, the Son of Man," he says (John 3:13). "For I have come down from heaven. . . . I am the bread that came down from heaven" (John 6:38, 41). In John's Gospel alone, Jesus says that he has been sent from heaven to earth no less than thirty-nine times, and he is unique among the founders of world religions in making this claim. Muhammad did not claim to come from heaven, neither did Buddha nor Krishna.

Secondly, notice that Jesus claims to be Israel's God specifically. His use of the phrase "I am" in John 8:58, while a veiled reference to modern readers unfamiliar with Hebrew, was quite clear to his audience. "I am" is not Jesus using bad grammar. He could have said, "Before Abraham was, I *was*" and emphasized his preexistence, but instead he says, "I am." This is a *name for God that Jesus is applying to himself.* Which is a really big deal.

At the beginning of the book of Exodus, God appears to Moses in a burning bush, commanding him to tell Pharaoh to set the Israelites free. Moses says to God: "If I come to the people of Israel and say to them, 'The God of your fathers has sent me to you,' and they ask me, 'What is his name?' what shall I say to them?" God said to Moses, tell them "I AM WHO I AM" sent you. "Say this to the people of Israel, he continues. "I AM has sent me to you" (Exodus 3:13–14). "I am" was one of the most sacred names for God in the Old Testament, used thousands of times in the Hebrew Scriptures to refer to the one and only God of the universe—and now Jesus scandalously takes that name and applies it to himself. In essence, he tells the people, "I am the God who appeared to Moses at the burning bush, who met him on the mountain, whose presence filled the temple. I am the God who called Abraham and entered into covenant with him."

Some modern scholars have suggested that this interpretation is reading too much into the claim. They wonder whether Jesus' original hearers would have deduced all of this from one phrase. And it's a legitimate question. But you do not need to go very far to find the answer. The story tells us exactly how the people responded: "They picked up stones to throw at him," the Gospel writer says (John 8:59). In that culture, throwing rocks at people was not something you did to bully them but to kill them, in this case because he was claiming to be God.

As recorded three chapters prior to this incident, and again two chapters later, the people do the same thing for the same reason. Jesus healed a man on the Sabbath and a debate arose whether this act was considered "working" on the Sabbath and should be punished as such. Jesus enters the debate and says, "My Father is working until now, and I am working" (John 5:17). Modern readers may read that and not see the underlying meaning, but the Jewish response makes it clear what Jesus meant: "This was why the Jews were seeking all the more to kill him, because not only was he breaking the Sabbath, but he was even calling God his own Father, *making himself equal with God*" (v. 18, emphasis added). In case we miss the point, John wants us to know that they rightly understood his meaning.

> Not from the mere words "My Father," but from His claim of right to act as His Father did in the like high sphere. It is beyond all doubt that we have here an assumption . . . of participation in the Father's essential nature.[257]

Later, in John 10, as Jesus is walking in the temple on one of the Jewish holidays, he says, "My Father . . .is greater than all. . . . I and the Father are one" (vv. 29–30). What Jesus means by this last phrase is not that he and the Father are the same *person*.[258] Jesus uses the plural form "are" ("I and the Father *are*") but follows it up with the singular word "one" or "one thing." This means that they are *one in essence* and *nature*, but they are not the same (identical) person.[259] We may miss the deeper meaning here, but again the Jewish response leaves no doubt as to what he intended: they pick up stones to stone him and say, "It is not for a good work that we are going to stone you but for blasphemy, because *you, being a man, make yourself God*" (vv. 31–33, emphasis added).

There are yet other examples in the Gospels of people accusing Jesus of claiming to be God. When Jesus is given the opportunity to recant, apologize, or correct them, he simply does not (Matthew 26:63–65; John 5:17–23; 8:58–59; 19:7–10). In addition, there are many things Jesus *teaches* that also imply that he is God, things we don't always pick up on as modern readers:

- Jesus teaches people to *pray to him* (John 14:13–14; 15:16; 16:24), and subsequently we see others, including Stephen (Acts 7:59–60), Paul (1 Corinthians 1:2; 2 Corinthians 12:7–9; Ephesians 5:19–21), and John (Revelation 22:20) teaching the same thing.
- Jesus *accepts worship*, something reserved for God alone (John 20:28–29).
- Jesus *claims a number of titles* that are used in the Old Testament for YHWH: the shepherd of Israel (John 10:14; see Isaiah 40:11), I AM (John 8:58), the Alpha and Omega (Revelation 1:8; 22:13), and the Almighty (Revelation 1:8), among others.

That Which Only God Can Do

Jesus claims to be God through what he says, as seen above, but he also demonstrates that he is God by what he *does*—through his actions. Miracles are the obvious examples of this. Jesus does what only God can do: turning water into wine, walking on water, healing the sick, raising the dead. Jesus has complete sovereign control over the natural world as only God does. But there are a number of other things Jesus does that also demonstrate to the world that he is God, all of which revolve around him *replacing* and *redrawing* the *incarnational* symbols of Judaism around himself. *Incarnation* simply means "into meat" or "in the flesh." So when people talk of God, who is immaterial spirit, becoming human and taking on flesh and blood, it is called "incarnation."

In Judaism, God is not a created being, but there were symbols in first-century Judaism that pointed to God's *incarnational presence in the world*, namely, (1) the temple, (2) the Torah (the law of the Hebrew Bible), and (3) the understanding that God had promised to return to

Jerusalem one day.[260] Jesus claims to be the fulfillment of each and every one of these three formative symbols within Jewish life, and that he is bringing the final and climactic fulfillment of all that these symbols meant and were ever meant to mean.

THE TEMPLE

The temple in Jerusalem had two major purposes: (1) it was where *God's presence resided*, and (2) it was where people's *sins were forgiven* through the sacrifices they made there. Jesus claims to be the fulfillment of both purposes in his ministry, repeatedly acting as if the temple is no longer necessary because of his presence. Which is why near the end of his ministry, Jesus enters the temple and overturns the money changers' tables, declaring judgment on the institution itself and its role in Israel's religious life (Mark 11:15–19). It is an enacted parable of the temple's destruction and a confrontation, of sorts, between it and its maker. Jesus is saying the world isn't big enough for the two of them (and what they represented) any longer. The time had come for God to judge the temple and set it aside for good. It had done its job, and now God has come to accomplish what the temple always pointed to accomplishing.

TORAH

The second incarnational symbol Jesus fulfills and replaces is the Torah, the Old Testament Law. Jewish scholar Jacob Neusner has demonstrated that the way in which Jesus upstages the Torah in his teachings, most notably in the Sermon on the Mount (Matthew 5–7), indicates that he regards himself as authoritative over it. Jesus issues a new Torah, and he does it not as a replacement for Moses or as a new Moses, but in *taking the role of YHWH himself*.[261] Neusner says:

> Here is a Torah-teacher who says in his own name what the Torah says in God's name. Sages say things in their own names,

but without claiming to improve upon the Torah. The prophet Moses speaks not in his own name but in God's name, saying what God has told him to say. Jesus speaks not as a sage nor as a prophet . . . so we find ourselves . . . with the difficulty of making sense, within the framework of the Torah, of a teacher who stands apart from, perhaps above, the Torah. . . . We now recognize that at issue is the figure of Jesus, not the teachings at all.[262]

Jesus is not setting the Torah aside; he is saying that he is the end or fulfillment of the Torah—the reason it existed. With his arrival in human history, Jesus inaugurated the new age toward which the Torah had pointed but for which it was not adequate. Salvation was not possible through obedience to the Torah any longer, but is available to all people by responding to Jesus' summons to "Follow me" and trust in him (Matthew 4:19; 8:22; 9:9). Loyalty to God and his law, astonishingly, now takes the form of loyalty to Jesus.

GOD'S RETURN TO ZION

The final incarnational concept that Jesus reinterprets as fulfilled in himself is the expectation of God's long-awaited return to Zion (Jerusalem). The Jewish people had a long-held expectation that God would one day return to Zion (Jerusalem), bringing both judgment and salvation to Israel and the whole world. The book of Isaiah contains many such passages, for example:

> The LORD Almighty will reign on Mount Zion and in Jerusalem, and before its elders—with great glory. . . . "[H]e will come with vengeance . . . he will come to save you." Then will the eyes of the blind be opened and the ears of the deaf unstopped. Then will the lame leap like a deer, and the mute tongue shout for joy.
>
> (ISAIAH 24:23; 35:4–6 NIV)

As we read the Gospels, we see Jesus teaching that the coming of YHWH to Zion is now happening with him—but in a way no one expected. Jesus tells his followers a story (Matthew 25:14–30) about a nobleman (God) who gives his servants (Israel) a task and then goes away for a time. The nobleman eventually returns and asks the servants for an accounting. He tells this story not as some kind of "end times," "second coming" parable of the fact that one day Jesus will come back and ask the church what they did with their stuff, but about his *first coming*—that he as the "nobleman" has come to see how his servants have done. His journey to Jerusalem being the embodiment of God's return to Zion to succeed where his people have failed. The "nobleman" has returned and how a person responds to his return defines whether one is blessed or judged. Everything about his entry into Jerusalem the week prior to his death is about "a new encoding, in an acted narrative, of the widespread and well-known biblical prophecies" of God's return.[263]

Philippians 2:5–11 and the Early Christians

For these reasons, the earliest Christians came to believe that Jesus was God, and amazingly, they did so *without* ever abandoning their base of Jewish monotheism. They spoke about Jesus using "precisely those categories which Jews over the previous centuries had developed for speaking of the presence and action of the one true God in the world: Presence (as in the Temple), Torah, Word, Wisdom. The early Christians had no intention of departing from Jewish-style monotheism. They would have insisted that they were searching out its true meaning."[264] They had found that meaning in Jesus. The early Christians remained monotheistic but put Jesus in the place of Israel's God. "In the beginning was the Word," the apostle John writes in his gospel, referring to Jesus, "and the Word was with God, and the Word was God . . . and the Word became flesh and dwelt among us" (John 1:1, 14).

Paul, likely writing the earliest Christian letters and theology, would often take a key monotheistic text of the Old Testament and apply it directly to Jesus. For instance, God announces that he alone, unlike the pagan gods of the nations, is the one and only true God of the universe and "To me every knee shall bow, every tongue shall swear allegiance" (Isaiah 45:23). But Paul, writing his letter to the Philippian church, explains the nature of Jesus by redrawing this monotheistic text around him: "Your attitude should be the same as that of Christ Jesus: who, *being in very nature God*, did not consider *equality with God* something to be grasped, but made himself nothing . . . at *the name of Jesus every knee should bow*, in heaven and on earth and under the earth, and *every tongue confess that Jesus Christ is Lord*, to the glory of God the Father" (Philippians 2:5–11 NIV 1984, emphasis added)

Paul aligns Jesus with the Jewish Scripture's concept of God. He says that every knee and every tongue will confess that *Jesus* is Lord. This God who, all through history, has never shared glory and identity with anyone, is sharing it unabashedly with Jesus. Paul says that Jesus is "in very nature God" (Philippians 2:6 NIV 1984), and that in him "all the fullness of the Deity lives in bodily form" (Colossians 2:9 NIV).

In this way Philippians 2:6 is the strongest possible statement about the deity and divinity of Jesus. It is much stronger than if Paul came right out and said "Jesus is God" because, as we have already discovered, to say that could have meant a lot of things. New Age religion teaches that we are all gods or a part of God. But, of course, that's not what Paul means by the word *God*. As we have said, he's a first-century Jew who uses the word to mean the one and only true God of the whole world. He says that Jesus is the *morphe* of the one and only God of the universe; that he has the unique qualities that God possesses. He is the very substance and very being of God. And if that wasn't enough to square it away for his hearers, Paul explains further: Jesus "did not consider *equality with God* something to be grasped" (v. 6 NIV 1984). The word *grasp* here means "to be kept, or held on to." In other words, Jesus is the same in substance and being as the Father. He is *equal* with God, but Jesus doesn't see that equality as something to be "held on to," inferring that it is something *he already has*.

Furthermore, Paul claims that this one who is equal with God actually died (v. 8). People often wonder why Paul (and Christians) makes such a big deal out of the death of Christ. But this reaction is yet another example of how far removed we are from the scandal of Christian thought in the marketplace of ideas. Celebrated historian and atheist Robert Wright says, "We can be pretty sure the Crucifixion [actually] *happened*, in part because it made so *little* theological sense."[265] Why? Because, he says, "throughout history, gods had been beings to whom you made sacrifices. Now here was a god that not only demanded no ritual sacrifices from you but himself made sacrifices— indeed the ultimate sacrifice—for you."[266] Such was the beauty and the power of the gospel in the ancient world and, I would argue, in the modern world as well. *God* has done for us what we could not do for ourselves.

All of Paul's statements are amazing in light of the fact that Jews are the last people in the world who would believe that God had become a human being (and one who died on a cross, at that). The Greeks, the Romans, and the Eastern religions of that time could all conceive of the idea of a god-man, but Jews didn't think that way. Yet Paul and John and thousands of other Jews came to do so; they some-how came to believe that Jesus was God incarnate. With Thomas they said, "My Lord and my God" (John 20:28).

All of which leaves us with a final important question: *Why* did they do this? Why did they, against all odds, come to change their entire religious worldview around this Galilean preacher almost overnight? Why did they come to worship him and, as we will see, go on to suffer many awful things because they claimed he was their God? It doesn't make much sense. Unless there is some legitimacy to it all.

The Resurrection

Other people throughout history have claimed to be God, and the world deemed them delusional. When I started studying Christianity, I wondered: *Why did anyone actually believe Jesus? Why take him seriously? Why bother writing it down? Why have people over the last two thousand years been willing to die for this, including several people who had seen him killed on the cross?* There must have been something more than his teachings, his miracles, and living a good moral life. *Why believe Jesus at such risk to yourself?*

It became clear to me that it couldn't be his *death*. Others have died, even claiming to be a savior, and that didn't change people in a very significant way beyond a kind of martyr example. Then I discovered the thing that makes Jesus unique, that vindicates all of his claims and forces us to make a different choice about him than we would make about any other person, namely *the resurrection*. The crazy claim that Easter actually happened. When the earliest followers of Jesus saw him alive again after he died—talked with him, touched him, ate meals with him, and then watched him leave this earth—it convinced them that he was no ordinary man. The resurrection showed them that Jesus was who he claimed to be, and it led to the birth of the most powerful movement the world has ever seen, a movement that has outlasted empires and spread to almost every language and culture on the planet: the church.

The resurrection is at the center of Christianity. It's the most important celebration each year for Christians. If the resurrection didn't happen, then Christianity falls apart. The apostle Paul says it this way: "If Christ has not been raised, your faith is futile; you are still in your sins. Then those also who have fallen asleep in Christ are lost. If only for this life we have hope in Christ, we are of all people most to be pitied" (1 Corinthians 15:17–19 NIV). The connection he makes is clear: if the resurrection didn't happen *historically*, in real time and space, then Jesus' sacrifice didn't do what Christians believe it did. Sin, death, and evil have *not* really been defeated. But Paul and all the early Christians believed the resurrection *did* happen, and this was why they had certainty about the rest. You can't sit on the fence about the resurrection. If Jesus really did rise from the dead, we must believe and follow him. We have no other options. He defeated death, the one thing no one has ever defeated. The thing so powerful and absolute the Greek gods even claimed they couldn't reverse. Rejecting him if he really rose from the dead, which historians agree has a lot of support and evidence, is then a rejection of God himself, and what he had planned for your life.

Four Pushbacks

All of which leads us to the final question I want to explore with you: *Should* we believe this claim? In my own study I found many reasons that historians and scholars tell us, yes, we should. Here we will focus on just a few that come together in one big idea. There is no better explanation than the resurrection being true that makes sense of (1) the *claims* of the early church, (2) the unexplainable phenomena of the quick and unique *birth of the early church*, and (3) the fact that *the body of Jesus has never been found.*

As we have seen in previous chapters, non-Christian historians of the first century, including Josephus and others, wrote that the

Jews were claiming their leader, Jesus of Nazareth, had risen from the dead. The rise of the early church was unique and surprising because it happened so quickly, emerging among frightened Jews who went from monotheistic worship of God on the Sabbath (Saturday) to bold, courageous worship of *a man* just weeks later, changing their worship day to Sunday to commemorate his resurrection, and being willing to be tortured and killed as his followers for these things. Historians are admittedly baffled by all of this. What caused these conservative Jews to change so radically and so quickly? The explanation that makes the most sense of the data is that Jesus really did come back from the dead, visited them for forty days, and sent them on a mission to change the world at the cost of their own lives.

Of course, there has been pushback to the resurrection—alternative explanations for the threefold evidence just mentioned—though much of it has been shown to be weak and not very rational. What are the most common arguments *against* the resurrection?

OBJECTION #1: JESUS DIDN'T REALLY DIE

The first explanation offered by skeptics for the "supposed" resurrection of Jesus is that *he didn't really die*. This is the official position of Islam, but it isn't all that different from the position of the average atheist. Because the claims of people saying they saw Jesus after his crucifixion are historically difficult to deny, this position doesn't even try denying them. Instead, it admits that the appearances likely happened, but . . . Jesus didn't really die; he simply passed out and was thrown in a shallow grave or dirt pile. After a few days, *voila!* He came to, healed, and started walking around appearing to people, claiming to have risen from the dead. Makes sense, right?

Most scholars and historians write off this explanation immediately. Why? They consider the historical context of the Roman Empire and the way the Romans treated criminals. If there was one thing the

Romans knew how to do, it was kill people! They would crucify up to six thousand people on a single day. They didn't put guys up on crosses and take them down only to have them head home a few days later by mistake! No, they made sure they were dead. The idea that the Romans just "messed it up" is wishful thinking that does not hold up under historical scrutiny.

OBJECTION #2: THE BODY WAS STOLEN

So let's agree that Jesus died. He wasn't mostly dead—he was truly dead. Perhaps his *disciples were involved in an elaborate hoax and stole Jesus' body.* This isn't an original idea—it was actually the first thing the disciples themselves thought when told that Jesus had been raised. The Bible itself records this explanation: "Early on the first day of the week," the Gospel of John says, "while it was still dark, Mary Magdalene went to the tomb and saw that the stone had been removed from the entrance. So she came running to Simon Peter and the other disciple, the one Jesus loved, and said, 'They have taken the Lord out of the tomb, and we don't know where they have put him!'" (20:1–2 NIV). If you are slow to believe that Jesus was raised from the dead, you are in good company, because that's what all the early disciples first believed!

Scholars point out that the resurrection narratives are trustworthy when judged by the critical methods of historical study applied to all ancient writings. Because they contain unflattering content portraying the disciples as scared and slow to believe, even exposing Thomas as a doubter, this suggests they are not fabrications. There was no precedent for this in the ancient world.

In addition, the Gospels tell us that *women were the key eyewitnesses* to the resurrection. In that culture, women were not allowed to testify in a court of law because their testimony was considered untrustworthy. So, if you wanted to convince people in the ancient world that your leader was raised from the dead—and you are making up the story—you *do not* make women the eyewitnesses of the resur-rection. It would be counterproductive. And yet, here, pushing against common sense, against tradition and culture, the testimony is given by women (John 20:1–2, 11–18). In fact, amazingly, *in all four gospel narratives* the first ones to arrive at the empty tomb are women. There would have been tremendous pressure to eliminate them from the story, but the writers do not, as if to say, "Take it or leave it. This is just what happened."

Third, and perhaps most convincingly, is the need to explain why the disciples would create such an elaborate hoax and then be *will-ing to die for it.* This action irrationally subverts everything we know about human nature. We'd have to believe that these followers of Jesus unanimously held to something they knew was not true and suffered torture, pain, and death without a peep. Lots of people die for lies they think are true. But who dies for a lie *they know isn't true,* for something they made up? Jesus' own brother was tortured and killed, all of which could have been stopped if he had recanted. But he never did. Either he died for something he was convinced was true to the core and was worth dying for, or he died for a lie he himself made up. I find the former far more convincing than the latter. Don't you?

OBJECTION #3: THEY WENT TO THE WRONG TOMB

A third pushback of skeptics is that the women, and later the other disciples, were so distraught in their grief that they *showed up at the wrong tomb.* Yes, they found an empty tomb, the theory says, but it was simply the wrong one. They visited the place where they thought their body was laid, but there was never a body there.

I traveled to Israel a few years ago, and our guide took us to what they think is the location where Jesus was crucified and the location where they believe he was placed after his death. I walked into the empty tomb and stood there for a second. Rock. A small surface where a body would be laid, but nothing else. I thought, *Yay! Nothing is here!* I had just spent thousands of dollars and flown halfway around the world to stand in an empty room . . . and couldn't be happier. It was the most beautiful emptiness. I am not saying that is for sure where Jesus' body was laid, who knows? I *am* saying that in that culture of small-town family connections, they knew where people were buried.

So did the disciples just go to the wrong tomb? I don't think so. I mean I've gotten lost before, as I'm sure you have too. My little girl sits in the back seat of my car and routinely says, "You're lost, Dad," to which I smile and tell her to go back to watching *Bubble Guppies* and let me drive. Yes, people make mistakes about where they are going. People even make mistakes about dead people. The worst mistake I ever made as a pastor was the day I told a woman that her husband was dead and sat grieving with her for forty-five minutes before I realized that I had the wrong guy. Whoops, my bad! I tried to soften the blow by joking with her that it was all kind of a gift, because she kind of got her husband back from the dead—you know, like Jesus.

She didn't laugh.

So, I know better than anyone that mistakes happen. But again, let's be honest with the evidence: there is nothing to suggest that this is what happened with Jesus. It's an objection based on nothing. Historians don't buy the wrong tomb theory because those in power could have easily used the dead body to expose the hoax. When rumors of a resurrected hero started, they would have simply rolled out his body. "Look, guys, here is Jesus and he's clearly dead. You just went to the wrong tomb. End of story." End of hoax. End of Christianity.

But they didn't do that, because there was *no body* to be found. People today are still looking for the bones of Jesus, digging up old ossuaries in Israel and Palestine hoping to find him, because if they do, then it's all over. Christianity crumbles, because unlike other religions and worldviews, Christianity is "all in" on the resurrection. It's not a set of teachings or a philosophy of life; it's about a historic moment, a real event that actually happened, that if proven false makes the whole thing fall apart.

OBJECTION #4: THE DISCIPLES BORROWED THE IDEA OF RESURRECTION

The final objection is that the disciples and the early church simply *adapted an existing religious idea*—the resurrection—and projected it onto Jesus. But contrary to popular myth, nobody in the surrounding culture actually believed in a present-day human resurrection. Greeks followed Plato and Homer who, as dualists, believed that the goal of life was to *escape* the material world to the spiritual world. A return to the physical world (in the form of a new body) was undesirable. Once a person was dead and gone, Greeks never wanted to come back to this world—they had finally escaped the prison of the soul. For Jews, resurrection was a real hope but not in the way the disciples claimed had happened to Jesus. According to Old Testament teaching, *all the people of Israel together*, at the *end of time*, would be resurrected from the dead (Ezekiel 36–37). But it would have been very, very unusual to claim that the resurrection was going to happen to just *one person in the middle of time*. That is why all the early disciples doubted the resurrection when they were first told about it (John 20:3–10). They weren't borrowing an existing idea; the idea itself *didn't* fit their worldview at all. That's the point. Their existing faith was blown up!

What Now? Liar, Lunatic, or Lord

Millions hold the position that Jesus was a great moral teacher, but they do not believe that he was God. Those who are not willing to accept Jesus' claim to be God, or who do not believe in the resurrection, are left with two possibilities. Perhaps Jesus was lying or maybe he was a lunatic. Richard Dawkins has also suggested that maybe Jesus was sincerely mistaken. But this simply puts Jesus in the category of lunatic—people who sincerely believe they are other people are usually under surveillance in psychiatric institutions. We don't take what they say seriously. That's why it's safe to say that if Jesus were "sincerely mistaken" about his identity, he is not to be celebrated at the end of the day, and neither is he to be trusted.

The point of reviewing these options is to show, as C. S. Lewis points out, that a middle-of-the-road option is not a *rational* option when it comes to the problem of Jesus:

> A man who was merely a man and said the sort of things Jesus said would not be a great moral teacher. He would either be a lunatic—on the level with a man who says he is a poached egg—or he would be the devil of hell. You must take your choice. Either this was, and is, the Son of God, or else a madman or something worse. You can shut Him up for a fool or you can fall at His feet and call Him Lord and God. But let us not come with any patronizing nonsense about His being a great human teacher. He has not left that open to us.[267]

People who claim Jesus was only a good teacher haven't really read Jesus' teachings. If they had (and they understood the historical context of what he is saying), they would immediately be confronted by the fact that he is far more than a good teacher.

Given this, I hope you see that many people do not become a Christian because it's easy or because it is a crutch or a form of wishful thinking. My own life would be far easier (and likely far more indulgent) if I *weren't* a Christian. If I went with how I felt and what I selfishly wanted for myself when I was seventeen, I would likely not be a Christian at all. As a seventeen-year-old who thought about little else but girls, partying, and the next drug I could try, I wasn't drawn to Jesus for personal benefit. No. I was compelled by a conviction that the story of Jesus was true, and if it was, I had to abandon my life and plans for his.

At the end of the day I'm a Christian because the tomb is empty, not because of wishful thinking. I'm a Christian because Jesus is God. All religions, in some way, tell us that we have to work our way to God, that we have to impress God, whoever or whatever he might be. Help old ladies across the street, avoid watching certain movies, pray so many times a day, and maybe God will be impressed at your commitment to him. He will look at all those good works and deem you worthy to save. But that's not what Jesus says. Jesus comes along and his whole life, ministry, and message is that nothing we do will ever work. We need help, and he has come to help us. We need life, and his is the life we need.

"I came to cast fire on the earth," Jesus said, "and would that it were already kindled! I have a baptism to be baptized with, and how great is my distress until it is accomplished!" (Luke 12:49–50). Here Jesus is speaking of his death. The fire did come down on *him*, the fire of God's judgment, so that those who belong to Jesus would be saved, passed over on the day of judgment when God comes back to town. All of the fires of sacrifice lit throughout history were pointers to the fire he underwent on the cross to save us. He got what we deserve, accomplishing for us what we could never do for ourselves. And he didn't stay dead. He let evil do its worst, and then he rose again victorious. This is not fan-fiction, a myth, or a symbol. It's reality.

And *that's* why I am a Christian.

This is the crisis of faith that we all must face. You and I have been confronted by the possibility that all of this may be true. If you aren't a Christian, Jesus says that two things are necessary for you to become one: "*Repent* and *believe* in the gospel" (Mark 1:15, emphasis added). We first need to "repent," turn from all the things we're trusting to justify ourselves, the things that have replaced God in our lives. All the things in the world we look to for our joy, eternal significance, pleasure, and identity that aren't Jesus Christ. Maybe that's money or sex or relationships or power or reputation or family. We need to turn from ways of thinking and living that are not in line with how God made us to live. In knowing God, we find that he must be our ultimate satisfaction, and that once we drink of his grace, we will never thirst for all the God-substitutes we look to (John 4:14).

Secondly, Jesus says we need to "believe," to put our faith and trust in him and what he did for us: what his death and his resurrection accomplished for us. On the cross Jesus died for us, because of our sin; he absorbed the wrath of God meant for us. This is the invitation Jesus makes to each one of us: turn away from sin and turn toward him. The apostle Paul, in his letter to the Roman church, climaxes his argument about God's amazing work in Jesus with these astounding words: "If you confess with your mouth that Jesus is Lord and believe in your heart that God raised him from the dead, you will be *saved*" (Romans 10:9, emphasis added).

This is where Christianity hits real life. The objections we have explored—all of the problems we might have with God—all come down to Jesus. And when we look closely at him, we find that he came not for the sake of people who are merely adopting a worldview or finding out which beliefs are better than others, but for a more profound purpose. That we will be what the Bible calls *saved*—restored, reconciled to God, loved, free, and given joy forevermore. In other words, facing the problem of God is about far more than getting the right *information for ourselves*; it's about *a transformation of ourselves*. He has real power to create new life and new desires and new futures for anyone. Because the resurrection is true, Jesus changes not just what we *do* (that's the approach of religion) but what we *want* to do. And that is the key. As J. R. R. Tolkien writes of Samwise Gamgee, pondering the journey ahead for the hobbits: "Sam was the only member of the party who had not been over the river before. He had a strange feeling as the slow gurgling stream slipped by: his old life lay behind in the mists, dark adventure lay in front." When a person decides to follow Jesus, to trust him with the biggest questions in life and death, there is a shift from old to new, a crossing of the river into a new adventure. When I opened my life to Christ, everything was just . . . different. There were things I left behind that used to shine like silver to me and now were as dull as rust. The veil was pulled back, and I could see and feel in ways I had not before. I had direction and purpose that was not there before.

Saved. It's not how I would have put it at the time, but as I look back—yes. That's what happened. I was saved from a life without God. But also I was saved from *myself.* Saved from what I had thought was a meaningful and joyful life.

Maybe, that's what you need saving from today: the philosophies and worldviews you have chosen to adopt in your life, not because they make the most sense or are the most historical and scientific, but for other reasons. Other motives, that if asked to explain, you couldn't—or maybe wouldn't want to—but nonetheless have driven your life to this point. Things you have believed because of comfort or pleasure or because you didn't want to live differently than you do right now. A way I understand completely. I see it every day in myself and in the people I pastor. But we must understand that, in reality, this approach to life is the opposite of freedom, even though it may feel like freedom. And this fact, beyond everything else, may be the hardest thing to come to terms with.

The Abduction of My Grandfather

A few years ago my brother and I went to visit my grandfather, who in his nineties had, out of nowhere, sold his apartment where he had lived for over fifty years, and was all of a sudden living in a brand-new large home with a young couple. We only found out where he had gone by pure luck, and thus we were pretty suspect of the whole situation, as this is a popular scam among couples who can't afford homes in expensive neighborhoods: they befriend an older, usually quite lonely person, someone close to death, and convince him to leave his home and come live with them, usually emptying his bank account in the process. We arrived at the house in order to save him. To tell him the truth and set him free from his captivity.

We pictured ourselves rolling in, grabbing him, and running out the door. But when we got there, he told us he didn't want to leave. He said that he liked the people, they loved him well and cared for him, and that he liked his new home. So . . . we left. I was mad, frustrated, and confused. I couldn't understand why he didn't want to come with us. Didn't he see that this was a scam? Couldn't he recognize that he was being used? We had told him plainly. But he just stared at us, smiling, as if he *knew* but was okay with it anyway. He didn't *want* to be saved. He didn't care. He was happy. He was comfortable; everything was in its place; things were stable. And that was enough. He didn't want to ask deeper questions. He didn't want to go down the rabbit hole that might change things. In his way of thinking, if he had a few years left, he might as well live with this couple in *comfort and luxury*—even if it was all based on a lie. He saw it as a worthy trade.

In other words, my grandfather didn't *want* his life to be different. But how is that possible? How could he not completely rearrange everything because of this newfound truth? The truth sets us free, doesn't it? I think this is a picture of the way many people think about the things we have explored in this book. If God is real, if the claims of Jesus are true, if there really is a heaven and hell, if Jesus is exclusively the way to know God—then that's a problem. God upsets our comfortable lives where we have the illusion of being in control. But as long as our needs are met, we don't want to question too deeply because it will mean changing things, and we aren't sure we'll like it. The prospect of a different reality frightens us. It feels like anything *but* freedom. In other words, some people would rather *not* be saved. The truth sets us free only if we want it to.

But what if our feelings and desires are betraying us? What if we can't trust how we *feel* in a given moment because we can't push past what keeps us comfortable and preoccupied? What if we sense that this longing, if we follow it, will change everything, so we ignore it and choose the comfort of the shore? What if the reason God is a problem is that he causes us to come face to face with the fact that he has a claim on our lives? He challenges the status quo we've created for ourselves.

Sure, he offers us an opportunity to change and be transformed, but if we are honest, that scares us too. If we take him up on it, he promises it will cost us. We don't realize that God's rewiring of our hearts prepares us for a greater glory than any of us can imagine, and that that freedom, beauty, and joy, however disorienting to begin with, leads to the fullest life.

So, each of us must decide. Will we trust the one who comes to save us? The one who will lead us, however shakily, to the true harbor? Sometimes by telling us to take the boat to the other side—as he did his own disciples—where a storm will kick up now and then, just to give us the opportunity to see him walking out to save us, to trust him and glory in it. The kind of opportunity that forces us to look inside—our beliefs, our motives, our lives—as scary as that may be, and actually see reality. And then to have the courage to let that truth carry us forward, as much as we may want to cling to falsehood because it's familiar.

Such is the invitation from, and the hope found in, Jesus Christ. And such has been the point of the journey of this book. I realize that the arguments I've presented may not fully convince you to become a follower of Jesus. But it is my prayer that in the journey, you have seen that Christianity offers a compelling, alternative vision of the world. And I invite you to open yourself up to this vision. I pray you'd be willing to listen and go where the evidence leads, to question your questions, and doubt your doubts. Even if it brings you to the end of yourself and to believe in things that scare you, that you never thought you would. To follow him to places you never dreamed of, places he wants to lead you, rather than places you've agreed to go on your own terms.

For such is the risk, and the adventure, of Christianity.

Notes

INTRODUCTION

1. Reginald Bibby, *Beyond the Gods* (Project Canada Books, 2011), 53.

CHAPTER 1: THE PROBLEM OF SCIENCE

2. A lecture by Richard Dawkins extracted from *The Nullifidian* (December 1994), http://www.simonyi.ox.ac.uk/dawkins/WorldOfDawkins-archive/Dawkins/Work/Articles/1994-12religion.shtml. Emphasis added.

3. Sam Harris, *The End of Faith* (New York: W. W. Norton, 2004), 72.

4. Nancy Pearcey, *Total Truth* (Wheaton, Ill.: Crossway, 2004), 58.

5. Nick Van Til, "Modernizing the Case for God: A Review of *Time's* Review," *Time*, April 7, 1980.

6. Nancy Pearcey, *Total Truth*, 58.

7. David Bentley Hart, *The Experience of God: Being, Consciousness, Bliss* (New Haven: Yale University Press, 2013), 16.

8. Ibid.

9. David Lindberg, "Medieval Science and Religion," in *Science and Religion*, Gary Ferngren, ed. (Baltimore: Johns Hopkins University Press, 2002), 70.

10. Alister McGrath, *The Twilight of Atheism: The Rise and Fall of Disbelief in the Modern World* (New York: Doubleday, 2004), 85–86.

11. Quoted in Dinesh D'Souza, *What's So Great about Christianity* (Washington, D.C.: Regnery, 2007), 104. Emphasis added.

12. Ibid., 110.

13. Ibid.

14. Ibid., 103.

15. Alister McGrath, *The Twilight of Atheism*, 87.

16. Alvin Plantinga, "Darwin, Mind and Meaning," November 17, 1997, 8. http: hid-www.ucsb.edu.

17. Kenneth Richard Samples, *Without a Doubt: Answering the 20 Toughest Faith Questions* (Grand Rapids: Baker, 2004), 188. Emphasis added.

18. Ibid., 192–194.

19. Alvin J. Schmidt, *Under the Influence: How Christianity Transformed Civilization* (Grand Rapids: Zondervan, 2001), 190.

20. Richard C. Lewontin, "Billions and Billions of Demons," *The New York Review of Books* (January 9, 1997), 28.

21. Nancy Pearcey, *Total Truth*, 170–171.

22. Nicholas Wolterstorff, *Reason Within the Bounds of Religion* (Grand Rapids: Eerdmans, 1988), 20.

23. Brian J. Walsh and J. Richard Middleton, *The Transforming Vision: Shaping a Christian World View* (Downers Grove, Ill.: InterVarsity Press, 1984), 35.

24. Ibid., 17, 31.

25. Gregory A. Boyd, *Benefit of the Doubt: Breaking the Idol of Certainty* (Grand Rapids: Baker, 2013), 47.

26. Sam Harris, *Letter to a Christian Nation* (New York: Vintage, 2008), 51.

27. Timothy Keller, *The Reason for God: Belief in an Age of Skepticism* (New York: Penguin Group, 2008), xvii.

28. Marcus Borg, *Jesus: A New Vision: Spirit, Culture, and the Life of Discipleship* (Canada: HarperCollins, 1991), 33–34.

29. Craig S. Keener, *Miracles: The Credibility of the New Testament Accounts* (Grand Rapids: Baker, 2011), 194–195.

30. See for instance, Dr. Stephen C. Meyer's, *Signature in the Cell* (which explores the biological weaknesses of Darwin's theory) and *Darwin's Doubt* (which explores the paleontological weaknesses of Darwin's theory in respect to the Cambrian explosion, etc.,). Stephen C. Meyer, *Signature in the Cell: DNA and the Evidence for Intelligent Design* (San Francisco: Harper One, 2009); *Darwin's Doubt: The Explosive Origin of Animal Life and the Case for Intelligent Design* (New York: Harper One, 2013).

31. Stephen Jay Gould, "Evolution's Erratic Pace," *Natural History* 86, no. 5 (May 1977), 14.

32. Charles Darwin, *The Origin of Species* (London: John Murray, 1859), 280.

33. Ronald N. Giere, "Naturalism," in *The Routledge Companion to Philosophy of Science*, eds. Stathis Psillos and Martin Curd (London: Routledge, 2008), 216.

34. Dinesh D'Souza, *What's So Great about Christianity*, 14.

35. C. S. Lewis, *Miracles* in *The Complete C. S. Lewis Signature Classics* (New York: HarperOne, 2002), 313.

36. Quoted in C. S. Lewis, *Miracles* in *The Complete C. S. Lewis Signature Classics*, 313.

37. Mitch Stokes, *A Shot of Faith (to the Head): Be a Confident Believer in an Age of Cranky Atheists* (Nashville: Thomas Nelson, 2012), 44.

38. Alvin Plantinga, *Where the Conflict Really Lies: Science, Religion, and Naturalism* (Oxford: Oxford University Press, 2011), xiv.

39. John Piper, "C. S. Lewis, Romantic Rationalist: How His Paths to Christ Shaped His Life and Ministry," Plenary 1, 2013 National Conference. http://www.desiringgod.org/messages/c-s-lewis-romantic-rationalist-how-his -paths-to-christ-shaped-his-life-and-ministry.

40. Charles Darwin to W. Graham, July 3, 1881, in *The Life and Letters of Charles Darwin*, ed. Francis Darwin (1897; reprint, Boston: Elibron, 2005), 1:285.

41. Lesslie Newbigin, *The Gospel in a Pluralist Society* (Grand Rapids: Eerdmans, 1989), ch.17.

42. Stanley J. Grenz, *A Primer on Postmodernism* (Grand Rapids: Eerdmans, 2006), 1–10.

43. Quoted in Lee Strobel, *The Case for a Creator: A Journalist Investigates Scientific Evidence That Points Toward God* (Grand Rapids: Zondervan, 2004), 70.

44. Lesslie Newbigin, *The Gospel in a Pluralist Society*, 214.

45. Stephen Jay Gould, *Rocks of Ages: Science and Religion in the Fullness of Life* (New York: Ballantine, 1999), 195.

CHAPTER 2: THE PROBLEM OF GOD'S EXISTENCE

46. Immanuel Kant, ed. Mary Gregory, *Critique of Practical Reason* (Cambridge: Cambridge University Press, 1997).

47. C. S. Lewis, *Mere Christianity* in *The Complete C.S. Lewis Signature Classics*, 15.

48. Richard Dawkins, *The God Delusion* (Boston: Houghton Mifflin Harcourt, 2006), 226.

49. John Calvin, *Romans–Galatians: Calvin's Commentaries* (Associated Publishers and Authors, 1980), 1358.

50. Richard Dawkins, *The God Delusion*, 216.

51. Ibid., 221.

52. Ibid.

53. Timothy Keller, *The Reason for God*, 153.

54. Ibid.

55. Charles Darwin, *The Descent of Man*, various publishers, ch. 21–General Summary and Conclusion.

56. J. B. S. Haldane, *Possible Worlds and Other Essays* (London: Chatto & Windus, 1927), 190–197.

57. Alister McGrath, *C. S. Lewis—A Life: Eccentric Genius, Reluctant Prophet* (Wheaton, Ill.: Tyndale, 2016, reprint ed.), 235–236.

58. For more, see Harry Bruinius, *Better for All the World: The Secret History of Forced Sterilization and America's Quest for Racial Purity* (New York: Knopf, 2006).

59. Adolf Hitler, *Mein Kampf*, 4th printing (London: Hurst & Blackett, 1939), 239–240, 242.

60. David Hume, *Argument Against Miracles: A Critical Analysis* (New York: University Press of America, 1989), 75.

61. Dinesh D'Souza, *What's So Great about Christianity*, 117–118.

62. William Lane Craig, *On Guard: Defending Your Faith with Reason and Precision* (Colorado Springs: David C. Cook, 2010), 88.

63. Ibid., 90. This is why the ancient question of why God didn't create the universe *sooner* is meaningless. In the early fifth century AD, Augustine was asked this and answered rightly that God did not make the universe at

a point in time but "simultaneously with time," and thus the question is a category mistake.

64. J–M Wersinger, "Genesis: The Origin of the Universe," *National Forum* (Winter 1996), 9–12.

65. Robert Jastrow, *God and the Astronomers* (New York: W.W. Norton, 1992), 107.

66. Francis S. Collins, *The Language of God: A Scientist Presents Evidence for Belief* (New York: Free Press, 2006), 67.

67. Ibid.

68. Norman L. Geisler and Frank Turek, *I Don't Have Enough Faith to Be an Atheist* (Wheaton, Ill.: Crossway, 2004), 105.

69. Ibid., 106.

70. Quoted in Timothy Keller, *The Reason for God*, 134.

71. Fred Hoyle, "The Universe: Past and Present Reflections," *Engineering and Science* (November 1981), 12.

72. Stephen Hawking, *A Brief History of Time* (New York: Bantam, 1988), 121–122.

73. Richard Dawkins, *The God Delusion*, 144.

74. Ibid., 145.

75. Ibid.

76. Alvin Plantinga, "Darwin, Mind and Meaning," https://www.calvin.edu/academic/philosophy/virtual_library/articles/plantinga_alvin/darwin_mind_and_meaning.pdf.

77. Richard Dawkins, *The God Delusion*, 146.

CHAPTER 3: THE PROBLEM OF THE BIBLE

78. Sam Harris, *The End of Faith* (New York: W. W. Norton, 2004), 19.

79. F. F. Bruce, *The Books and the Parchments: How We Got Our English Bible* (Old Tappan, N.J.: Fleming H. Revell, 1950), 178; Ravi Zacharias, *Can Man Live Without God* (Dallas: Word Publishing, 1994), 162.

80. Chaim Potok, *In the Beginning* (New York: Knopf, 1975), 360.

81. Bart D. Ehrman, *Misquoting Jesus: The Story Behind Who Changed the Bible and Why* (New York: HarperSanFrancisco, 2005), 10.

82. Quoted in Norman L. Geisler, *When Skeptics Ask: A Handbook on Christian Evidences*, rev. updated ed. (Grand Rapids: Baker, 2013), 172.

83. Josh McDowell, *The New Evidence That Demands a Verdict* (Nashville: Thomas Nelson, 1989), 36–37.

84. Josh McDowell, *More Than a Carpenter* (Wheaton, Ill.: Tyndale, 1977), 47–48; *The New Evidence That Demands a Verdict*, 38.

85. Karen Armstrong, *A History of God: The 4,000-Year Quest of Judaism, Christianity, and Islam* (New York: Ballantine/Epiphany, 1993), 82.

86. Frederic G. Kenyon, *Handbook to the Textual Criticism of the New Testament* (London: Macmillan and Company, 1901), 4.

87. F. F. Bruce, *The New Testament Documents: Are They Reliable?* (Leicester, UK: InterVarsity Press, 1981), 43.

88. Ibid.

89. Richard Bauckham, *Jesus and the Eyewitnesses: The Gospels as Eyewitness Testimony* (Grand Rapids: Eerdmans), 52.

90. Ibid.

91. Timothy Keller, *The Reason for God* (New York: Penguin Group, 2008), 107.

92. A. A. Ruprecht, "Slave, Slavery" in *Dictionary of Paul and His letters*, eds. Gerald F. Hawthorne, Ralph P. Martin, Daniel G. Reid (Downers Grove, Ill.: InterVarsity Press, 1993), 881–882.

93. Nelson Glueck, *Rivers in the Desert: A History of the Negev* (New York: Farrar, Strauss & Cudahy, 1959), 31.

94. N. T. Wright, *The New Testament and the People of God* (Minneapolis: Fortress Press, 1992), 36.

95. Ibid.

CHAPTER 4: THE PROBLEM OF THE CHRIST MYTH

96. Walter P. Weaver, *The Historical Jesus in the Twentieth Century, 1900–1950* (Harrisburg, Pa.: Trinity, 1999).

97. Bart D. Ehrman, *Did Jesus Exist?: The Historical Argument for Jesus of Nazareth* (San Francisco: HarperOne, 2013), 2.

98. Acharya S., *The Christ Conspiracy: The Greatest Story Ever Sold* (Kempton, Ill.: Adventure Unlimited Press, 1999), 125.

99. Edwin Yamauchi, "Jesus Outside the New Testament: What Is the Evidence?" in *Jesus Under Fire: Modern Scholarship Reinvents the Historical Jesus*, ed. Michael Wilkins and J. P. Moreland (Grand Rapids: Zondervan, 1995), 212.

100. Rodney Stark, *The Rise of Christianity: A Sociologist Reconsiders History* (Princeton, N.J.: Princeton University Press and San Francisco: Harper SanFrancisco, 1996), 7.

101. N. T. Wright, *The Resurrection of the Son of God* (Minneapolis: Fortress Press, 2003), chs. 18–19.

102. Acharya S, *The Christ Conspiracy*, 167.

103. Tom Harpur, *The Pagan Christ: Recovering the Lost Light* (Markham, Ont.: Thomas Allen, 2005), 6.

104. Acharya S, *The Christ Conspiracy*, 115.

105. Craig S. Keener, *The Gospel of Matthew: A Socio-Rhetorical Commentary* (Grand Rapids: Eerdmans, 1999), 99.

106. C. M. Daniels, "The Role of the Roman Army in the Spread and Practice of Mithraism," in John Hinnells, ed., *Mithraic Studies: Proceedings of the First International Congress of Mithraic Studies* (Manchester: Manchester University Press, 1975), vol. 2, 250.

107. Manfred Clauss, *The Roman Cult of Mithras: The God and His Mysteries* (Edinburgh: Edinburgh University Press, 2000), 118.

108. Louis Bouyer, *The Christian Mystery: From Pagan Myth to Christian Mysticism* (New York: T & T Clark, 1990), 70; Fritz Graf, "Baptism and Graeco-Roman Mystery Cults," in "Rituals of Purification, Rituals of Initiation," in David Hellholm, Tor Vegge, Øyvind Norderval, Christer Hellholm, *Ablution, Initiation, and Baptism: Late Antiquity, Early Judaism, and Early Christianity* (Walter de Gruyter, 2011), 105.

109. Craig A. Evans, *Jesus and His Contemporaries: Comparative Studies* (Leiden, Netherlands: Brill, 2001), 48.

110. Bruxy Cavey, "Duped? Questioning the Logic of Pop Spirituality. Part 6: Jesus–Christ or Copycat?" http://media.themeetinghouse.ca/podcast/handouts/2009-05-24-650-notes.pdf.

111. St. Augustine, *Retractations* (1.13.3) quoted in "Part 1: Salvation History," by William G. Most in *Basic Catholic Catechism*. http://www.ewtn.com/library/catechsm/mostcat.htm.

112. Cited in Humphrey Carpenter, *J. R. R. Tolkien: A Biography* (Boston: Houghton Mifflin, 2000), 151–152.

113. Humphrey Carpenter, *J. R. R. Tolkien*, 151.

114. Ibid.

115. C. S. Lewis, "Myth Became Fact," in *God in the Dock: Essays on Theology and Ethics* (Grand Rapids: Eerdmans, 1994). Emphasis added.

CHAPTER 5: THE PROBLEM OF EVIL AND SUFFERING

116. Ronald H. Nash, *Faith and Reason: Searching for a Rational Faith* (Grand Rapids: Zondervan, 1988), 177.

117. Randy Alcorn, *If God Is Good: Faith in the Midst of Suffering and Evil* (Colorado Springs: Multnomah, 2009), 11.

118. David Bentley Hart, *The Experience of God* (New Haven: Yale University Press, 2013), 16.

119. Ibid.

120. David Hume, *Dialogues Concerning Natural Religion* (London: William Blackwood, 1907), 134.

121. David Bentley Hart, *The Experience of God*, 16.

122. Randy Alcorn, *If God Is Good*, 21.

123. See Rhonda Byrne, *The Secret* (New York: Atria Books/Beyond Words, 2006).

124. Ibid.

125. Alvin Plantinga, *God and Other Minds: A Study of the Rational Justification of Belief in God* (Ithaca, N.Y., and London: Cornell University Press, 1967), 118.

126. J. L. Mackie, "Evil and Omnipotence," *Mind*, 64, no. 254 (1955), 200–201. Emphasis added.

127. Alvin Plantinga, *God and Other Minds*, 120.

128. Ibid.

129. C. S. Lewis, *Mere Christianity* (San Francisco: Harper San Francisco, 2001), 38–39.

130. Charles Darwin to W. Graham, July 3, 1881, in *The Life and Letters of Charles Darwin*, 1:285.

131. Steven Pinker, "Why They Kill Their Newborns," *The New York Times*, November 2, 1997.

132. Ibid.

133. Timothy Keller, *The Reason for God* (New York: Penguin Group, 2008), 26.

134. J. L. Mackie, "Evil and Omnipotence," *Mind*, 64, no. 254 (1955).

135. Malcolm Muggeridge, *In a Valley of This Restless Mind* (London: Collins, 1978), 72.

136. Malcolm Gladwell, *David and Goliath: Underdogs, Misfits, and the Art of Battling Giants* (New York: Little, Brown and Company, 2013), 110.

137. Ibid., 106–107.

138. Ibid.

139. Alvin Plantinga, *Warranted Christian Belief* (Oxford: Oxford University Press, 2000), 466-467.

140. Max Scheler, "The Meaning of Suffering," in *On Feeling, Knowing and Valuing: Selected Writings*, ed. Harold J. Bershady (Chicago: University of Chicago Press, 1992), 98.

141. Timothy Keller, *Walking with God through Pain and Suffering* (New York: Dutton, 2013), 30. Emphasis added.

142. John G. Stackhouse Jr., *Can God Be Trusted: Faith and the Challenge of Evil* (Oxford: Oxford University Press, 1998), 80. Emphasis added.

143. Timothy Keller, *The Reason for God*, 32.

144. Jürgen Moltmann, *The Trinity and the Kingdom* (Minneapolis: Augsburg Fortress Press, 1993), 115.

CHAPTER 6: THE PROBLEM OF HELL

145. Peter Kreeft and Ronald K. Tacelli, *Handbook of Christian Apologetics* (Downers Grove, Ill.: InterVarsity Press, 1994), 282.

146. Bertrand Russell, *Why I Am Not a Christian and Other Essays on Religion and Related Subjects* (New York: Simon and Schuster, 1957), 17.

147. Charles Darwin, *The Autobiography of Charles Darwin: 1809–1882*, ed. Nora Barlow, with original omissions restored (New York: W. W. Norton, 1993), 87.

148. C. S. Lewis, *The Problem of Pain* (New York: Macmillan, 1962), 118.

149. Bertrand Russell, *Why I Am Not a Christian*, 17.

150. D. A. Carson, "God's Love and God's Wrath," *Bibliotheca Sacra* 156 (1999), 388–390.

151. Annihilationism was an idea I was introduced to early on that I adopted for a time, but it proved wanting for a number of reasons both philosophical and biblical: (1) God made human beings with souls that are eternal by definition (Ecclesiastes 3:11), (2) annihilationism violates the intrinsic value of a human being who, as an image bearer of God, not only was designed to live forever but deserves to have his or her choices honored and held in tact forever, (3) the biblical texts that describe eternal life and eternal punishment (Matthew 25:31–46; Daniel 12:1–3) are meant to describe experiences of parallel quantity (time) with different qualities, (4) the extensive amount of biblical texts teaching the eternal *conscious* punishment of people (Matthew 13:50; 25:46; Mark 9:48; John 5:28; Revelation 14:11), (5) there are, in my estimation, better exegetical explanations for every text that annihilationists use to support their case (John 3:16, Revelation 20:14; 2 Thessalonians 1:9). For a detailed study of these things, see G. K. Beale, *The Book of Revelation* (Grand Rapids: Eerdmans, 1999), 1030; Wayne Grudem, *Systematic Theology: An Introduction to Biblical Doctrine* (Grand Rapids: Zondervan, 1995), 1150–1151.

152. Miroslav Volf, *Exclusion and Embrace: A Theological Exploration of Identity, Otherness, and Reconciliation* (Nashville: Abingdon Press, 1996), 304. Emphasis added.

153. J. P. Moreland in Lee Strobel, *The Case for Faith: A Journalist Investigates the Toughest Objections to Christianity* (Grand Rapids: Zondervan, 1998), 174.

154. Miroslav Volf, *Exclusion and Embrace*, 303.

155. G. K. Chesterton, quoted in Cliffe Knechtle, *Give Me an Answer that Satisfies My Heart and Mind: Answers to Your Toughest Questions about Christianity* (Downers Grove, Ill.: InterVarsity Press, 1986), 42.

156. Randy Alcorn, *If God Is Good* (Colorado Springs: Multnomah, 2009), 318.

157. D. A. Carson, "The Profile Evidence" in Lee Strobel, *The Case for Faith*, 221–222.

158. John M. Frame, *Systematic Theology: An Introduction to Christian Belief*

(Phillipsburg, N.J.: P&R Publishing, 1083. This hints to part of the answer to the question of those who have never heard.

159. Charles Templeton quoted in Lee Strobel, *The Case for Faith*, 172.

160. N. T. Wright, *The New Testament and the People of God* (Minneapolis: Fortress Press, 1992), 282–284. See also *Jesus and the Victory of God* (Minneapolis: Fortress Press, 1997, 6th ed.), ch. 8.

161. See G. K. Beale, *The Book of Revelation*, 50–55; see also 1029.

162. Timothy Keller, *The Reason for God* (New York: Penguin Group, 2008), 259–260.

163. Thomas F. Torrance, quoted in Darrell W. Johnson, *Discipleship on the Edge: An Expository Journey through the Book of Revelation* (Vancouver: Regent College Publishing, 2004), 354.

164. C. S. Lewis, *The Problem of Pain* in *C. S. Lewis: The Complete Signature Classics* (New York: HarperOne, 2002), 627.

165. C. S. Lewis, *Mere Christianity* in *C.S. Lewis: The Complete Signature Classics*, 144.

166. Miroslav Volf, *Exclusion and Embrace*, 299.

167. C. S. Lewis, *The Great Divorce* (Grand Rapids: Baker, 1979), n.p.

168. Thomas Chalmers, "The Expulsive Power of a New Affection," https://www.monergism.com/thethreshold/sdg/Chalmers,%20Thomas%20-%20The%20Exlpulsive%20Power%20of%20a%20New%20Af.pdf, 3, 6.

169. Ibid., p. 5.

170. Ibid., p. 10.

171. C. S. Lewis, "Hell" in Millard J. Erickson, ed. *The New Life: Readings in Christian Theology* (Grand Rapids: Baker, 1979), 500.

CHAPTER 7: THE PROBLEM OF SEX

172. Bertrand Russell, *Why I Am Not a Christian and Other Essays on Religion and Related Subjects* (New York: Simon and Schuster, 1957), 26.

173. Margaret Sanger, *The Pivot of Civilization* (Elmsford, N.Y.: Maxwell Reprint Co., 1969).

174. Christopher Hitchens, *God Is Not Great: How Religion Poisons Everything* (New York: Twelve Books, 2007), 283.

175. Darrell L. Guder, ed. *Missional Church: A Vision for the Sending of the Church in North America* (Grand Rapids: Eerdmans, 1998), 25.

176. Ibid. Herein lies the foundation for the call to freedom and people waging battle with civil and religious authority structures.

177. Nicholas Boyle, *Who Are We Now? Christian Humanism and the Global Market from Hegel to Heaney* (Edinburgh: T & T Clark, 1998), 80.

178. Mark Driscoll and Grace Driscoll, *Real Marriage: The Truth about Sex, Friendship, and Life Together* (Nashville: Thomas Nelson, 2012), ch. 6.

179. Mark Driscoll, "Part 1: Let Him Kiss Me," The Peasant Princess, Mars Hill Church, MP3 audio file, http://marshill.se/marshillmedia/the-peasant-princess.

180. The Roman Catholic Church teaches Mary was a virgin her whole life, even though the Bible teaches that Jesus had brothers and sisters (Mark 6:1–6) and Matthew goes out of his way to say that Mary didn't sleep with Joseph until she had Jesus (Matthew 1:18, 25).

181. Mark Driscoll and Grace Driscoll, *Real Marriage*, 162.

182. Ibid.

183. Ibid.

184. Linda J. Waite and Maggie Gallagher, *The Case for Marriage: Why Married People Are Happier, Healthier, and Better Off Financially* (New York: Doubleday, 2000), chs. 3 and 6.

185. Robert T. Michael, John H. Gagnon, Edward O. Lauman, and Gina Kolata, *Sex in America: A Definitive Survey* (Boston: Little, Brown & Co., 1994), 124.

186. Juli Slattery, *No More Headaches: Enjoying Sex and Intimacy in Marriage* (Wheaton, Ill.: Tyndale, 2009), 25.

187. Kevin Leman, *Sheet Music: Uncovering the Secrets of Sexual Intimacy in Marriage* (Wheaton, Ill.: Tyndale, 2008), 95–99.

188. Dan B. Allender and Tremper Longman III, *Intimate Allies: Rediscovering God's Design for Marriage and Becoming Soul Mates for Life* (Wheaton, Ill.: Tyndale, 1999), 253–254.

189. C. S. Lewis, *The Screwtape Letters* in *The Complete C. S. Lewis Classics* (New York: HarperOne, 1942/1996), 249.

190. As quoted in Nancy Pearcey, *Total Truth* (Wheaton, Ill.: Crossway, 2004), 143.

191. Ibid., 144.

192. Ibid., 145.

193. Steven D. Levitt and Stephen J. Dubner, *SuperFreakonomics: Global Cooling, Patriotic Prostitutes, and Why Suicide Bombers Should Buy Life Insurance* (Toronto: HarperCollins Publishers LTD, 2009), 23.

194. Ibid., 30.

195. Ibid.

196. Ibid.

197. Philip G. Zimbardo and Nikita Duncan, "The Demise of Guys: Why Boys Are Struggling and What We Can Do About It" (New York: Ted Conferences, 2012), http://www.contentreserve.com/TitleInfo.asp?ID=%7BE7E5D67C -E030-4902-AA9C-43122E53BB79%7D&Format=50. Emphasis added.

198. Rob Bell, *Sex God: Exploring the Endless Connections Between Sexuality and Spirituality* (Grand Rapids: Zondervan, 2007), 13.

199. See N. T. Wright, *The New Testament and the People of God* (Minneapolis: Fortress Press, 1992), 123–124.

200. Peggy Noonan, "You'd Cry Too If It Happened to You," *Forbes*, September 14, 1992. Italics added.

201. John Piper, *What Jesus Demands from the World*, reprint ed. (Wheaton, Ill.: Crossway, 2011), 322.

202. Ibid.

203. Nancy Pearcey, *Total Truth*, 218.

204. Richard Dawkins, "The Evolution of Bill Clinton: Sex and Power," *The Observer*, March 22, 1998.

205. Peter Singer, "Heavy Petting," review of *Dearest Pet: On Beastiality*, by Midas Dekkers, http://www.nerve.com/Opinions/Singer/heavyPetting/main.asp. Emphasis added.

206. Randy Thornhill and Craig Palmer, "Why Men Rape," *The New York Academy of Sciences* (January/February 2000): 20–28.

207. D. S. Bailey, quoted in Timothy Keller, "The Gospel and Sex," 6. http:// www.christ2rculture.com/resources/Ministry-Blog/The-Gospel-and-Sex -by-Tim-Keller.pdf.

208. Ibid.

209. D. A. Carson, *Christ and Culture Revisited* (Grand Rapids: Eerdmans, 2008), 127.

210. Brian J. Walsh and Sylvia C. Keesmat, *Colossians Remixed: Subverting the Empire* (Downers Grove, Ill.: InterVarsity Press, 2004), 82. Emphasis added.

211. Neil Postman, *Amusing Ourselves to Death: Public Discourse in the Age of Show Business* (New York: Viking, 1985), vii–viii.

212. Brian J. Walsh and Sylvia C. Keesmat, *Colossians Remixed*, 82.

213. Richard B. Hays, *Interpretation: A Bible Commentary for Teaching and Preaching: First Corinthians* (Louisville, Ky.: Westminster John Knox Press, 1997), 98. Emphasis added.

214. Timothy Keller with Kathy Keller, *The Meaning of Marriage: Facing the Complexities of Commitment with the Wisdom of God* (New York: Penguin, 2013), 236.

215. C.S. Lewis, *Miracles* (New York: Macmillan, 1960), 160.

CHAPTER 8: THE PROBLEM OF HYPOCRISY

216. David Kinnaman and Gabe Lyons, *unChristian: What a New Generation Really Thinks about Christians . . . And Why It Matters* (Grand Rapids: Baker, 2007) 27.

217. Steven Weinberg, *Facing Up: Science and Its Cultural Adversities* (Harvard University Press, 2001), 242.

218. Steven Pinker, quoted in Dinesh D'Souza, *What's So Great about Christianity* (Washington, D.C.: Regnery, 2007), 204.

219. Robert Kuttner, "What Would Jefferson Do?" *The American Prospect,* October 17, 2004, 31.

220. Dan Brown, *The Da Vinci Code* (New York: Doubleday, 2003), 125.

221. David Kinnaman, and Gabe Lyons, *unChristian*, 46–47.

222. Ibid., 47.

223. Alister McGrath, *Intellectuals Don't Need God and Other Modern Myths: Building Bridges to Faith through Apologetics* (Grand Rapids: Zondervan, 1993), 75–76.

224. Cited in Dinesh D'Souza, *What's So Great about Christianity*, 207.

225. Malcolm Gaskill, *Witchcraft: A Very Short Introduction* (Oxford: Oxford

University Press, 2010), 76. See also William Monter, "Witch Trials in Continental Europe," in Bengt Ankarloo and Stuart Clark eds., *Witchcraft and Magic in Europe: The Period of the Witch Trials* (Philadelphia: University of Pennsylvania Press, 2002), 12ff.

226. Dinesh D'Souza, *What's So Great about Christianity*, 214–215.

227. Christopher Hitchens, *God Is Not Great* (New York: Twelve Books, 2007), 36.

228. Alister E. McGrath, *The Twilight of Atheism* (New York: Doubleday, 2004), 230.

229. Dinesh D'Souza, *What's So Great about Christianity*, 215.

230. Daniel C. Dennett, *Breaking the Spell: Religion as a Natural Phenomenon* (New York: Viking, 2006), 5.

231. Miroslav Volf, *Exclusion and Embrace* (Nashville: Abingdon Press, 1996), 302. Emphasis added.

232. C. S. Lewis, "The Abolition of Man," in *The Complete C. S. Lewis Signature Classics* (New York: HarperCollins, 2002), 730.

233. Dietrich Bonhoeffer, *The Cost of Discipleship* (New York: Simon and Schuster, 1995), 111.

234. Ibid., 112–113.

235. Benjamin Fernando, "The Evangel and Social Upheaval (part 2)" in *Christ Seeks Asia*, ed. W. Mooneyham (Charlestown, Ind.: Rock House, 1969), 118–119.

236. T. Edward Damer, *Attacking Faulty Reasoning: A Practical Guide to Fallacy-Free Arguments*, 3rd ed. (Belmont, Calif.: Wadsworth, 1995), 159–161.

237. C. S. Lewis, *Mere Christianity* (San Francisco: Harper San Francisco, 2001), 170.

CHAPTER 9: THE PROBLEM OF EXCLUSIVITY

238. See Joe Boot, *How Then Shall We Answer? Overcoming Objections to the Christian Faith* (London: New Wine Press: 2008), 178.

239. John G. Stackhouse Jr., *Making the Best of It: Following Christ in the Real World* (Oxford: Oxford University Press, 2008), 288–289.

240. Ibid. Emphasis added.

241. Richard J. Mouw, *Uncommon Decency: Christian Civility in an Uncivilized World* (Downers Grove, Ill.: InterVarsity Press, 1992), 20.

242. Fritz Ridenour, *So What's the Difference: A Look at 20 Worldviews, Faiths, and Religions and How they Compare to Christianity* (Ventura, Calif.: Regal, 2000), 99–100.

243. Tim Keller, *The Reason for God* (New York: Penguin Group, 2008), 14.

244. Alvin Plantinga, "A Defense of Religious Exclusivism," in *The Analytic Theist: An Alvin Plantinga Reader*, ed. James F. Sennett (Grand Rapids: Eerdmans, 1990), 205.

245. Timothy Keller, *The Reason for God*, 4.

246. Ibid.

247. N. T. Wright, *Simply Christian: Why Christianity Makes Sense* (New York: Harper One, 2006), 61.

248. Lesslie Newbigin, *The Gospel in a Pluralist Society* (Grand Rapids: Eerdmans, 1989), 9–10.

CHAPTER 10: THE PROBLEM OF JESUS

249. N. T. Wright, *The New Testament and the People of God* (Minneapolis: Fortress Press, 1992), 123–124. A worldview *provides* the stories, *answers* the questions, is *expressed* in the symbols, and *results* in a "praxis"—action, behavior, and a way of being in the world.

250. C. S. Lewis, *Mere Christianity* (Nashville: Broadman and Holman, 1980), 55. Emphasis added.

251. Ibid.

252. Having said this, there is a surprisingly short list of people throughout history who have actually claimed to be God. Religious leaders such as Buddha, Krishna, Muhammed, and Gandhi did not claim to be God. In fact, they assured their followers they were not God.

253. http://thefreedictionary.com/blasphemy.

254. N. T. Wright, *Jesus and the Victory of God* (Minneapolis: Fortress Press, 1997, 6th ed.), 187.

255. J. I. Packer, *Knowing God* (Downers Grove, Ill.: InterVarsity Press, 1979), 45.

256. Mark Driscoll and Gerry Breshears, *Vintage Jesus: Timeless Answers to Timely Questions* (Wheaton, Ill.: Crossway Books, 2007), 14–15.

257. Robert Jamieson, A. R. Fausset, and David Brown, "John 5:18," in *A Commentary, Critical and Explanatory, on the Old and New Testaments* (Oak Harbor, Wash.: Logos Research Systems, Inc., 1997).

258. See Mathew 28:16–20 where Jesus' vision of God is the Father, and the Son and the Holy Spirit.

259. St. Augustine was right in saying this passage counters two heresies of the early church: the "we are" condemns the Sabellians (who denied the distinction of persons in the Godhead), while the "one" condemns the Arians (who denied the unity of their essence).

260. N. T. Wright, *The Challenge of Jesus: Rediscovering Who Jesus Was and Is* (Downers Grove, Ill.: InterVarsity Press, 1999), 111.

261. Jacob Neusner, *A Rabbi Talks with Jesus: An Intermillennial, Interfaith Exchange* (New York: Doubleday, 1993), 30.

262. Ibid., 30.

263. N. T. Wright, *Jesus and the Victory of God*, 639.

264. N. T. Wright, *Simply Christian* (New York: Harper One, 2006), 117.

265. Robert Wright, *The Evolution of God* (New York: Back Bay Books, 2009), 245–246.

266. Ibid.

267. C. S. Lewis, *Mere Christianity*, 56.

CPSIA information can be obtained
at www.ICGtesting.com
Printed in the USA
LVHW02s0736260718
584940LV00004B/4/P